Privatization

Antipode Book Series

General Editor: Noel Castree, Professor of Geography, University of Manchester, UK

Like its parent journal, the Antipode Book Series reflects distinctive new developments in radical geography. It publishes books in a variety of formats – from reference books to works of broad explication to titles that develop and extend the scholarly research base – but the commitment is always the same: to contribute to the praxis of a new and more just society.

Published

Privatization: Property and the Remaking of Nature-Society Relations
Edited by Becky Mansfield

Decolonizing Development: Colonial Power and the Maya
Joel Wainwright

Cities of Whiteness
Wendy S. Shaw

Neoliberalization: States, Networks, Peoples
Edited by Kim England and Kevin Ward

The Dirty Work of Neoliberalism: Cleaners in the Global Economy
Edited by Luis L. M. Aguiar and Andrew Herod

David Harvey: A Critical Reader
Edited by Noel Castree and Derek Gregory

Working the Spaces of Neoliberalism: Activism, Professionalisation and Incorporation
Edited by Nina Laurie and Liz Bondi

Threads of Labour: Garment Industry Supply Chains from the Workers' Perspective
Edited by Angela Hale and Jane Wills

Life's Work: Geographies of Social Reproduction
Edited by Katharyne Mitchell, Sallie A. Marston and Cindi Katz

Redundant Masculinities? Employment Change and White Working Class Youth
Linda McDowell

Spaces of Neoliberalism
Edited by Neil Brenner and Nik Theodore

Space, Place and the New Labour Internationalism
Edited by Peter Waterman and Jane Wills

Forthcoming

Grounding Globalization: Labour in the Age of Insecurity
Edward Webster, Rob Lambert and Andries Bezuidenhout

Privatization

Property and the Remaking of Nature–Society Relations

Edited by
Becky Mansfield

© 2008 by the Author.
Book compilation © 2008 Editorial Board of Antipode and Blackwell Publishing.
First published as Volume 39, Issue 3 of *Antipode*

BLACKWELL PUBLISHING
350 Main Street, Malden, MA 02148-5020, USA
9600 Garsington Road, Oxford OX4 2DQ, UK
550 Swanston Street, Carlton, Victoria 3053, Australia

First published 2008 by Blackwell Publishing Ltd

1   2008

Library of Congress Cataloging-in-Publication Data

Privatization: property and the remaking of nature-society relations/edited by Becky Mansfield.
    p. cm. – (Antipde book series)
    Includes bibliographical references and index.
    ISBN 978-1-4051-7550-0 (pbk.: alk. paper) 1. Privatization. 2. Neoliberalism. I. Mansfield, Becky.
    HD3850.P749 2008
    338.9'25–dc22

A catalogue record for this title is available from the British Library.

Set in 10.5pt Times
by Aptara, New Delhi, India

The publisher's policy is to use permanent paper from mills that operate a sustainable forestry policy, and which has been manufactured from pulp processed using acid-free and elementary chlorine-free practices. Furthermore, the publisher ensures that the text paper and cover board used have met acceptable environmental accreditation standards.

For further information on
Blackwell Publishing, visit our website at
www.blackwellpublishing.com

Contents

Introduction:
Property and the Remaking of
Nature–Society Relations

Becky Mansfield

Privatization is an increasingly prevalent and polarizing theme within broad political debates about economic development, inequality, and social justice. This book contributes to developing a geographical analysis of privatization by examining its role within the larger project of neoliberalism and analyzing its significance for remaking contemporary nature–society relations. The term privatization is often used to describe a transfer in control and/or ownership of business and industry from the public realm to the private. The privatization of Russian state-owned enterprises in oil, electricity, telecommunications, and so on in the post-Soviet era is a prime example. This type of privatization is really a variant of a more general process of limiting access to resources through enclosure, in which things are made into property that can be owned, controlled, and transferred. The enclosure of land in England and Scotland in the eighteenth century, as described by Marx, is the archetypal example of this form of privatization. While these two processes (ie a shift from public to private and a more general process of enclosure) appear in some ways distinct, what connects them is that they are both about allocation of resources through practices of ownership and control, and in particular control vested in private entities.

Privatization has particular salience for understanding contemporary nature–society relations because property has become the central mode of regulating multiple forms of nature. Efforts to create and impose new private property regimes are remaking ecosystems, livelihoods, and identities, creating what Diana Liverman has called a "massive transformation of the human–environment relationship" (2004:734). One significant trend in privatization of nature is the ongoing and intensified worldwide enclosure of land and resources necessary for individual, household, and community livelihoods (eg Goldman 1998). Surviving commons—in forests, fisheries, wildlife, and so on—are steadily being transformed into private property as the exploitation of nature continues to be a crucial accumulation strategy. Another trend is the extension of the property relation to new forms of nature, particularly genetic information and biological processes (eg McAfee 2003; see also Prudham this volume). This extension means that property relations structure our relationship not only to resources necessary for life, but to life itself and even ourselves. A third trend comprises efforts to privatize environmental management through market-based instruments (eg Bakker 2003; Mansfield 2004b; Robertson 2004). Examples include conservation easements, tradable pollution credits and wetland mitigation banking (see Robertson this volume), and transferable fishing quotas (see St Martin this volume; Mansfield this volume). While enclosure of resources has been a centuries long process, these efforts to privatize environmental management constitute a recent attack on the state-based regulatory approach to environmental protection pioneered over the past century (McCarthy and Prudham 2004). In these ways, privatization is a process of remaking nature–society relations, and the essays in this book all address one or more aspects of this process.

Within critical scholarship, contemporary privatization is receiving increased attention, in particular when conceptualized in terms of primitive accumulation and dispossession (Glassman 2006; Harvey 2003; Perelman 2000). This book contributes to this growing investigation of privatization by attending especially to its property dimensions, investigating what property is, what it is meant to do, and how it actually works. Together, the essays in this volume make two overarching contributions, each of which is discussed further below. The first is to make clear the importance of privatization, as a set of property relations, for political economic change broadly and neoliberalization more specifically. While privatization is often taken as one of many aspects of neoliberalism, and should be distinguished from others, the essays in this book show that privatization is not only linked to these other aspects, but helps hold them together. The second is to illustrate and show the importance of the complexity of property relations which comprise privatization. While "property" is often taken to mean private property, and private property is often taken to mean ownership, this book contributes to a reconceptualization of property as a social relation of interdependence that, in practice, yields mixed and often contradictory results. The importance and complexity of these property relations makes privatization an especially important, if vexing, site for progressive politics. By giving attention throughout to the role of privatization in the remaking of nature–society relations, this volume casts light not only on people's use of the environment, but also on more general processes of political economic change constituted by and through privatization. Nature–society relations are not just "a case" but are part of how privatization is itself produced.

A central goal of this book is to extend current geographical scholarship on neoliberalism, including but not exclusively scholarship on neoliberalism and nature. In this context, privatization is generally treated as one of several aspects of neoliberalism, alongside others such as

liberalization of trade, deregulation, commodification, and marketization. In short, neoliberalism is often defined in terms of these other
aspects, and there has been extensive focus in particular on dynamics of
de/re-regulation (McCarthy and Prudham 2004; Peck and Tickell 2002).
As Bakker argues in this volume, analytical precision about these multiple processes of neoliberalism—what each aspect entails and how it
is distinct from others—is a means to more carefully describe and explain actual phenomena (see also Castree 2005). To make distinctions
among these processes, Bakker develops a typology in which she distinguishes not only between the target and type of neoliberal reform,
but also whether these reforms are undertaken on institutions, organizations, or governance practices. Treating these aspects of neoliberalism
as analytically distinct processes allows for finer-grained analysis and
comparison of specific neoliberal projects, their goals, their strengths
and weaknesses, and their outcomes. Thus, Bakker applies her framework in analysis of global neoliberalization of water and resistance
to it, arguing in particular that opposition to the commodification of
water should be posed not in terms of a human right to water but instead in terms of a water commons. In this book Guthman, too, uses
these analytical distinctions to describe product labels (such as organic
or fair trade) as a form of neoliberalization. Her essay shows that the
power of labels comes from how they manage to articulate multiple processes of neoliberalism into a seemingly defetishizing form of consumer
information.

Given the existing body of geographical scholarship on neoliberalism,
it is now taken as given (among critics, at any rate) that neoliberal platitudes about free markets, small government, and deregulation are ideological constructs that manage to obscure the actual disciplinary work
(by the state, market, and individuals themselves) required to make markets function. Analysis of privatization in this context is enlightening
not least because the imposition of myriad private property relations is a
particularly important and deeply transformative form of re-regulatory
discipline that cuts across multiple sites and scales. Privatization does
not just happen through some natural, evolutionary process, as is often implied by "free market" proponents. States must not only enforce
property rights—one of the few functions allowed the state by liberal
theorists from Adam Smith to Friedrich von Hayek—but they participate in creating and defining the property they are going to enforce. At
the same time, private property relations require individuals not only to
act in new ways, but to become different kinds of subjects. Following
Marx, the most obvious version of this is that private property is a form
of dispossession that separates individuals from the means of production
and forces them into wage labor. But the converse is also true; private
property creates owners and makes them efficient, profit-seeking,
"rational" individuals. In other words, property disciplines both owners

and non-owners to become market subjects. Privatization does not simply mark an institutional shift, but instead entails a more fundamental restructuring of political–economic and nature–society relations, including people's senses of themselves as subjects (eg subject as owner). Privatization, then, is a key moment in neoliberalism as governmentality (Barry, Osborne and Rose 1996; Larner 2000).

In this book, the disciplinary, regulatory dimensions of privatization are touched on in all the essays. For example, Wolford shows that recipients of land through land reform in Brazil are faced with the need to then justify their ownership, and to find ways to enforce their property rights against the still landless. These beneficiaries of land reform have to use their land productively to create this justification. In my essay I show that giving exclusive fishing rights to Native Alaskans is one way of requiring them to participate in capitalist markets and become self-disciplining capitalist subjects. Exclusive fishing rights are to be used as a form of capital, and are allocated to those groups who best do this. Robertson's analysis of wetland mitigation banking, however, shows that this disciplining is not always successful. Property owners may not act in ways assumed by market proponents—who then must turn to a political process for basic functions like setting prices.

Perhaps paradoxically, what all this highlights is that attending to analytical distinctions among different processes of neoliberalization only gets us so far. What does it mean to carefully delimit privatization as *separate from* deregulation when we can also talk about privatization as a *form of* regulation? Each essay in this volume attends to the relationship between privatization and other aspects of neoliberalism, but what analysis of privatization of nature reveals is these multiple processes are intimately interrelated. Further, examining these interrelationships shows that privatization plays a special role in neoliberalism. Privatization is not merely one of several shifts promoted under neoliberalism, but instead is the central assumption and precursor to other market-based reforms. The premise of the "free market" seems to be deregulation, but underlying this are private property relations, and in particular a privatized nature–society relation.

Debates about property and its disciplinary dimensions are in no way new. They play a central role in the approaches of both John Locke and Karl Marx, each of whom addresses property explicitly. Discussion of the similarities and differences between their approaches brings into focus the underlying importance of privatization as precursor to and economic justification for neoliberalism. For Locke, the seventeenth century liberal theorist, property is the natural outcome of people's labor (ie that bit of nature which I improve through labor is my property). But his theory of property also builds on ways that property subsequently disciplines owners, turning them into civilized and rational individual subjects. That is, for Locke protection of property is right and necessary not only because it is natural, but because of the effect that it has on people. People will only labor if they are guaranteed to benefit from that labor, and this can only be assured through private property. Further, once something is private property, individuals will apply their labor to "improve" it (ie use it productively) only because they are able to profit directly from their efforts. Both wealth and poverty become the sole responsibility of the individual; wealth is the outcome of using property properly, while poverty can be ascribed to individual mismanagement. Therefore, property is the outcome of labor, but also property rights are the incentive for labor, efficiency, accumulation, and so on. Property rights thus serve critical functions in making capitalist markets possible. Privatization, in the sense of enclosure, is the premise on which commodification, marketization, and deregulation are built.

It is worth noting that some scholars have recently tried to argue that Locke includes a "sustainability constraint" such that under conditions of scarcity, property is no longer justified (Judge 2002:332; see also Haddad 2003). However, this misses the fundamental point of Locke's liberal argument, which is that private property always leads to abundance (Buckle 1991). Scarcity will be overcome through "improvement" inspired by the possibility of endless accumulation, so therefore private property can only lead to the greater good. This sounds remarkably similar to contemporary proclamations that "the market" makes everyone better off than they would be otherwise, and it also shows that underlying this free market argument is one about private property. It is this economic logic of property that underpins privatization of nature today. Proponents justify privatization in terms of its disciplinary dimensions, ie people will only protect that from which they are guaranteed to benefit, and it is only private property that can provide that guarantee. This, of course, is Garret Hardin's "tragedy of the commons" (now a truism in environmental management), which is fundamentally, and explicitly, an argument about property and its ability to shape nature–society relations.

The direct counter to these liberal accounts of property, of course, is Marxian analysis of primitive accumulation (see Glassman 2006), which also makes the importance of the property relation quite clear—but with rather different implications from Locke. Marx and Locke both treat enclosure of the commons as necessary for accumulation. For Marx, however, privatization is not simply the stimulus to accumulation, but is simultaneously its opposite: dispossession, or the social production of scarcity. While property may create abundance for some, it is this produced scarcity—separating people from the means of production— that is analytically significant. Scarcity, as created by privatization, leads not only to the capitalist labor relation, but also to capitalist commodities and markets. What makes privatization more than just an institutional shift from public to private management is that it creates new objects of property that can be bought and sold; privatization is a key moment for creating commodified things. As Prudham argues in this volume, it is important to recognize the "relational character of privatization and commodification"; privatization enhances capital by creating commodities through which capital can circulate, thus helping to displace crisis. Highlighting these dimensions of privatization is not meant to prioritize commodification and exchange relations over production and labor relations. Rather it is to offer the reminder that dispossession, as the necessary precursor to capitalist accumulation, "is a process which operates two transformations" in that in the same moment it creates both the capitalist commodity and the wage labor relation (Marx 1976:874). Further, the commodity has to be logically first; it is the produced necessity for individuals to buy what they need that requires them to sell their labor for a wage. Privatization, then, is a disciplinary process that creates new kinds of subjects (both owners and workers) and turns nature into commodities (though false ones, because they are not produced by capitalists; Polanyi 1957). The deeply transformative nature of the property relation indicates that contemporary privatization is not just one aspect of neoliberalism among many, but instead privatization is the necessary precursor. It is through privatization that neoliberalism becomes possible.

Just as the regulatory dimensions of privatization are touched on in all the essays in this book, so is the importance of the property relation as necessary for neoliberalization, and capitalist accumulation more generally. For example, Prudham makes these connections explicit, and then uses this framework to analyze legal rulings over intellectual property in genes and, by extension, organisms in the cases of the "oncomouse" and canola seed. He shows that these new enclosures are attempts to find new ways to circulate capital, but also that this process of privatization can never be complete. Robertson's analysis of new markets in water quality credits highlights the importance—and difficulty—of first defining just what is the object to be traded. His essay shows us not property as given in the market, but property in the making as the precursor to the market. Guthman's analysis of product labeling as a neoliberal accumulation strategy hinges not just on how such labels individualize responsibility, but on the fact that the right to use labels becomes a form of property right; as such, they are scarce. This scarcity calls into question their overall potential for transforming commodity systems. St Martin's analysis of New England fisheries shows that attempts to institutionalize property rights as a management system are attempts to alter class processes. The existing, non-capitalist share system of labor, in which boat owners and crew split the proceeds of each fishing trip, is premised on fish as a common property resource, and privatization would undermine this labor relation and remove one barrier to capital accumulation. Property is not inherently capitalist, but it is linked relationally to a capitalist class process.

Along with the *importance* of the property relation, it is crucial to attend to *complexity* in the meaning and practice of property. Privatization plays such a pivotal role in the constitution of neoliberalism in part because of the ways it mystifies property relations by erasing complexity. Neoliberal privatization elides "property" with "private property" and ownership (Blomley 2005; Waldron 1988). The (neo)liberal rationale for property is based on this idea of complete control: the ability to use an object however one pleases, including the ability to exclude others from using it and the ability to transfer it to others (eg selling it). Drawing on this simplistic notion of private property, privatization provides political legitimacy for neoliberal projects, in that it is used to link capital accumulation and individual freedom. For private property to enable capital accumulation and market exchange in ways envisioned by liberals and neoliberals, private property rights must be relatively strong and unfettered by broader social restriction, state based or otherwise; ie private property is that to which the owner can do whatever s/he wants. Thus, neoliberal privatization is linked and even considered as equivalent to greater individual freedom. Obviously missing from this formulation of property and freedom is the question of whose freedom is enhanced by privatization, and ways that inequality is created through privatization, with its enclosures and dispossessions, as discussed above. Freedom and inequality are not allowed in the same discursive plane, nor can other kinds of freedoms—including economic, political, and social freedoms—be articulated in this plane.

What is increasingly clear is that the neoliberal conception of property is faulty not just for its failure to take into account inequality, but also for its misunderstanding of how property itself works. Legal scholarship, in particular, yields several useful insights on what property is and how it works. First, property is not a thing (the object being controlled) but a social relation (Cohen 1927; Macpherson 1978). It is a social arrangement that allows one certain rights to certain objects, and these social arrangements can change. As Carol Rose notes, it is not so much the declaration of property ("this is mine") that matters, but the decision by other people to acknowledge that declaration ("I agree to act as though that is yours") (Rose 1994). Therefore, any "freedom" is one that is given by others, and is not inherent in the property itself. Prudham's essay in this book on patents for genetically modified organisms not only illustrates the necessity of an entity claiming property to get others to acknowledge that claim, but shows that acquiring that acknowledgement is difficult and not assured. Not only have Monsanto's claims to GMO canola and Harvard's claims to the genetically modified "oncomouse" been challenged in courts in both the US and Canada, but the Canadian Supreme Court ultimately denied Harvard's patent on the oncomouse, thus calling into question the ability to own intellectual property in organisms (even while it upheld the patent on GMO canola). The enclosure of intellectual property in general, and intellectual property in genes and organisms in particular, is still contested, and just what such property ultimately will entail is an open question.

Second, as a social relation, property need not be defined in terms of individual control. Despite the neoliberal insistence on individual ownership, there exist other kinds of property, including state and collective (or communal) (Macpherson 1978). In the neoliberal view, these other forms of property and their particular social relations are rendered contradictory and largely invisible. When they are recognized, they are treated as the problem, as in the "tragedy of the commons". Developing a typology of forms of property is one of the core contributions of the common property literature, which undermines the tragedy of the commons approach by emphasizing that common property is not the same thing as no property (or "open access") and therefore there is no necessary tragedy (eg Berkes et al 1989). This typology does concede the neoliberal perspective that property of some kind is essential for environmental protection (Mansfield 2004a), yet it is also one means to counter neoliberal platitudes about the necessity of privatization. Thus, for St Martin (this volume), the share system of labor in New England fisheries is premised on the distinction between private and common property. St Martin presents the now familiar story of attempts to erode common property through privatization schemes (in this case in the form of individual transferable quotas) that would lead to the entrenchment of capitalist economic activity. What St Martin's analysis shows, however, is that opposition to privatization can occur not because people want to avoid wage labor through subsistence use of the commons—the classic story—but because alternative forms of property support alternative, non-capitalist labor relations. Diversity of property contributes to diversity of economic relations.

Third, even private property does not conform to its representation within economic theory. In the most simple sense, ownership does not entail full rights to do anything with that which is owned, but instead involves individual strands of rights (eg to use or transfer) that need not go together (think of the simple example of a leased house) and that in practice often conflict (Cohen 1927; Hohfield 1913; Waldron 1988). This basic insight about ways that property rights can conflict recently has yielded a more profound criticism of the concept of private property. As I discuss further in my essay in this book, legal scholars have begun to theorize private property not solely in terms of entitlement and freedom, but simultaneously in terms of obligation and responsibility (Singer 2000; Underkuffler 2003). US case law shows that while the ownership model of property is rhetorically dominant, there always have been other more social models of property that exist in practice. Beyond this legal realm, empirical research is revealing a huge diversity of ways that people have conceptualized and practiced even private property relations both today and in the past (Islamoglu 2004; Verdery and Humphrey 2004). The geographer Nick Blomley has put this diverse conception of private property to work in his research, describing, for example, multiple ways that activists have been able to use property language to make a public claim on private (and privatized) spaces (Blomley 2004a, 2000b). Efforts such as these begin to break apart the category of private property from the inside, challenging it not for what it leaves out, but for not being forthright about the complex relations it embodies.

The essays in this book push these ideas about complexity of property in a number of directions. One way of thinking about this complexity and what it means is by linking it to the diverse economies approach (Gibson-Graham 2006; Leyshon 2005). From a diverse economies perspective, capitalism is never as complete as it seems because there are always already alternatives that are neither completely capitalist nor completely outside capitalism. Similarly, the complexity of property shows that privatization is never as complete as it seems. In a deconstructive mode, this complexity shows that privatization (and by extension neoliberalism) contains within it that which it denies—and as such cannot be what it appears or what proponents assert. Drawing explicitly on this perspective, St Martin shows that New England fisheries are an already existing form of non-capitalism in which labor has not been fully proletarianized. While this non-capitalist economic activity would be undermined by privatization in the form of transferable quotas, he shows that such activity has been able to survive not just at the periphery but even in what is supposed to be the heart of capitalist relations. Prudham, too, alludes to this diversity by arguing that privatization and commodification are never complete; while the privatization of genetic material and organisms is an attempt to privatize life, this process will never be finished. Attempts to privatize nature are premised on a fictional notion of nature as a unique object that can be atomized into bits to be owned. If external and autonomous nature, as such, does not exist (but is always nature–society), then this simple definition of property cannot hold. In Robertson's essay on the work that market proponents must do to define both the object of property and its price, he makes a similar argument about the incompleteness of neoliberal marketization. Property and markets are always more than they seem, and these other elements are actively obscured by neoliberal proponents. In these ways, acknowledging the complexity of property shows that alternatives to it already exist; it is never complete.

Another way to theorize the complexity of property and the alternatives that always already inhere is through examining property in terms of the relationship between freedom and oppression, protection and violence. As the discussion above indicated, it is quite easy to cast privatization as a form of violent dispossession. The essays in this book support this view in various ways, identifying how privatization is imposed and how it supports capitalist accumulation. At the same time, however, several essays call this basic formulation into question, showing that privatization—by creating new property rights—has protective and not just violent aspects. In one sense, this is a truism. That establishment of property rights is protective has never been questioned; it is protective for its owners while being a form of violence against those who no longer have access to resources. These aspects of the property relation are easy to see when adopting a simple, ownership definition of property.

However, if complexity of property is recognized, so that property means not just individual control but also interconnection, other aspects of protection come into focus. In my essay I analyze the advent of fishing quotas for Alaska Natives as a form of privatization. While it is possible to interpret this privatization as a form of neoliberal violence that disciplines these people to capitalism, I find that it is equally plausible to interpret this privatization as a form of protection for the dispossessed, providing them protections from capitalism in the name of social justice. Similarly, Wolford's analysis of land reform in Brazil finds this form of privatization to be both neoliberal and populist. For the World Bank, land reform is a neoliberal project of assigning property as a precursor to markets. For the rural landless, land reform is a populist project of assigning property as a means to social justice. This tension is reflected in an incompatibility in Brazilian law between the simple notion of private property and the sense that property serves non-market social functions. Guthman's essay on product labels, too, can be taken to illustrate this dynamic. Her central argument is that these labels are perverse, in that what is meant to be a form of resistance to market ideology ends up being a form of it. But she also argues that these labels have indirect consequences that could lead to collective action that would provide real protections from the market. These three examples all highlight ways that neoliberalization contain alternatives within it—property is not just protective or just violent, but both, and these are linked.

What analysis of privatization finds, then, is that which is progressive is linked to that which is problematic. First, the deeply transformative nature of privatization is itself a spark to more general resistance. By reworking people's basic relationship to themselves, each other, their livelihoods, and nature, privatization can create powerful opposition. Bakker makes this clear in her analysis of resistance to the privatization of water. Enclosure of both local and global water commons has tremendous effects on ecosystems, livelihoods, personal and public health, spiritual values, and so on. It is the multiple ways in which enclosure of water remakes nature–society relations that inspires the broad-based and multi-faceted resistance that Bakker documents. Bakker's intervention is to suggest that to be most effective, resistance strategies should be formulated to address the particulars of privatization.

Second, this issue demonstrates the futility of essentializing either neoliberalism or resistance to it. Resistance is often framed within dominant discourses and practices of neoliberalism (in part attesting and contributing to their power), but this also shows that neoliberal discourse and practice can be turned inside-out, yielding results that are unintuitive on their face. While such findings could be taken as support for neoliberalism (e.g. privatization can be good for the poor), what these findings do instead is undermine simplistic notions about how property works and what effects it has. Property transforms people's relationships to themselves, others, and nature through ownership and market discipline, but in so doing, property simultaneously forms interconnections that constantly threaten to undermine—or exceed—such discipline. This means that there is no "pure" form of resistance, completely on the outside of processes of privatization and neoliberalization—but this should not be cause for despair but for hope. Just as the impossibility of "getting back" to "pure" nature does not necessitate abandoning efforts to create healthier and more just nature–society relations, the impossibility of creating a nature–society relation outside of neoliberalism need not mean acceding to what neoliberal proponents have to offer. What we see in the essays in this issue is that privatization is the remaking of nature–society relations as property, and that this process underpins neoliberalism more generally. But just what this process means, and where it leads, is not a closed question. In this sense, these findings on the depth and complexity of what property actually does help us recognize already existing alternatives that can contribute to possible new futures.

Acknowledgements

I would like to thank all the authors in this book for their creativity, intellectual energy, and willingness to work on a timeline. I would also like to thank Noel Castree and Melissa Wright for their invitation to put this volume together, and Jo Kitching for her able assistance in making it happen. I also wish to acknowledge my graduate students—especially Johanna Haas, Jason Davis, and April Luginbuhl—whose interests have intersected with mine in very productive ways. They have pushed me to read widely and think broadly about these issues related to privatization and property.

References

Bakker K (2003) *An Uncooperative Commodity: Privatizing Water in England and Wales*. Oxford: Oxford University Press
Barry A., Osborne T. and Rose N. (eds) (1996) *Foucault and Political Reason: Liberalism, Neo-liberalism, and Rationalities of Government*. Chicago: University of Chicago Press

Berkes F, Feeny D, McCay B J and Acheson J M (1989) The benefits of the commons. *Nature* 340:91–93

Blomley N (2004a) Un-real estate: Proprietary space and public gardening. *Antipode* 36(4):615–641

Blomley N (2004b) *Unsettling the City: Urban Land and the Politics of Property.* New York: Routledge

Blomley N (2005) Remember property? *Progress in Human Geography* 29(2):125–127

Buckle S (1991) *Natural Law and the Theory of Property.* Oxford: Clarendon Press

Castree N (2005) The epistemology of particulars: Human geography, case studies, and "context". *Geoforum* 36:541–544

Cohen M R (1927) Property and sovereignty. *Cornell Law Quarterly* 13:8–30

Gibson-Graham J K (2006) *A Postcapitalist Politics.* Minneapolis: University of Minnesota Press

Glassman J (2006) Primitive accumulation, accumulation by dispossession, accumulation by "extra-economic" means. *Progress in Human Geography* 30(5):608–625

Goldman M. (ed) (1998) *Privatizing Nature: Political Struggles for the Global Commons.* New Brunswick: Rutgers University Press

Haddad B M (2003). Property rights, ecosystem management, and John Locke's labor theory of ownership. *Ecological Economics* 46:19–31

Harvey D (2003) *The New Imperialism.* Oxford: Oxford University Press

Hohfield W N (1913) Some fundamental legal conceptions as applied in juridical reasoning. *Yale Law Journal* 23:16–59

Islamoglu H. (ed) (2004) *Constituting Modernity: Private Property in the East and West.* London: I B Taurus

Judge R P (2002) Restoring the commons: Toward a new interpretation of Locke's theory of property. *Land Economics* 78:331–338

Larner W (2000) Neo-liberalism, policy, ideology, governmentality. *Studies in Political Economy* 63(autumn):5–25

Leyshon A (2005) Intervention: Diverse economies. *Antipode* 37(5):856–862

Liverman D (2004) Who governs, at what scale and at what price? Geography, environmental governance, and the commodification of nature. *Annals of the Association of American Geographers* 94(4):734–738

Macpherson C B (ed) (1978) Property: Mainstream and Critical Positions. Toronto: University of Toronto Press

Mansfield B (2004a) Neoliberalism in the oceans: "Rationalization," property rights, and the commons question. *Geoforum* 35(3):313–326

Mansfield B (2004b) Rules of privatization: Contradictions in neoliberal regulation of North Pacific fisheries. *Annals of the Association of American Geographers* 94(3):565–584

Marx K (1976) *Capital: A Critique of Political Economy.* Translated by B Fowkes. Vol 1. London: Penguin Books

McAfee K (2003) Neoliberalism on the molecular scale: Economic and genetic reductionism in biotechnology battles. *Geoforum* 34:203–219

McCarthy J and Prudham S (2004) Neoliberal nature and the nature of neoliberalism. *Geoforum* 35:275–283

Peck J and Tickell A (2002) Neoliberalizing space. *Antipode* 34(3):380–404

Perelman M (2000) *The Invention of Capitalism: Classical Political Economy and the Secret History of Primitive Accumulation.* Durham: Duke University Press

Polanyi K (1957) *The Great Transformation: The Political and Economic Origins of Our Time.* Boston: Beacon Press

Robertson M (2004) The neoliberalization of ecosystem services: Wetland mitigation banking and problems in environmental governance. *Geoforum* 35:361–373

Rose C M (1994) *Property and Persuasion: Essays on the History, Theory, and Rhetoric of Ownership*. Boulder: Westview Press

Singer J W (2000) *Entitlement: The Paradoxes of Property*. New Haven: Yale University Press

Underkuffler L S (2003) *The Idea of Property: Its Meaning and Power*. Oxford: Oxford University Press

Verdery K. and Humphrey C. (eds) (2004) *Property in Question: Value Transformation in the Global Economy*. Oxford: Berg

Waldron J (1988) *The Right to Private Property*. Oxford: Clarendon Press

Chapter 1

The Fictions of Autonomous Invention: Accumulation by Dispossession, Commodification and Life Patents in Canada

Scott Prudham

Introduction

On 5 December 2002, the Supreme Court of Canada ruled by a 5–4 decision to deny Harvard College a patent over its oncomouse, a rodent used in medical research and genetically engineered to contract cancer. The majority opinion argued that the mouse, as a higher life form, does not qualify as a "manufacture" or as a "composition of matter" under the Canadian Patent Act. In what seemed something of a reversal, however, only 17 months later on 21 May 2004 the same court ruled (again in a 5–4 decision) that Saskatchewan farmer Percy Schmeiser had violated a Monsanto Corporation patent over so-called "Roundup Ready" canola. In the latter ruling, the Court controversially refuted Schmeiser's right as a farmer to save seed derived from pollen drift, even if it came from Monsanto plants.

The decisions left Canada with a pair of landmark decisions that are, at least superficially, difficult to reconcile with one another. Moreover, the Harvard case leaves Canada directly at odds with the United States over intellectual property rights vis-à-vis genetically modified organisms (GMOs), conflicting as it does with a US patent issued in 1987 covering the same mouse. While Canada has generally been in league with the US in aggressively pursuing the commercialization of biotechnology, and in tandem, the restructuring of intellectual property rights to over genes and GMOs, the two SCC cases point to very real and potentially significant divergences over so-called genetic enclosures (Bridge, McManus and Marsden 2003) in the very heartland of biotech. This alone makes the cases noteworthy.

In this paper, I wish to read and interpret these cases as singular moments in the ongoing struggle to define property rights over the products of the so-called new biotechnologies, including ways in which exclusive patent and property rights act as instruments for the privatization of individual genes, biological processes, and indeed, whole organisms. I am certainly not the first to link the new biotechnologies to issues of the privatization and commodification of life (Busch 1991; Buttel 1989, 2003; Kenney 1986; Kloppenburg 2004; Thackray 1998). More generally, considerable recent literature has explored the distinct ways in which biophysical nature is commodified, a distinctness arising not least from the materiality of biophysical processes (eg Bakker 2003; Bridge 2000; Cronon 1991; Mansfield 2003; Prudham 2005). Drawing on and seeking to contribute to this literature, my goal in the paper is to use the cases (and particularly arguments mobilized by judges as well as by social and environmental activist groups) in order to better understand in particular: (i) how capital is made to circulate through biophysical nature; (ii) how this turns on the creation of new property rights and relations through so-called "extra-economic" means; and (iii) what are the politics (and political ambiguities) of resisting these various commodifications of nature?

The paper proceeds as follows. I first sketch in slightly more detail some of the basic essentials of the two cases. Subsequently, I elaborate conceptually on a set of themes related to the questions above in order to establish a more rigorous basis for examining the cases. Following this, I trace some of the historical lineage of the cases in question, linking them to the development of the new biotechnologies as key (neoliberal) strategies for expanding the scale and scope of capital accumulation. Subsequently, I visit in some detail specific arguments made for and against the extension of patent rights over full organisms in both cases. In a strictly formal sense, tensions between the cases are reconciled by the consistency with which the SCC limited life patents to discrete genes and processes and refused to extend them over whole organisms (a point of enduring disagreement on the court, but not between the two majority opinions). However, this consistency is sustained only at the costs of constructing parts of organisms as completely separable from their wholes, and their wholes as solely the sum of their parts. More fundamentally, it requires accepting that discrete bits of socionature can be viewed as "autonomous inventions", the products of single authors separate from prior social and biophysical contributions. This in turn, I argue, begs questions not only about the commodification of nature, but about the foundations of private property. I conclude with some reflections on some of the more explicitly normative questions and challenges posed by these cases.

The Cases in Brief
The formal history of the SCC oncomouse decision began on 21 June 1985 when the President and Fellows of Harvard College applied for a Canadian patent over "transgenic animals" genetically engineered to be

susceptible to cancer. Harvard applied for a patent to cover the process of inserting the cancer causing genes into the mice, but also to cover the resulting whole mouse and, for that matter, *any* non-human mammal genetically engineered to develop cancer. The whole organism or product claims were rejected in 1993 by the Canadian Patent Office because the Examiner determined that whole organisms were outside the scope of the definition of "invention" in section 2 of the Canadian Patent Act. The Examiner did, however, grant the *process* claims (to the genes and their method of insertion). This decision was eventually overturned by the Federal Court of Appeals which granted the product patent. The Canadian government appealed, and the case went to the SCC.

Among the interesting dimensions of this decision is that it follows on and ultimately conflicts with Harvard's US oncomouse patent (see Haraway 1997). This controversial patent was awarded by the US Patent Office in 1988 and assigned to Harvard College by the principal researchers who developed it. Harvard licensed the patent to Du Pont in order to commercialize it. Rather remarkably, in the US case, a patent covering *any non-human mammal* genetically engineered to develop cancer was granted (see also Kevles 1998; Rifkin 1998). However, divergence between the US and Canadian patent decisions over the oncomouse was highlighted in the Canadian Federal Court, Trial Division where a Canadian judge took issue with the majority opinion in the (in)famous Diamond v Chakrabarty decision of the US Supreme Court in 1980. Siding with the minority in Chakrabarty, the Canadian judge reasoned that because separate plant breeders' protections were legislated by the 1930 US Plant Patent Act and the 1970 US Plant Variety Protection Act, Congress must have intended to keep life forms outside the scope of the US patents. The SCC majority opinion later upheld this reasoning, noting further that the mouse, as a higher life form, does not qualify as a "manufacture" or as a "composition of matter" under the Canadian Patent Act's definition of invention. Specifically:

> The sole question in this appeal is whether the words "manufacture" and "composition of matter", within the context of the Patent Act, are sufficiently broad to include higher life forms. It is irrelevant whether this Court believes that higher life forms such as the oncomouse ought to be patentable. The words of the Patent Act "are to be read in their entire context and in their grammatical and ordinary sense harmoniously with the scheme of the Act, the object of the Act, and the intention of Parliament".

The second case involved a suit brought by Monsanto against Percy Schmeiser, a conventional (ie non-organic, non-alternative) farmer from the province of Saskatchewan. According to the Court record, by 1996, about 600 farmers in Canada had embraced the use of Monsanto's Roundup Ready canola, covering approximately 50,000 acres in total.

This includes many farmers in the area of Mr Schmeiser's farm. Monsanto licensed GM canola seed to farmers at a cost of $15 per acre, and required the farmers to enter into a Technology Use Agreement. One of the terms of this agreement was that the farmers would not save seed, despite their traditional right to and practice of doing so.

By 1996, five of Mr Schmeiser's immediate neighbours in Saskatchewan were growing Roundup Ready canola on their fields. Mr Schmeiser saved seed that year from his fields, as he normally does. He planted the seed in the spring of 1997. Later that same season, he sprayed a public right of way near his field with Roundup, and found to his apparent surprise that 60% of the canola plants survived. In the fall of 1997, Mr Schmeiser harvested seed from the plants in this patch, and he stored the seed over the winter, and planted it the following year despite warnings from Monsanto against growing Roundup Ready canola without a license. Under court order, samples of Schmeiser's 1998 crop were taken, and it was confirmed that 95–98% of the canola grown in these fields was Roundup Ready. Monsanto filed suit.

In its decision against Schmeiser, the Court upheld the validity of the Monsanto patent, which Schmeiser had challenged based on his claim of the right to save seed. A trial judge first upheld the patent in Monsanto Company Inc v Schmeiser, finding the patent did not contravene the Canadian Plant Breeder's Rights Act of 1990 (an act that upheld farmers' rights to save seeds), despite the fact that the GM canola can be replicated through normal plant reproduction. Upholding this reasoning, the majority argued:

> The patent is valid. The respondents did not claim protection for the genetically modified plant itself, but rather for the genes and the modified cells that make up the plant. A purposive construction of the patent claims recognizes that the invention will be practiced in plants regenerated from the patented cells, whether the plants are located inside or outside a laboratory. *Whether or not patent protection for the gene and the cell extends to activities involving the plant is not relevant to the patent's validity.* (Emphasis added)

and subsequently:

> Case law shows that infringement is established where a defendant's commercial or business activity involving a thing of which a patented part is a component necessarily involves use of the patented part. Infringement in this case therefore does not require use of the gene or cell in isolation. (Percy Schmeiser and Schmeiser Enterprises v Monsanto Canada and Monsanto Inc 2004, SCC 34, Per MacLachlin C J and Major, Binnie, Deschamps and Fish J J)

Critically, the dissenting opinion cited the oncomouse decision in questioning whether patents on genes and cells, reproduced as part of whole organisms, could be protected without creating de facto property rights over whole organisms:

> The heart of the issue is *whether the Federal Court of Appeal's decision can stand in light of this Court's ruling that plants as higher life forms are unpatentable.* A purposive construction that limits the scope of the respondents' claims to their "essential elements" leads to the conclusion that the gene claims and the plant cell claims should not be construed to grant exclusive rights over the plant and all of its offspring. (Emphasis added) (Percy Schmeiser and Schmeiser Enterprises v Monsanto Canada and Monsanto Inc 2004, SCC 34, Per Iacobucci, Bastarache, Arbour and LeBel J J)

The end result however, was that Schmeiser, by this time an international cause celebre among anti-GM activists and defenders of farmers' rights to save seed, was found to have violated Monsanto's patents. Monsanto's award in the case was financially insignificant, perhaps some sign of the Court's sympathy. Still, the case bolstered the company's proprietary claims over a variety of one of the more commercially successful GM crops in the world, all the more significant since it took place in Canada, the world's leading producer of GM canola (Clive 2004).

Stretching and Deepening: Accumulation by Dispossession and the Commodification of Nature

These cases together comprise two landmark Canadian Supreme Court decisions that both reflect but also shape the ways patent and other intellectual property rights delineate and designate discrete genes, biological processes and whole organisms as exclusive forms of individuated, alienable (and saleable) property. One case upholds the rights of Monsanto to claim at least discrete bits of GM canola as its exclusive property, constrains the power of farmers to save GM seed, and makes farmers responsible for the random pollen drift of corporate canola. The other case constrains Harvard's (and DuPont's) capacity to claim (and market) outright ownership over the oncomouse. The cases also seem in tension with one another based on the reasoning of the minority in the Schmeiser case, ie that patents to parts provide de facto patents to wholes. More definitively, the decisions contravene US precedent in granting outright patents over whole organisms even as they help to internationalize the private ownership of genes.

Before discussing the cases, their historical context, and some of the arguments mobilized in the course of the Court's deliberations, I wish to discuss in greater detail a set of overarching themes, both theoretical and political, to which I believe these cases speak, specifically in relation to debates, again both theoretical and political, about the privatization and commodification of nature, and more specifically, of life. The first of these themes is that of the relational character of privatization and commodification.

Bakker (2005) has recently warned of a need to distinguish between commercialization, privatization, and commodification. In a certain sense, I agree, it is important not to collapse discrete and potentially quite different dynamics into overly broad generalizations; the term commodification, whether mobilized analytically or polemically, carries this risk. And these cases, at least directly, concern private property claims over living organisms and parts thereof as inventions. At the same time, there is a danger of overemphasizing the distinctions between privatization and commodification. Thus, I argue it is more useful conceptually and politically to see these cases as relational moments in commodification, and specifically as instances of accumulation by dispossession (Harvey 2003). That is, rather than privatization per se, the specifics of the cases, including the technologies involved, and the lineage from which they emerge make them highly consistent in important ways with the notion of accumulation by dispossession as a means to expand the scale and scope of capital accumulation via so-called 'extra-economic' means. Viewed in this manner, attempts to privatize life forms as exclusive, alienable, and saleable property are critical junctures in the creation and augmentation of the capacity for capital, as value[1] in motion, to circulate in and through biophysical nature, propelled by the value expanding tendencies of generalized and specifically capitalist commodity circulation. Privatization, and for that matter, exchange, are relational moments in specifically *capitalist* commodification.

I have no wish to review and debate the dynamics of capital accumulation and commodity circulation here. However, it is important to remember that capitalism is not distinguished as a form of social organization by production for exchange per se, nor are commodities unique to capitalism. Rather, what distinguishes capitalist commodification is the general and expanding character of commodity production and circulation by capitalists who deploy wage labour in doing so (Marx 1977). While all commodities are embodied social relations, capitalist commodities are embodied capitalist relations (albeit in myriad specific forms). This gives rise to expansionary tendencies, and uneven geographical development (Harvey 1982; Smith 1984). That said, generalized commodity production and circulation expands in two interconnected ways (i) 'stretching', ie the extension of the spatial reach of particular commodities into new or larger markets; and (ii) 'deepening', ie the appearance of more and more things as commodities, including the tendency to commodify labour power itself (Lysandrou 2005).[2] These twin processes of expansion propel the tendency toward the (apparent) commodification of everything that exists, and the appearance that commodification under capitalism reaches into "every nook and cranny" (Thrift 2000). I say "apparent" because these tendencies of commodification are *necessarily* incomplete, not least because of the fictitiousness of money, labour and nature as key inputs whose reproduction cannot be fully incorporated into and coordinated by the circuits of accumulation and market exchange (Polanyi 1944).

In this context, accumulation by dispossession has been revised by Harvey from the classical Marxist notion of primitive accumulation in order to examine the ways in which the expansion of capital accumulation turns on the creation of new forms of private property and *through which capital can then more readily circulate and be realized*. This latter point is critical. As Glassman (2006) has recently discussed, accumulation by dispossession draws attention to such appropriations as ongoing features of capitalist dynamics, including in the most fully developed capitalist economies. Under accumulation by dispossession, privatization is a *means* by which the capacity of capital to circulate is enhanced. Privatization from this perspective is central to commodification as a dynamic expansionary process. Equally, while privatization may therefore be examined in and of itself, it may also be a relational moment in the broader processes of expanding the scale and scope of commodity circulation and capital accumulation. And given the myriad ways in which state, common, and open access property may be (and has been) turned into exclusive, private property essentially by fiat (see eg McCarthy 2004), there is no reason from a theoretical or empirical perspective to confine accumulation by dispossession in any strict or direct sense to proletarianization and the dissolution of petty commodity production in the manner in which primitive accumulation has often been interpreted (Glassman 2006). In fact, and somewhat paradoxically, individuated property rights over commodities as things helps allow for the dissolution of the very specificity of these things in the realm of exchange, which in turn allows for "capitalist commodification as a process where qualitatively distinct things are rendered equivalent and saleable through the medium of money" (Castree 2003:278). For example, if all oncomice are exclusively owned by Harvard (and licensed by DuPont) this is one basis by which their equivalence in exchange may be and has been determined. Thus, I argue that the specifics of these cases exemplify what Kloppenburg (2004) elegantly argued and demonstrated, namely that in the absence of state sanctioned, exclusive rights over discrete biological processes and entities, the self-reproducing character of biological organisms (typified by the seed in his analysis) poses a threat to the realization of exchange value. Without stringent protections of exclusive rights, pollen drifts, mice reproduce, and so on, potentially undermining the realization of invested capital.

My second theme, consistent with the first, is to locate these cases at the nexus of neoliberalism and nature. Harvey (2005) (along with others) has also argued that neoliberalism may be understood (at least in substantial measure) as a broad-based and diverse set of strategies oriented to reinvigorating accumulation in the advanced capitalist nations as well as on a world scale (see also Jessop 2002; Peck and Tickell 2002). The so-called "enterprising up of life" itself (Haraway 1997) represents a central and even constitutive role in this project. A proliferation of recent critical literature on neoliberalism, including its environmental dimensions, should not be confused with the longer history of the social processes involved, and strategies to reinvigorate the economic dynamism of leading capitalist economies in so-called knowledge sectors (including biotech) date to the early 1970s. These cases thus help exemplify the constitutive role in the emergence and consolidation of neoliberalism played by re-structuring social relations to biophysical nature (McCarthy and Prudham 2004). I attempt to fill out this argument somewhat in the next section by situating the cases in relation to an historical political economy of increasingly commercially oriented (bio)technoscience.

All this said, the cases also point to commodification as an inherently unfinished tendency. I agree with Donna Haraway that the oncomouse— and GM canola for that matter—is a complex assemblage of "signs and referents all rolled into one fleshy mystery in a secularized salvation history of civilian and military wars, scientific knowledge, progress, democracy, and economic power" (Haraway 1997:85). If accumulation by dispossession highlights an extra-economic dimension to extending the scale and scope of commodity production and circulation, this only highlights the existence of irreducibly extra-economic facets of the commodification of nature (or anything for that matter) more generally. I am unsatisfied with the dichotomy between "economic" and "extra-economic", not least because such terminology runs the risk of thinking of these as formally distinct realms. But as placeholders, they at least direct attention to the myriad ways in which what are generally received as economic processes necessarily rely upon processes not generally seen as economic. This is consistent with the argument that, where nature is concerned, "the process of commodification (or its effects) might operate rather differently depending on which particular natures are being commodified" (Castree 2003:275; on materiality more generally, see Bakker and Bridge 2006). And a key concern becomes attending to processes of abstraction, individuation, and alienation required to render discrete bits of biophysical nature available and equivalent for exchange in isolation from ecological context (Castree 2003).[3] Robertson (2000, 2004) has written compellingly about the discursive production of exchange under the US EPA wetland banking program, problematizing among other things the erasure of ecological difference in exchange. Most recently, he has carefully unpacked the scientific efforts of botanists and ecologists mobilized to sustain at least an appearance of scientific rigour in rendering commensurable (and exchangeable) geographically and ecologically distinct wetlands (Robertson 2006). As he notes (2006:369), the relations between capital and science here need to be understood as "as articulations between structurally closed but operationally open (that is, autopoietic) logical realms" (on autopoiesis and political economy, see also Jessop 2001).

In this paper, I am keen to profile similar discursive and institutional work necessary to render the messy materiality of life legible as discrete entities, individuated and abstracted from complex social and ecological integuments. In doing so, I look to the ways in which judges and interested activists deliberate over the economic, legal, ecological, ethical, and even metaphysical arguments and representations required to uphold discrete genes, processes, and whole organisms as inventions. Much of this turns on what Haraway (1997) calls the myth of "autonomous invention", the necessary fiction that despite complex social and biophysical contributions to the (re)production of mice and canola they can be legally sustained (and exchanged) as the inventions (and thus property) of single authors (and owners). It is, on its face, rather farcical, and yet it reinforces Proudhon's telling aphorism that "all property is theft". The question in the cases is then very much which thefts receive state sanction, how and why.

The self-evident fiction of autonomous invention suggests that nature does indeed comprise a special class of commodity. For many activists (including ones who mobilized around the cases discussed here) this is the basis of an argument against the commodification of nature, an argument with which I have considerable sympathy. The naked hubris that posits genes, biological processes, and whole organisms as alienable privatized inventions is quite evidently a multi-faceted theft and ought rightly to be named as such (McAfee 2003). And one might even extend this argument beyond Kloppenburg's reasoning, to see privatization not only as a way of resolving potentially conflicting social claims to nature, but also as a legal and institutional strategy aimed at repressing the self-reproducing character of life. That is, if life forms can reproduce themselves, they make for awkward forms of intellectual property to contain, posing a constant threat of ecological transgression! There is some hint of this anxiety in the cases too.

Yet, Proudhon's statement considered in relation to these cases points to potential limitations of this "nature as exception" argument. Perhaps nature is not as exceptional as might be supposed when considered as viable terrain for exclusive property claims. This is my fourth theme in reading the cases, and it is by no means my own idea. Put succinctly, if the supposedly ontologically stable and distinct category "nature" is better understood as a complex assemblage of semiotically and materially produced socionatures or hybrids (see eg Haraway 1991, 1997; Harvey 1996; Latour 1993; Smith 1984, 1996; Swyngedouw 1999), what implications does this have not only for the advocates of such privatizations and the fiction of autonomous invention, but also for critics? There are ambiguities here, not only in the potential reinscription of a transcendental, objective notion of nature, but also and somewhat paradoxically, in undermining the particularity of the ecological critique in the sense that complex assemblages of socio-ecological production underpin all commodities, and all inventions. The question then becomes whether to abandon the exceptionalism of the strictly ecological critique, or to expand the socionature critique to encompass all enclosures.

Nature, Neoliberalism, and the Political Economy of Biotechnology

If 1973 serves to punctuate histories of capitalist social regulation (Arrighi 1994; Harvey 1989), highlighted by fallout from the first oil shock and an emerging American fiscal crisis, it is also the year in which Stanley Cohen and Herbert Boyer "discovered" recombinant DNA. This breakthrough was foundational to the transfer of genes and gene segments between different species (splicing), and as such perhaps more than any other single discovery underpins the era of the new biotechnologies. But the so-called Cohen–Boyer process was also foundational because the successful patenting of this process by university researchers—via a claim filed in 1974 and eventually granted in 1980 (Kenney 1998)—set important precedents in the privatization of life, but also in the patenting and licensing of federally funded university research (Hughes 2001). Indeed, by 1997 when the patent expired, the Cohen–Boyer process had become one of the first and certainly most lucrative technologies ever to be licensed from university research, and had at the same time been focal to re-working university–industry relations in technology transfer, in biotech or otherwise.

This conjuncture, that is, a crisis of American capitalism, the emergence of a suite of new biotechnologies, and the commercialization of these technologies via restructuring of university–industry–state relations, is indeed contingent, but in no way entirely incidental. Instead, it highlights the degree to which flagging national economic competitiveness, most importantly in the US and the UK, led to the aggressive targeting of biotech as one of the new, so-called "information" driven sectors that would fuel economic recovery and renewal (Wright 1994). Significantly, wrangling over the Cohen–Boyer process involving two universities (Stanford and the University of California), the National Institutes of Health, and would-be commercial users was paralleled by important changes underway at Harvard, precipitated in large part by its relationship with Monsanto. In 1974, Harvard granted Monsanto the right to an exclusive worldwide license over commercial applications of specific research conducted at the university and funded (in part) by the company, departing from its historic practice of opposing exclusive commercial licensing. In the following year, Harvard made a more general policy shift by ending its commitment to making health science related discoveries available free of charge. The purpose was explicitly to pursue more of the kinds of exclusive arrangements it had signed with Monsanto to capitalize on potential licensing revenues (Kevles 1998).

These precedents were central to a sea-change in university–industry–state relations in the US precipitated in large part by the commercial maturation of the new biotechnologies. They acted as templates for the Bayh-Dole Act of 1980 (PL 65-517) and its subsequent refinements, encouraging American university and government researchers to patent their federally funded discoveries while enshrining biotech as a new commercial frontier for capital accumulation (ie deepening). The result has been only too successful, particularly in the most commercially immediate of the life sciences which have been substantially subordinated to capital. For example, one estimate is that drug companies were contributing about 60% of the total costs of continuing education in the medical field in the United States by the early 1990s (Angell 2004). Moreover, there is considerable evidence of growing commercial influence on research findings (Krimsky 2003), not least via the widespread practice of ghost writing.[4] Again, these tendencies are particularly evident in the lucrative medical and pharmaceutical fields.

Canada is by no means to be understood as the passive recipient of US-led technological and institutional changes in these arenas, but neither is the Canadian experience less characterized by tightly coordinated industry and state action aimed at developing a basis for national economic competitiveness through biotech. Again, I cannot do justice to this history, which to my knowledge remains to be chronicled in detail. Yet, in Canada, strategic, commercially driven research alliances between universities and private capital in the health and pharmaceuticals sectors have come to increasingly characterize the social relations of (research) production, evidenced not least at my own institution by controversy surrounding Nancy Olivieri's research partnership with Apotex, a pharmaceutical multinational.[5] The commercialization of rDNA and related technologies has been focal in efforts to renew the competitiveness of Canada's national economy (Slaughter and Leslie 1997). In particular, amidst persistent economic stagnation in the early 1980s and under the auspices of a neoliberal federal administration, the National Biotechnology Strategy was launched with the explicit goal of providing public support for the emergence of biotech as a new avenue for private accumulation, drawing in part on the nation's existing strength in the agriculture sector (Government of Canada Industry Canada 1998). Pursuit of commercial opportunities for emerging biotechnologies remained essentially the sole focus of federal biotech policy in Canada until increasing concerns about health and environmental impacts—not least in the food sector—led to a broadening of this mandate in 1999 under the Canadian Biotechnology Advisory (Prudham and Morris 2006). Yet the horses were out of the barn, Canada having already emerged as one of the leading nations to embrace GM crops in commercial agriculture; by 1998, Canada ranked behind only the US and the UK in the biotech sector, and had (according to boosters within Industry Canada) "more biotechnology companies per capita than any country" (Government of Canada Industry Canada 1998). And despite the oncomouse decision, Canada has largely moved to comply with US-led efforts on the internationalization of IPRs in the biotech arena by recognizing exclusive private claims (enclosures) over genes and gene constructs and by enacting stronger patent protections for commercial plant breeders.

This context situates the SCC oncomouse and Schmeiser cases as significant but hardly isolated moments, connecting them to now relatively longstanding tendencies in the commodification of nature via commercial development of the new biotechnologies. They specifically exemplify moments in both deepening and stretching, as new forms of private property rights over life are created, and as these rights are (unevenly) internationalized. The involvement of both Monsanto and Harvard as important players in the reconfiguration of US university–industry–state relations around commercial biotechnology as far back as the mid-1970s provides a source of continuity as well, connecting past and present. But these systemic tendencies in no way diminish the significance of political struggles over these and similar cases. Quite the opposite. Indeed, if the historical political economy of biotechnology indicates anything it is that time and again, active, extra-economic political intervention has been required to secure enclosures critical to accumulation by dispossession. Put simply, property rights do not merely evolve; they are made (Weaver 2003). Somewhat ironically and paradoxically, I found a moment when this contingency was on full display in the minority opinion in the oncomouse case, a moment where the judges were arguing for the sort of whole organism patent that Harvard had successfully obtained in the US. The judges turned to the extra-legal domain of capital investment and international economic competitiveness to argue:

> The mobility of capital and technology makes it desirable that comparable jurisdictions with comparable intellectual property legislation arrive at similar legal results. (Harvard College v Canada 2002, SCC 76, Per McLachlin C J and Major, Binnie and Arbour J J. Para B)

Though I am no lawyer or judge, I cannot imagine this recourse to mobile capital and technology is a sound basis of legal reasoning. It thereby provides a glimpse on the marshalling of broad rhetorical strategies in order to justify what is fundamentally a political intervention (whether the rights are granted or not), and thus to the open-ended character of both cases as judicial reviews of the scope of patent rights. This is also evident in the fact that, this minority opinion notwithstanding, in both decisions the SCC rejected whole organism patents of the sort endorsed in the US. How meaningful this difference is remains an open question for both speculation (see below) and subsequent observation, but it does exemplify that struggles precipitated by attempts to accumulate through dispossession can offer opportunities for openings as well as closures.

Inventing "Things"

The seemingly extra-legal reasoning evident in the minority opinion in the oncomouse case is in fact the tip of the iceberg when it comes to the collision of all manner of arguments in these cases, as the judges (and some of the interested observers) struggled to extend and limit patent rights to life. This speaks in turn to the considerable "work" required in privatizing and commodifying nature, and somewhat more abstractly, to the extra-economic ways in which discrete bits of socionature may be sustained as commodities. Some heavy discursive "lifting" (Robertson 2000, 2004) is specifically required in pursuit of the alienation, individuation, and abstraction involved in constructing the discrete "thingness" of genes and organisms, not least in order to geographically displace them (semiotically and materially) from their social and ecological context (Castree 2003). This is necessary for these discrete bits to be rendered equivalents and exchanged, but also for them to be seen as "things" invented and owned by individual inventors. Some of this work is indeed evident in the quote above, reducing what is at stake to issues of national economic competitiveness. Yet elsewhere in both decisions, both the majority and minority opinions reflect the highly complex biological, economic, political, legal, ethical and sometimes metaphysical questions surrounding exactly how a life form may be construed solely as the product and property of an autonomous inventor.

For example, in the Schmeiser case, a critical point of dissension between minority and majority opinions turned on the degree to which life forms can be considered analogous to non-biological, mechanical inventions more familiar to patent law. The issue was not only whether or not life or discrete elements of life forms (ie cells, genes, etc) can credibly be considered inventions, but also whether or not conferring exclusive rights to self-replicating organisms grants undue control over the whole. The majority argues that Schmeiser infringed upon Monsanto's patent in saving and using Roundup resistant seed because, although no patent claim can be recognized covering the whole organism

> by analogy, then, the law holds that a defendant infringes upon a patent when the defendant manufactures, seeks to use, or uses a patented part that is contained within something that is not patented ... [T]he patented genes are not merely a "part" of the plant; rather, the patented genes are present throughout the genetically modified plant ... In that

sense, the cells are somewhat analogous to Lego blocks: if an infringing use were alleged in building a structure with patented Lego blocks, it would be no bar to a finding of infringement that only the blocks were patented and not the entire structure. (Percy Schmeiser and Schmeiser Enterprises v Monsanto Canada and Monsanto Inc 2004, SCC 34, majority judgment, MacLachlin C J and Fish, para 42)

However, in the dissenting opinion authored by Justice Arbour, this analogy is rejected on the basis that life forms are distinct kinds of inventions.

there is no genuinely useful analogy between growing a plant in which every cell and every cell of its progeny are remotely traceable to the genetically modified cell and contain the chimeric gene and putting a zipper in a garment, or tires on a car or constructing with Lego blocks. The analogies are particularly weak when it is considered that the plant can subsequently grow, reproduce, and spread with no further human intervention. (Para 156)

Similarly, in the oncomouse case, the *nature* of life, and the manner in which elements of life forms may be individuated, abstracted, and alienated (discursively and legally) from the organisms of which they are a part became a subject of some disagreement. In the majority opinion, Justice Bastarache excludes Harvard's mouse, and higher life forms more generally, from the scope of the definition of invention as defined by any "art, process, machine, manufacture or composition of matter". He argues that this specific language, as opposed to defining what is patentable as "anything . . . made by man [sic]" indicates that Parliament had in mind a restrictive definition (para 158). He then writes:

Injecting the oncogene into a fertilized egg is the but-for cause of a mouse predisposed to cancer, but the process by which a fertilized egg becomes an adult mouse is a complex process, elements of which require no human intervention. The body of a mouse is composed of various ingredients or substances, but it does not consist of ingredients or substances that have been combined or mixed together by a person. Thus, I am not satisfied that the phrase "composition of matter" includes a higher life form whose genetic code has been altered in this manner. (Para 162)

The minority opinion dismisses these and related arguments with piercing sarcasm and wit:

The question, then, is what, in the Commissioner's view, is the "constituent material" of the oncomouse as a physical entity? If the oncomouse is not composed of matter, what, one might ask, are such things as oncomouse "minds" composed of? The Court's mandate is to approach this issue as a matter (that slippery word in yet another context!) of law, not murine metaphysics. In the absence of any evidence or expert assistance, the Commissioner now asks the Court to take judicial notice of the oncomouse, if I may use Arthur Koestler's phrase, as a "ghost in a machine" but this pushes the scope of judicial notice too far. (Harvard College v Canada 2002, SCC 76, Binnie dissenting opinion at para 45)

This exchange is singular. Clearly, there is a debate over life itself at stake here, and in particular, whether or not life is a mere "composition of matter" consistent with the patent act's definition. The somewhat predictable argument turns on one opinion opposed to patenting whole organisms because life must be more than the sum of its parts, and in counterpoint, an opinion embracing what might be conceptualized as a sort of high modernist or unbounded embrace of reductionist science. Indeed, the minority opinion in the same exchange goes on to chastise the majority opinion as presenting a threat to "the patentability of scientific invention at the dawn of the third Millennium" (ibid).

Yet, there is something distinctly dissatisfying about the terms of the debate as constituted here, debating metaphysics at the expense of considering the extent to which the materiality of life can be exhausted by human invention. That is, if life is a mere composition of matter, it does not follow that science can fully know, bound, or contain this matter in all its complexity, much less so if the changes in question amount to the insertion of individual genes and gene constructs. Add to this that prior human transformations of this "mere composition of matter" only make the myth of the autonomous inventor even harder to sustain. In this light, it is tempting to speculate over the majority opinion's note that "Researchers who wish to use a wild mouse can catch one in the parking lot. Harvard would have no complaint" (Harvard College v Canada 2002, SCC 76, Binnie dissenting opinion at para 97). Could patents be a way not only of protecting engineered natures against illicit human reproduction, but also as a way of reining in the potentially transgressive action of biophysical processes, lest unchecked reproduction lead to the trespass of an oncomouse in the parking lot?

Exception to the fictions of autonomous invention based on its discursive erasure of prior ecological production was a key theme among NGOs who opposed patent rights to life forms in these cases. This is exemplified by Michelle Swanarchuk, writing on behalf of the Canadian Environmental Law Association:

> An animal such as a transgenic mouse has been changed from its natural progenitors by human intervention, but the mouse into which a novel gene has been introduced, with its complexity and myriad natural qualities, *is a product of nature*. (Swanarchuk 2003:5, emphasis added)

One factum submitted in the Schmeiser case made similar points, but noted also how the contributions of prior *social* labour are ignored (dispossessed) by the heroic narrative of a single human inventor:

> When Monsanto's chimeric gene is inserted into a canola plant cell, it becomes one of approximately 40,000 genes that comprise the genome of that plant. The genetically modified genes and cells at issue contribute nothing to the germination, growth, maturation, or seed production of the plant into which they may be or become incorporated ... Indeed, it is plant breeding and selection by generations of farmers which has over time contributed to the value of an agricultural plant such as canola. In North America, the genome of many other agricultural plants are also the product of decades of public investment in plant selection and breeding. (Council of Canadians, Action Group on Erosion Technology and Concentration et al 2003, para 15 and 16).

One of the striking implications of this later quote is that it points (implicitly) to something akin to socionature, that is, a transformed and produced nature, as opposed to some transcendent, external, first, or universal connotation of nature. The lineage of Monsanto's canola but also of the oncomouse helps to fill this out. Canola is in some ways the archetypal Green Revolution crop, having been intentionally refined in the early 1970s by publicly supported Canadian agricultural breeding efforts seeking to generate a variety of rapeseed whose oil is digestible for humans and livestock alike (Busch et al 1994; Tanaka et al 1999). The term "canola" is a neologism derived from "Canadian Oil Low Acid", first registered as a trademark term by the Western Canadian Oilseed Crushers' Association. The canola variety of rapeseed has proved a boon to the processed food industry as well as to the industrial livestock feed business in some measure because of its specific material properties, including in particular high oil and protein content and low acidity in the seeds, as well as extremely low levels of saturation in oils derived from crushing the seeds. Though scarcely three decades old, canola is now the world's second most significant source of vegetable oil after soy (Food and Agriculture Organization of the United Nations 2006), and it is one of the staple crops of Canada's agro-industrial complex. Canada is far and away the world leader in acreage committed to GM canola, accounting for an estimated 89% of the world's total in 2004 (Clive 2004).

In parallel, the oncomouse, though significantly transformed by Harvard researchers, is but one variety of the legion of lab rodents bred specifically for research. Notwithstanding references in the minority opinion to catching mice "in the parking lot", the oncomouse is better understood as a special category of companion species whose existence is inextricably linked to our own (Haraway 1997), and specifically, to biomedical efforts to better understand disease in humans via proxy research. This nature is social in part because of the degree to which breeding and production of rodents for research is a business unto itself—and in this respect, who can quibble with Justice William Binnie when he noted that "mice are already commodities" (Harvard College v Canada 2002, SCC 76, Binnie dissenting opinion at para 100)? This is in itself a highly suggestive insight, though perhaps not only in the way it was intended to be. If mice are already commodities, then what makes Harvard's changes sufficient to warrant a patent where other mice breeders have been denied such rights?

Worrying over the *socionatures* at stake in these cases is important, but there are ambiguities in doing so as political strategy. Recognizing and contesting the alienation of ecological production as ostensibly discrete "things" are claimed as inventions by would-be exclusive patent holders is vital. It is an important check on the ways in which the autonomous invention deepens "genetic reductionism" (McAfee 2003), robbing biophysical processes of their rightful role in the production and reproduction of canola and oncomice. It also resonates with more populist and public concerns about the commodification of life, and it is important to support these struggles (see eg Rifkin 1998). And yet, in addition to prior and ongoing biophysical contributions to reproducing canola and the oncomouse, there are also prior and ongoing social contributions, including purchased labour power. These too render problematic any claim of exclusive invention and thus ownership.

Seeing both the "matter" of non-human nature but also the socially constructed meanings ascribed to this non-human world as socionatures has become a widespread preoccupation in critical environmental scholarship (see eg Cronon 1995; Demeritt 2002; Whatmore 2002), but the issue is more than a language problem surrounding the description of discrete socionatures like canola and the oncomouse. Rather, problematizing the mythology of the autonomous inventor by recourse to *socionature* as opposed to an external, objective, or universal sense of non-human nature has far-reaching consequences if all inventions and commodities are in part embodiments of prior social and biophysical contributions, as they surely must be. And while considerable difference of judicial opinion is apparent in both cases, this is based on substantial agreement that the issue is whether or not life presents special problems for patent doctrine; the doctrine itself is not in question. Thus, for Justice Arbour, the crucial difference between canola and Lego is that canola is self-reproducing. But can this distinction truly hold if a more relational and expansive notion of socionature is embraced? Proudhon's observation of the fine line between property and theft (dispossession) remains a productive entrée.

Conclusion

By way of conclusion, I would like to reflect somewhat on the specifics of these cases, and to consider some of the more explicitly normative issues raised by them. One of the most striking aspects of the oncomouse case is the way in which commodification seems to make for strange bedfellows. Here, the vanguard of a more complete privatization of life forms is Harvard College. Certainly, Harvard's role here is emblematic of neoliberal era reconfigurations of university–industry–state relations, and of social relations to nature via the commercialization of biotechnology and associated realms of technoscience. Yet it is also a caution against overly simplistic and economistic suggestions that would flatten the ideas of commodification and accumulation by dispossession by seeing them as things that "capitalists" do. Commodification, privatization, and accumulation by dispossession are irreducibly social and political processes, contingent upon and conditioned by complex configurations of social actors, including the state. In the Harvard case, the College has on the one hand sought to develop the technology and to patent it in order to leverage funds for research, both through direct royalties to be gained from licensing, and on the other hand, by awarding commercial partnerships and inviting new ones through the promise of shares in these same royalties. If the mouse is to be used by Harvard researchers and their exclusive partners, seeking patent protection is hardly classic capital accumulation in as much as the mouse represents not only exchange but also use value to its producer. At the same time, Harvard's controversial arrangement with DuPont in providing (aka selling) the latter an exclusive right to license the oncomouse for use in research suggests that "academic capitalism" (Slaughter and Leslie 1997) is hardly a stretch (see Marshall 2002).

In the Schmeiser case, romantic depictions of Percy Schmeiser as the hero in his fight against Monsanto, particularly vis-à-vis his defense of farmers' rights to save seed, somewhat disguise the degree to which this case can also be read as a fight over the dissolution of petty commodity production. The conventional canola grown by Schmeiser before 1996 was also a commodity, and he a commodity producer, albeit in the vein characteristic of intensive, (nominally) independent family farming. The shift, then, from a more common to a more closed property regime vis-à-vis canola germplasm is more of a consolidation of nature's commodification and the capacity for capital to circulate through biophysical nature in agriculture, tendencies that are longstanding and uneven (Goodman, Sorj and Wilkinson 1987; Kautsky 1988; Kloppenburg 2004) but by no means wholly new. In short, this is not the commodification of nature de novo.

Finally, and also somewhat in response to Castree's (2003) urge for more explicit normative argumentation regarding the commodification of nature, I would like to close with some (brief) discussion of more personal views on these specific cases. In one sense, it is easy to be critical of efforts to privatize and commodify genes and whole organisms, and I doubt very much that many of this volume's readers will find it hard to be skeptical of the efforts at enclosure mounted here by Monsanto and Harvard. Each offers normative arguments in their defense. Monsanto, in response to critics of its global biotechnology strategy, has rolled out a slick campaign around retaining profitability and improving efficiency in the agriculture sector (and thus invoking the sacred cow of agrarian populism, the family farm), while at the same time claiming to reduce the economic and environmental costs of food production (see http://www.monsanto.com/monsanto/layout/default.asp). The claim that commercial biotechnology is actually increasing yields and reducing the costs of food has been subject to serious critique by activists and academics alike, and although there are nuances, Monsanto's claims to legitimacy fly in the face of reason given the company's role in deepening productivist agriculture, and of reinforcing the industrial appropriation of on-farm production, subordinating farmers to agro-industrial capital. Moreover, Monsanto's PR campaign contradicts serious scholarship indicating time and again that food shortages are socially mediated by (mal)distribution, and that on a global basis, there is no shortage of food. In this context, I do not find it hard to oppose Monsanto's claims not only that the company has invented whole organisms, but also specific gene constructs, and I do not feel at all ambivalent in my opposition to efforts at enclosing the genetic foundations of the global food system led by agricultural and pharmaceutical companies. It strikes me that, if anything, Monsanto's own championing of the possibilities opened by genetic engineering, including a new generation of so-called "pharm" crops, reinforce what for some has been an old theme in the biotech debate: the problem is not the technologies themselves, but rather the social relations and imperatives that develop and sustain them (see eg Kloppenburg 2004).

   If there is ambivalence I feel in relation to the Monsanto case, it has to do with the particularisms seemingly required to oppose the company's claims. While some opinions on the Court and among the civil society groups that mobilized around this case found comfort in differentiating between patents over genes, and patents over organisms, exclusive ownership of genes seems to me to be a thin edge to the wedge for exclusive ownership of plant and animal varieties. I find little comfort that neither Monsanto nor Harvard obtained whole organism patents in these cases, and indeed whether or not their product and process patents give each de facto rights over whole organisms remains a tension evident within the cases. Schmeiser's lawyers pushed this issue unsuccessfully, but a strong minority opinion held that Monsanto's product and process patents effectively conferred whole organism ownership in all but name. The issue may not be fully resolved from a legal standpoint in Canada, and time will tell if patents to parts inseparable from (or useless without) the wholes are any difference from patents to the wholes. But it bears repeating that this renders patents over specific genes no less problematic. These are discoveries, not inventions. I thus support the important work being done by environmentalists, farm groups, religious organizations, academics and others around the world who oppose the corporate biotechnology agenda of enclosing genetic diversity as private property. Nevertheless, I am ambivalent about the longer term efficacy of this exceptionalism if it requires recourse to ideas of an external and universal nature, as noted above. Opposition to life patents as domains of exception tends to leave unexamined the thorny issue of how *any* patent is justified given the fictions of autonomous invention. To me these cases strongly suggest that the entire exercise of awarding patents turns on hair-splitting in order to discursively and institutionally produce discrete "things", sever them from contending use values via state sanction of exclusive property rights, and thereby allow them to circulate as exchange values. These may be necessary fictions, but they are no less fictions.

In the Harvard case, it is slightly more difficult to feel clearly about what is "the right thing". I am cynical of Harvard's intentions here, driven as they are by a degree of entrepreneurialism that seems crass to say the least. Looking back to 1975 when Harvard reversed its commitment to open access provision of health-related research findings, one can argue this reversal is about securing adequate return for the university's investments in research during an era of declining and threatened public commitments to research, particularly of the basic variety (Wright 1994). In this sense, how is Harvard's insistence on profiting from its oncomouse wrong? In addition, advocates for granting the oncomouse patent argue that Canada will suffer in relation to the United States if denial of the patent means that potentially path-breaking cancer research will not be conducted in Canada because Harvard will not make the mouse available. I lost a close friend to cancer recently. It may well be that additional deaths or morbidity from cancer, a disease that increasingly touches most of our lives, will result if Harvard does indeed deny the use of the oncomouse in Canada. At the same time, there is no evidence so far that Harvard has actually withdrawn the mouse from circulation north of the border, likely because the process patents governing production of the oncomouse in Canada upheld in the case will suffice to protect their investment. And anyone who wants to defend Harvard's insistence on profiting from the oncomouse will have to address whether or not the University's financial or academic standing was really under threat in 1975, not to mention whether an institution with an endowment now just shy of US$26 billion can credibly cry poor.

Acknowledgements

This research was supported by the Social Sciences and Humanities Research Council of Canada under a standard research grant as well as via a Major Collaborative Research Initiative entitled "Globalization and

Autonomy". Thanks to William Coleman for conversations specifically regarding biotech and property rights, and to Morgan Robertson, Noel Castree, and Erik Swyngedouw for (hopefully ongoing) conversations about the commodification of nature. I am grateful to Emily Eaton, Paul Jackson, Mark Kear, Becky Mansfield, Melissa Wright, Kathy McAfee, Roger Picton, Neil Smith, Tom Young and two anonymous reviewers for helpful comments on an earlier draft. Any errors or ambiguities in this version are my exclusive responsibility.

Endnotes

[1] I remain agnostic about the ontological character of value, and in particular, about the labour theory of value. For my purposes here, I would argue this is not crucial. What is crucial is Marx's view that the competitive dynamics of capital accumulation are inherently expansionary and propel a constant search for new avenues of circulation and realization. For concise elaboration, see Harvey (1982).

[2] Lysandrou actually places considerable emphasis on deepening as the tendency toward commodification of labour power. However, as he also notes (and drawing on Marx), dispossession of the means for reproducing labour power, requisite for the commodification of labour power, turns in large part on the provision of the means of social reproduction as commodities.

[3] I take these terms from Castree's (2003) discussion of some of the different facets of the commodification of nature. He also argues that privatization, displacement and valuation are required. Obviously, privatization is a key concern in the paper. I leave the questions of displacement and valuation largely unexplored.

[4] Ghost writing involves staff with private firms writing up all or significant portions of journal articles and publishing them under the authorship of academics. The practice is widespread in medicine.

[5] Olivieri discovered health risks associated with a drug called deferiprone in the course of conducting her industry-sponsored clinical trials of the drug involving patients suffering from thalassemia, a serious blood disease. Apotex, the manufacturer of the drug and sponsor of the trials, threatened legal action against Olivieri should she disclose the information. She published her findings in 1998 and was then subjected to a public campaign aimed at discrediting her. The University of Toronto rather belatedly came to her defense after being pressed by the University of Toronto Faculty Association and the Canadian Association of University Teachers. See Thompson, Baird and Downie (2005).

References

Angell M (2004) *The Truth about Drug Companies: How They Deceive Us and What to Do About It.* New York: Random House

Arrighi G (1994) *The Long Twentieth Century: Money, Power, and the Origins of Our Times.* London and New York: Verso

Bakker K (2003). *An Uncooperative Commodity: Privatizing Water in England and Wales.* Oxford and New York: Oxford University Press

Bakker K (2005) Neoliberalizing nature? Market environmentalism in water supply in England and Wales. *Annals of the Association of American Geographers* 95(3):542–565

Bakker K and Bridge G (2006) Material worlds? Resource geographies and the "matter of nature". *Progress in Human Geography* 30(1):5–27

Bridge G (2000) The social regulation of resource access and environmental impact: Nature and contradiction in the US copper industry. *Geoforum* 31(2):237–256

Bridge G, McManus P and Marsden T (2003) The next new thing? Biotechnology and its discontents. *Geoforum* 34(2):165–174

Busch L (1991) *Plants, Power, and Profit: Social, Economic, and Ethical Consequences of the New Biotechnologies*. Cambridge, MA: Blackwell

Busch L, Gunter V, Mentele T, Tachikawa M and Tanaka K (1994) Socializing nature: Technoscience and the transformation of rapeseed into canola. *Crop Science* 34(3):607–614

Buttel F (1989) How epoch-making are high technologies? The case of biotechnology. *Sociological Forum* 4(2):247–261

Buttel F (2003) The global politics of geos: The Achilles' heel of the globalization regime? In Schurman R and Kelso D D T (eds) *Engineering Trouble: Biotechnology and its Discontents* (pp 152–173). Berkeley, CA: University of California Press

Castree N (2003) Commodifying what nature? *Progress in Human Geography* 27(3):273–297

Clive J (2004) Global status of commercialized transgenic crops: 2003. http://www.agbiotechnet.com/ Accessed 18 February 2005

Council of Canadians, Action Group on Erosion Technology and Concentration, Sierra Club of Canada, National Farmers Union, Research Foundation for Science Technology and Ecology and I. C. f. T. Assessment (2003) Factum of the intervenors. Percy Schmeiser and Schmeiser Enterprises Ltd v Monsanto Canada Inc and Monsanto Company. Supreme Court of Canada, Court File Number 29437

Cronon W (1991) *Nature's Metropolis: Chicago and the Great West*. New York: W W Norton

Cronon W (1995) The trouble with wilderness or getting back to the wrong nature. In Cronon W (ed) *Uncommon Ground: Toward Reinventing Nature* (pp 69–90). New York: W W Norton & Co

Demeritt D (2002) What is the "social construction of nature"? A typology and sympathetic critique. *Progress in Human Geography* 26(6):767–790.

Food and Agriculture Organization of the United Nations (2006) Faostat. http://faostat.fao.org/ Accessed 2 April 2006

Glassman J (2006) Primitive accumulation, accumulation by dispossession, accumulation by "extra-economic" means. *Progress in Human Geography* 30(5):608–625

Goodman D, Sorj B and Wilkinson J (1987) *From Farming to Biotechnology: A Theory of Agro-industrial Development*. Oxford and New York: Blackwell

Government of Canada Industry Canada (1998) *The 1998 Canadian Biotechnology Strategy: An Ongoing Renewal Process*. Ottawa: Industry Canada

Haraway D J (1991) *Simians, Cyborgs and Women: The Reinvention of Nature*. New York: Routledge

Haraway D J (1997) *Modest Witness@Second millennium FemaleMan Meets Oncomouse: Feminism and Technoscience*. New York: Routledge

Harvey D (1982) *The Limits to Capital*. Oxford: Blackwell

Harvey D (1989) The Condition of Postmodernity: An Enquiry into the Origins of Cultural Change. Oxford, UK and Cambridge, MA: Blackwell

Harvey D (1996) *Justice, Nature, and the Geography of Difference*. Cambridge, MA: Blackwell

Harvey D (2003) *The New Imperialism*. Oxford and New York: Oxford University Press

Harvey D (2005) *A Brief History of Neoliberalism*. Oxford: Oxford University Press

Hughes S (2001) Making dollars out of DNA: The first major patent in biotechnology and the commercialization of molecular biology, 1974–1980. *Isis* 92(3):541–575

Jessop B (2001) Regulationist and autopoieticist reflections on Polanyi's account of market economies and the market society. *New Political Economy* 6(2):213–232

Jessop B (2002) Liberalism, neoliberalism, and urban governance: A state–theoretical perspective. *Antipode* 34(3):452–472

Kautsky K (1988) *The Agrarian Question*. London and Winchester, MA: Zwan Publications

Kenney M (1986) *Biotechnology: The University–Industrial Complex*. New Haven: Yale University Press

Kenney M (1998) Biotechnology and the creation of a new economic space. In Thackray A (ed) *Private Science: Biotechnology and the Rise of the Molecular Sciences* (pp 131–143). Philadelphia: University of Pennsylvania Press

Kevles D (1998) Diamond v. Chakrabarty and beyond: The political economy of patenting life. In Thackray A (ed) *Private Science: Biotechnology and the Rise of the Molecular Sciences* (pp 65–79). Philadelphia: University of Pennsylvania Press

Kloppenburg J R (2004) *First the Seed: The Political Economy of Plant Biotechnology*. 2nd ed. Madison, WI: University of Wisconsin Press

Krimsky S (2003) *Science in the Private Interest*. Lanham: Bowman and Littlefield

Latour B (1993) *We Have Never Been Modern*. Brighton: Harvester Wheatsheaf.

Lysandrou P (2005) Globalisation as commodification. *Cambridge Journal of Economics* 29(5):769–797

Mansfield B (2003) From catfish to organic fish: Making distinctions about nature as cultural economic practice. *Geoforum* 34(3):329–342

Marshall E (2002) Dupont ups ante on use of Harvard's oncomouse. *Science* 296(5571):1212

Marx K (1977) *Capital: A Critique of Political Economy*. New York: Vintage Books

McAfee K (2003) Neoliberalism on the molecular scale. Economic and genetic reductionism in biotechnology battles. *Geoforum* 34(2):203–219

McCarthy J (2004) Privatizing conditions of production: Trade agreements as neoliberal environmental governance. *Geoforum* 35(3):327–341

McCarthy J and Prudham S (2004) Neoliberal nature and the nature of neoliberalism. *Geoforum* 35(3):275–283

Peck J and Tickell A (2002) Neoliberalizing space. *Antipode* 34(3):380–404

Polanyi K (1944) *The Great Transformation: The Political and Economic Origins of Our Time*. Boston: Beacon Press

Prudham S and Morris A (2006) Making the market "safe" for GM foods: The case of the Canadian Biotechnology Advisory Committee. *Studies in Political Economy* 78(Autumn): 145–175

Prudham W S (2005) *Knock on Wood: Nature as Commodity in Douglas-Fir Country*. New York: Routledge

Rifkin J (1998) *The Biotech Century: Harnessing the Gene and Remaking the World*. New York: Jeremy P Tarcher/Putnam

Robertson M (2000) No net loss: Wetland restoration and the incomplete capitalization of nature. *Antipode* 32(4):463–493

Robertson M (2004) The neoliberalization of ecosystem services: Wetland mitigation banking and problems in environmental governance. *Geoforum* 35:361–373

Robertson M (2006) The nature that capital can see: Science, state, and market in the commodification of ecosystem services. *Environment and Planning D: Society and Space* 24:367–387

Slaughter S and Leslie L L (1997) *Academic Capitalism: Politics, Policies, and the Entrepreneurial University*. Baltimore: Johns Hopkins University Press

Smith N (1984) *Uneven Development: Nature, Capital, and the Production of Space*. Oxford: Basil Blackwell

Smith N (1996) The production of nature. In Robertson G, Mash M, Tickner L, Bird J, Curtis B and Putnam T (eds) *Future/Natural: Nature/Science/Culture* (pp 33–54). London: Routledge

Swenarchuk M (2003) *The Harvard Mouse and all That: Life Patents in Canada.* Toronto: Publisher Canadian Environmental Law Association Publication #454

Swyngedouw E (1999) Modernity and hybridity: Nature, regeneracionismo, and the production of the Spanish waterscape, 1890–1930. *Annals of the Association of American Geographers* 89(3):443–465

Tanaka K, Juska A and Busch L (1999) Globalization of agricultural production and use: The case of the rapeseed sector. *Sociologia Ruralis* 39(1):54–77

Thackray A (ed) (1998) *Private Science: Biotechnology and the Rise of the Molecular Sciences.* Philadelphia: University of Pennsylvania Press

Thompson J, Baird P and Downie J (2005) The Olivieri case: Context and significance. *Ecclectica,* December

Thrift N (2000) Commodity. In Johnston R J, Gregory D, Pratt G and Watts M (eds) *The Dictionary of Human Geography* (pp 95–96). Malden, MA: Blackwell

Weaver J C (2003) *The Great Land Rush and the Making of the Modern World, 1650–1900.* Montreal: McGill-Queen's University Press

Whatmore S (2002) *Hybrid Geographies: Natures, Cultures, Spaces.* Thousand Oaks, CA: Sage

Wright S (1994) *Molecular Politics: Developing American and British Regulatory Policy for Genetic Engineering, 1972–1982.* Chicago: University of Chicago Press

Chapter 2

The "Commons" Versus the "Commodity": Alter-globalization, Anti-privatization and the Human Right to Water in the Global South

Karen Bakker

Prologue

On a rainy Friday in 2003, the world's Water and Environment Ministers met in Kyoto to discuss the global water crisis. While Ministers met behind closed doors, participants at the parallel public World Water Forum were presented with alarming statistics: water scarcity had been growing in many regions; and over 20% the world's population was without access to sufficient supplies of potable water necessary for basic daily needs. In response, conference organizers had drafted an Inter-Ministerial declaration, based upon the view that the best response to increasing scarcity was the commercialization of water. International support for the commercialization of water supply had been growing since the controversial Dublin Statement on Water and Sustainable Development in 1992.[1] In light of endemic "state failure" by governments supposedly too poor, corrupt, or inept to manage water supply systems, increased involvement of the private sector in water supply management was openly advocated by many conference participants.

Reflecting this shift in international water policy, private water companies had been invited to meet with government delegations, international financial institutions, and bilateral aid agencies to develop solutions to the world's water problems. Yet many of the governments represented at the conference had themselves been accused of irresponsible water management by their citizens. The government of South Africa, for example, had continued to support the Lesotho Highlands Water Project (the largest in Africa), despite the participation of its then-Minister for Water Affairs in the high-profile World Commission on Dams which comprehensively reviewed—and condemned—the social, environmental, and economic record of large dams around the world (Bond 2002). The private water companies in attendance at Kyoto were similarly targeted by activists, with corporations such as Enron under attack by an international alliance of anti-dam activists, environmentalists, public sector unions, international "bank-watcher" and "anti-globalization" think tanks, indigenous peoples, and civil society groups. These self-named "water warriors" protested both inside and outside the Forum, critiquing the Forum co-organizers (the Global Water Partnership and the World Water Council) for their close ties to private water companies and international financial institutions, and for an unrepresentative, opaque, and illegitimate process (ironically, similar critiques were directed by the Forum organizers at activists).

Activists' protests culminated with the disruption of a planned highlight of the Forum—a plenary session chaired by Michel Camdessus (former head of the IMF) promoting active government support for increased private sector involvement in the water sector in the South (Winpenny 2003). Chanting "water is life", activists stormed the stage and demanded the withdrawal of the private sector, a return to local "water democracy", a rejection of large dams as socio-economically and environmentally unsound, and a recognition of water as a human right. Yet activists' calls fell largely on deaf ears. Southern and northern ministerial delegates reached consensus; including, controversially, support for private sector financing, new mechanisms for private sector involvement in water supply management, and a conspicuous failure to refer to water as a human right.

Introduction: The Triumph of Market Environmentalism?

The Kyoto Declaration embodies an increasingly dominant philosophy of development, variously termed "liberal environmentalism" (Bernstein 2001), "green neoliberalism" (Goldman 2005), or market environmentalism (Bakker 2004): a mode of resource regulation which aims to deploy markets as the solution to environmental problems (Anderson and Leal 2001). Market environmentalism offers hope of a virtuous fusion of economic growth, efficiency, and environmental conservation: through establishing private property rights, employing markets as allocation mechanisms, and incorporating environmental externalities through pricing, proponents of market environmentalism assert that environmental goods will be more efficiently allocated if treated as economic goods—thereby simultaneously addressing concerns over environmental degradation and inefficient use of resources.

Critical research on market environmentalism frames this paradigm as the "neoliberalization of nature" (Bridge 2004; Mansfield 2004a; McAfee 2003; McCarthy 2004; McCarthy and Prudham 2004; Perrault 2006; Prudham 2004). The majority of this research focuses on the negative impacts of neoliberal reforms, including both environmental impacts and the distributional implications of the various forms of "accumulation by dispossession" enacted by neoliberalization (Glassman 2006), although some research also suggests that states can rationally administer environmental degradation and resource appropriation from local communities (Scott 1998), or that environmental improvements can occur in the context of state re-regulation which accompanies privatization (Angel 2000; Bakker 2005).

This debate is particularly acute in the water sector. The increasing involvement of private, for-profit multinational water corporations in running networked water supply systems around the world has inspired fierce debate internationally (see, for example, Finger and Allouche 2002; Johnstone and Wood 2003; Laurie and Marvin 1999; Swyngedouw 2005).[2] Proponents of market environmentalism in the water sector argue that water is an increasingly scarce resource, which must be priced at full economic and environmental cost if it is to be allocated to its highest-value uses, and managed profitably by private companies whose accountability to customers and shareholders is more direct and effective than attenuated political accountability exercised by citizens via political representatives (Rogers et al 2003; Winpenny 1994). Opponents of market environmentalism argue that water is a non-substitutable resource essential for life, and call for water supply to be recognized as a human right, which (they argue) both places an onus upon states to provide water to all, and precludes private sector involvement (see, for example, Bond 2002; Goldman 2005; Johnston, Gismondi and Goodman 2006; Laxer and Soron 2006; Morgan 2004b).

Several conceptual questions underlie this debate. Is water a human right? If so, is private sector provision incompatible with the human right to water? What is the relationship between property rights regimes and privatization? And how can we best conceptualize and mobilize alternatives to neoliberalization? This paper explores these questions, documenting the different constructions of property rights adopted by pro- and anti-privatization advocates, questioning the utility of the language of "human rights", and interrogating the accuracy of the (often unquestioned) binaries—rights/commodities, public/private, citizen/customer—deployed by both sides of the debate. In doing so, the paper undertakes two tasks: the development of a conceptual framework of market environmentalist reforms; and the application of this framework to the case of water supply.

The first part of the paper develops a typology of market environmentalist reforms in resource management, arguing that conceptual confusion frequently arises due to a lack of analytical precision about the wide range of ongoing reforms that are often over-simplified into a monolithic (and inaccurately labelled) "neoliberalism". The second section examines one example of these conceptual confusions: the positioning of "human rights" as an antonym to "commodities" by anti-privatization campaigners. After documenting the tactical failures of such an approach, the paper contrasts "anti-privatization" campaigns with "alter-globalization" movements engaged in the construction of alternative community economies and culture of water, centred on concepts such as the commons and "water democracies". In this third section of the paper, an attempt is made to complicate the public/private, commodity/rights, citizen/customer binaries underpinning much of the debate, through exploring the different socio-economic identities of citizens, and different property rights, invoked under different water management models around the world. In the concluding section, the conceptual and political implications of this analysis are teased out, focusing on the implications of this analysis for our understandings of "neoliberal natures".

Neoliberal Reforms and Resource Management: Clarifying the Debate

Much of the literature on "neoliberalizing nature" is concerned with the creation of private property rights for resources previously governed as common pool resources.[3] Of particular interest have been the impacts of "neoliberalism" on specific resources (Bakker 2000, 2001; Bradshaw 2004; Bridge 2004; Bridge and Jonas 2002; Bridge, McManus and Marsden 2003; Gibbs and Jonas 2000; Johnston 2003; Maddock 2004; Mansfield 2004a, 2004b; McAfee 2003; Robertson 2004; Smith 2004; Walker et al 2000). As Noel Castree notes in his review of this literature (Castree 2005), much of this work has emphasized case-specific analyses of very different types of processes broadly grouped under the rather nebulous banner of neoliberalization: privatization, marketization, deregulation, reregulation, commercialization, and corporatization, to name just a few.

Although Castree acknowledges the utility of this work in illustrating that "neoliberalism" is actually constituted of a range of diverse, locally rooted practices of neoliberalization, he identifies two analytical traps: failure to identify criteria by which different cases of neoliberalizing nature can be deemed sufficiently similar in order to conduct comparisons; and the occlusion of distinct types of neoliberal practices when subsumed under the broad (and overly general) label of neoliberalism. This paper responds to Castree's call for analytical frameworks with which to clarify these issues. As Sparke notes in a recent review (2006), this task is both analytically and politically crucial, insofar as the ideal types to which some of this work falls prey risk reinforcing or even reproducing the idealism of neoliberalism itself.

In developing such an analytical framework, an iterative approach is required which articulates (and revises) conceptual frameworks of neoliberalization (as a higher-order abstraction) and empirical analysis of the contingent mediation of neoliberal agendas by historically and geographically specific material conditions and power relations. In undertaking this analysis, it is important to distinguish between three categories of resource management upon which neoliberal reforms can be undertaken. Resource management *institutions* are the laws, policies, rules, norms and customs by which resources are governed. Resource management *organizations* are the collective social entities that govern resource use. And resource management *governance* is the process by which organizations enact management institutions; the practices by which, in other words, we construct and administer the exploitation of resources (Table 1).

As illustrated in Table 1, reforms can be undertaken in distinct categories, and are not necessarily concomitant; one may privatize without deregulating; deregulate without marketizing; and commercialize without privatizing, etc (Bakker 2004). To give a simple example: privatization of the water supply industry in England and Wales in 1989 did not entail marketization; that is, it did not entail the introduction of markets in water abstraction licenses. This example illustrates one of the main confusions which arises in the literature: reforms to institutions, organizations, and governance are all subsumed under the general term "neoliberalization", despite the fact that they often involve very different types of reforms, applied to different aspects of resource management. Another source of confusion arises when different types of reforms are assumed to be interchangeable, and when distinct terms (marketization, privatization) are assumed to be synonymous, when they are not.

How is such a typological exercise helpful in either analysis or activism? First, the failure to distinguish between categories of resource management, and between targets and types of reforms, obscures the specificity of the reform processes which are the object of analysis, and limits our ability to compare cases, as Castree has noted. For example, comparing the introduction of water rights for "raw" water (water in nature) (Haddad 2000) in California to private sector participation in water supply management in New York (Gandy 2002) is of limited interest, because two distinct processes are at work (marketization versus private sector participation). In contrast, comparing the introduction of water markets in Chile (Bauer 1998) and California (Haddad 2000) is worthwhile, because in both cases private property rights for water supply have been introduced via a process of marketization of water resource allocation. In short, the typology presented in Table 1 is analytically useful because it enables us to correctly compare different types of market environmentalist reforms, and to more accurately characterize their goals and evaluate their outcomes.

This typology is also useful in addressing the widespread failure to adequately distinguish between different elements of neoliberal reform processes, an analytical sloppiness that diminishes our ability to correctly characterize the aims and trajectories of neoliberal projects of resource management reform (Bakker 2005). Commercialization, for

Table 1: Resource management reforms: examples from the water sector

Category	Target of reform	Type of reform	Example drawn from the water sector
Resource management institutions	Property rights	Privatization (enclosure of the commons or asset sale)	Introduction of riparian rights (England; Hassan 1998); or sale of water supply infrastructure to private sector (England and Wales; Bakker 2004)
	Regulatory frameworks	De-regulation	Cessation of direct state oversight of water quality mechanisms (Ontario, Canada; Prudham 2004)
Resource management organizations	Asset management	Private sector 'partnerships' (outsourcing contracts)	French municipal outsourcing of water supply system management to private companies (Lorrain 1997)
	Organizational structure	Corporatization	Conversion of business model for municipal water supply: from local government department to a publicly owned corporation (Amsterdam, The Netherlands; Blokland, Braadbaart and Schwartz 2001)
Resource governance	Resource allocation	Marketization	Introduction of a water market (Chile; Bauer 1998)
	Performance incentives/ sanctions	Commercialization	Introduction of commercial principles (eg full cost recovery) in water management (South Africa; McDonald and Ruiters 2005)
	User participation	Devolution or decentralization	Devolving water quality monitoring to lower orders of government or individual water users (Babon River, Indonesia; Susilowati and Budiati 2003)

example, often precedes privatization in the water supply sector, which is sometimes followed by attempts to commodify water. The biophysical properties of resources, together with local governance frameworks, strongly influence the types of neoliberal reforms which are likely to be introduced: common-pool, mobile resources such as fisheries are more amenable to marketization, whereas natural monopolies such as water supply networks are more amenable to privatization (Bakker 2004). In other words, in failing to exercise sufficient analytical precision in analyzing processes of "neoliberalizing nature", we are likely to misinterpret the reasons for, and incorrectly characterize the pathway of specific neoliberal reforms.

As explored in subsequent sections of the paper, this typology may also be useful in clarifying activist strategies, and in structuring our analyses of activism and advocacy. For example, in much of the literature on "neoliberal nature" (and in many NGO and activist campaigning documents), water as a "commodity" is contrasted to water as a "human right". Careful conceptualization of the neoliberalization of water demonstrates that this is misleading, insofar as the term "commodity" refers to a property rights regime applicable to resources, and human rights to a legal category applicable to individuals. The more appropriate, but less widely used, antonym of water as a "commodity" would more properly be a water "commons". As explored in the following sections, this distinction has had significant implications for the success of "anti-privatization" and "alter-globalization" struggles around the world.

Debating Neoliberalization: Anti-privatization Campaigns and the "Human Right to Water"

The international campaign for a human right to water has grown enormously over the past decade. This campaign has its roots in the arguments of anti-privatization campaigners, who have fought numerous campaigns to resist, and then overturn water privatization projects around the world. Advocates of private sector involvement in water supply—private companies, bilateral aid agencies, and many governments—argue that it will increase efficiency, and deliver water to those who currently lack access. They point to the failure of governments and aid agencies to achieve the goal of universal water supply during the International Water and Sanitation Decade (1981–1990), and to the low efficiency and low levels of cost recovery of public utilities. Through efficiency gains and better management, private companies will be able to lower prices, improve performance, and increase cost recovery, enabling systems to be upgraded and expanded, critical in a world in which one billion people lack access to safe, sufficient water supplies. Privatization (the transfer of ownership of water supply systems to private companies) and private sector "partnerships" (the construction, operation and management of publicly owned water supply systems by private companies) have, it is argued, worked well in other utility sectors (see, for example, DFID 1998; Dinar 2000; Rogers et al 2002; Shirley 2002; Winpenny 2004).

This view has been strongly critiqued by those who argue that neoliberalization entails an act of dispossession with negative distributive consequences that is emblematic of "globalization from above"

(Assies 2003; Barlow and Clarke 2003; Bond 2004a; Hukka and Katko 2003; McDonald and Ruiters 2005; Petrella 2001; Shiva 2002). According to its opponents, the involvement of private companies invariably introduces a pernicious logic of the market into water management, which is incompatible with guaranteeing citizen's basic right to water. Private companies—answerable to shareholders and with the over-riding goal of profit—will manage water supply less sustainably than public sector counterparts. Opponents of privatization point to successful examples of public water systems, and on research that private sector alternatives are not necessarily more efficient, and often much more expensive for users, than well-managed public sector systems (see, for example, Estache and Rossi 2002). They assert the effectiveness of democratic accountability to citizens when compared with corporate accountability to shareholders; an argument less easy to refute following the collapse of Enron, which by the late 1990s had become one of the largest water multinationals through its subsidiary Azurix.

Opponents of water supply privatization frequently invoke a human right to water to support their claims (Gleick 1998; Hukka and Katko 2003; Morgan 2004b, 2005; Trawick 2003). The argument for creating a human right to water generally rests on two justifications: the non-substitutability of drinking water ("essential for life"), and the fact that many other human rights which are explicitly recognized in the UN Conventions are predicated upon an (assumed) availability of water (eg the right to food).

The claim to a human right to water rests on shaky legal ground: no explicit right to water is expressed in the most relevant international treaty,[4] although the UN Committee on Economic, Social and Cultural Rights[5] issued a comment in 2002, asserting that every person has a right to "sufficient, safe, acceptable, physically accessible, and affordable water" (ECOSOC 2002; Hammer 2004). Accordingly, a significant element of anti-privatization campaigning of NGOs in both the North and South has been a set of intertwined campaigns for the human right to water, beginning with a set of declarations by activists in both the North and the South,[6] and growing to include well-resourced campaigns hosted by high-profile NGOs such as Amnesty International, the World Development Movement, the Council of Canadians, the Sierra Club, Jubilee South, Mikhail Gorbachev's Green Cross and Ralph Nader's Public Citizen.[7] Activists have also focused on country-specific campaigns for constitutional and legal amendments, notably Uruguay's 2004 successful referendum resulting in a constitutional amendment creating a human right to water in 2004.

As the anti-water privatization campaign has transformed into a campaign for the human right to water, activists have gained support from mainstream international development agencies including the World Health Organization and the United Nations Development Programme

(ECOSOC 2002; UNDP 2006; UN Economic and Social Council 2003; WHO 2003). These agencies articulate several arguments in favour of the human right to water: higher political priority given to water issues; new legal avenues for citizens to compel states to supply basic water needs; and the fact that the right to water is implicit in other rights (such as the rights to food, life, health, and dignity) which have already been recognized in international law, and which are implicitly recognized through legal precedents when courts support right of non-payment for water services on grounds of lack of affordability (UNWWAP 2006).

Opponents have pointed out the difficulty of implementing a "right to water": lack of clear responsibility and capacity for implementation; the possibility of causing conflict over transboundary waters; and potential abuse of the concept as governments could over-allocate water to privileged groups, at the expense of both people and the environment. Others argue that a right to water will effect little practical change: the right to water enshrined in South Africa's post-apartheid constitution,[8] for example, has not prevented large-scale disconnections and persistent inequities in water distribution (Bond 2002; McDonald and Ruiters 2005). Another critique pertains to the anthropocentrism of human rights, which fail to recognize rights of non-humans (or ecological rights); providing a human right to water may, ironically, imply the further degradation of hydrological systems upon which we depend.

Another, more fundamental criticism is the argument that a human right to water does not foreclose private sector management of water supply systems. Critics of human rights doctrines argue that "rights talk" stems from an individualistic, libertarian philosophy that is "Eurocentric" (see, for example, Ignatieff 2003; Kymlicka 1995; Mutua 2002; Rorty 1993); as such, human rights are compatible with capitalist political economic systems. In other words, private sector provision is compatible with human rights in most countries around the world. A human right to water does not imply that water should be accessed free (although it might imply an affordable basic "lifeline" supply) (UNWWAP 2006), although this is at odds with cultural and religious views on water access in many parts of the world.[9] Indeed, the UN's Committee on Economic, Social and Cultural Rights recognized the ambivalent status which a human right conveys upon a resource when it defined water as a social, economic, and cultural good as well as a commodity (ECOSOC 2003).

Many citizens of capitalist democracies accept that commodities are not inconsistent with human rights (such as food, shelter), but that some sort of public, collective "safety net" must exist if these rights are to be met for *all* citizens. This is true for housing and food (as inadequate as these measures may be in practice). The situation with drinking water is more complicated, because drinking water is a non-substitutable resource essential for life, and because networked water supply is a natural monopoly subject to significant environmental externalities. In this case, strong market failures provide an overwhelming justification for public regulation and, in many cases, ownership of assets. Full privatization is thus inconsistent with a human right to water unless it is coupled (as it is in England) with a universality requirement (laws prohibiting disconnections of residential consumers), and with strong regulatory framework for price controls and quality standards.[10] Private sector participation in water supply, on the other hand, certainly fits within these constraints. In short rooted in a liberal tradition that prioritizes private ownership and individual rights, the current international human rights regime is flexible enough to be fully compatible with private property rights, whether for water or other basic needs.

In summary, pursuing a "human right to water" as an anti-privatization campaign makes three strategic errors: conflating human rights and property rights; failing to distinguish between different types of property rights and service delivery models; and thereby failing to foreclose the possibility of increasing private sector involvement in water supply. Indeed, the shortcomings of "human right to water" anti-privatization campaigns became apparent following the Kyoto World Water Forum, as proponents of private sector water supply management began speaking out in favour of water as a human right. Senior water industry representatives identified water as a human right on company websites, in the media[11] and at high-profile events such as the Davos World Economic Forum.[12] Right-wing think tanks such as the Cato Institute backed up these statements with reports arguing that "water socialism" had failed the poor, and that market forces, properly regulated, were the best means of fulfilling the human right to water (Bailey 2005; Segerfeldt 2005). Non-governmental organizations such as the World Water Council, regarded by anti-privatization campaigners as being allied with private companies also developed arguments in favour of water as a human right (Dubreuil 2005, 2006). Shortly after the Kyoto meeting, the World Bank released a publication acknowledging the human right to water (Salman and McInerney-Lankford 2004).

Two years later, at the Fourth World Water Forum in Mexico City in 2006, representatives of private water companies issued a statement recognizing the right to water, and recalling that the private sector had officially endorsed the right to water in 2005 at the 13th session of the UN's Commission on Sustainable Development (Aquafed 2006). At the Mexico City Forum, a somewhat contrived consensus across civil society, the private sector, and governments on the "right to water" emerged (Smets 2006). Despite dissenting views of Third World governments such as Bolivia, a "diluted" interpretation of the human right to water prevailed in the Ministerial Declaration of the Fourth World Water Forum, in regards to which private companies had an officially sanctioned role.

Ironically, this has occurred at the same time as private companies have been acknowledging the significant barriers to market expansion in the water supply sector in the South. Analysis of the discourse of the public statements of senior executives of water supply services firms reveals a retreat from earlier commitments to pursuing PSPs globally, with senior figures publicly acknowledging high risks and low profitability in supplying the poor (Robbins 2003). Some international financial institutions have begun officially acknowledging the limitations of the private sector (ADB 2003; UNDP 2003). High-profile cancellations of water supply concession contracts—including Atlanta, Buenos Aires, Jakarta, La Paz, and Manila—seem to bear out the hypothesis that water presents difficult, and perhaps intractable problems for private sector management. The private sector has indeed retreated from supplying water to communities in the South, but this has been largely due to the failure to achieve acceptable return on investment and control risk, not to anti-privatization, pro-human rights campaigns. Companies continue to insist that water is a human right, which they are both competent and willing to supply, if risk-return ratios are acceptable, but this not a condition which cannot be met by most communities.

Alter-globalization and the Commons

In reflecting on the failure of the "human right to water" campaigns to foreclose the involvement of the private sector in water supply management, we broach a question often raised by "alter-globalization" activists: how can we negotiate resistance to neoliberalization? In raising this question, alter-globalization (as distinct from anti-privatization) activists are often dismissive of human rights, arguing that "rights talk" resuscitates a public/private binary that recognizes only two unequally satisfactory options—state or market control: twinned corporatist models from which communities are equally excluded (see, for example, Olivera and Lewis 2004; Roy 1999; Shiva 2002). Instead, activists have turned to alternative concepts of property rights, most frequently some form of the "commons", to motivate their claims, juxtaposing this view to that of water as a commodity (Table 2).

At the risk of over-simplification, the commodity view asserts that private ownership and management of water supply systems (in distinction

Table 2: The commons versus commodity debate

	Commons	Commodity
Definition	Public good	Economic good
Pricing	Free or "lifeline"	Full-cost pricing
Regulation	Command and control	Market based
Goals	Social equity and livelihoods	Efficiency and water security
Manager	Community	Market

from water itself) is possible and indeed preferable. From this perspective, water is no different than other essential goods and utility services. Private companies, who will be responsive both to customers and to shareholders, can efficiently run and profitably manage water supply systems. Commercialization rescripts water as an economic good rather than a public good, and redefines users as individual customers rather than a collective of citizens. Water conservation can thus be incentivized through pricing—users will cease wasteful behaviour as water prices rise with increasing scarcity. Proponents of the "commodity" view assert that water must be treated as an economic good, as specified in the Dublin Principles and in the Hague Declaration,[13] similar to any other economic good—such as food—essential for life.

In contrast, the commons view of water asserts its unique qualities: water is a flow resource essential for life and ecosystem health; nonsubstitutable and tightly bound to communities and ecosystems through the hydrological cycle (Shiva 2002; TNI 2005). From this perspective, collective management by communities is not only preferable but also necessary, for three reasons. First, water supply is subject to multiple market *and* state failures; without community involvement, we will not manage water wisely. Second, water has important cultural and spiritual dimensions that are closely articulated with place-based practices; as such, its provision cannot be left up to private companies or the state. Third, water is a local flow resource whose use and health are most deeply impacted at a community level; protection of ecological and public health will only occur if communities are mobilized and enabled to govern their own resources. In particular, those who advance the "commons" view assert that conservation is more effectively incentivized through an environmental, collectivist ethic of solidarity, which will encourage users to refrain from wasteful behaviour. The real "water crisis" arises from socially produced scarcity, in which a short-term logic of economic growth, twinned with the rise of corporate power (and in particular water multi-nationals) has "converted abundance into scarcity" (Shiva 2002). As a response to the Dublin Principles, for example, the P7 Declaration (2000) outlined principles of "water democracy", of decentralized, community-based, democratic water management in which water conservation is politically, socio-economically and culturally inspired rather than economically motivated.

Despite their divergent political commitments, opponents and proponents of neoliberalization of water supply share some common conceptual commitments, including an understanding (lacking in many "neoliberalizing nature" analyses) that commodification is fraught with difficulty.[14] In the language of regulatory economists and political scientists, water is conventionally considered to be an imperfect public good (nonexcludable but rival in consumption) which is highly localized in nature, and which is often managed as a common-pool resource, for which relatively robust community-controlled cooperation and management mechanisms exist in many parts of the world (Berkes 1989; Mehta 2003; Ostrom 1990). It is the combination of public good characteristics, market failures and common property rights which makes water such an "uncooperative" commodity, and so resistant to neoliberal reforms, as neoclassical economists recognize when referring to the multiple "market failures" that characterize resources such as water supply[15] (Bakker 2004). To rephrase this analysis in political ecological terms: water is a flow resource over which it is difficult to establish private property rights; is characterized by a high degree of public health and environmental externalities—the costs of which are difficult to calculate and reflect in water prices; and is a partially non-substitutable resource essential for life with important aesthetic, symbolic, spiritual, and ecological functions which render some form of collective, public oversight inevitable. Private property rights can be established for water resources or water supply infrastructure, but full commodification does not necessarily, and in fact rarely follows.

A high degree of state involvement, therefore, is usually found even in countries that have experimented heavily with neoliberal forms to water management. Here lies the second point of convergence between "commodity" and "commons" proponents: both neoliberal reformers and defenders of the "commons" invoke dissatisfaction with centralized, bureaucratic state provision (cf Scott 1998). Whereas over much of the 20th century, "public good" would have been opposed to "economic good" in defense of the state against private interests by anti-privatization activists, alter-globalization movements—such as ATTAC and the Transnational Institute—explicitly reject state-led water governance models (Shiva 2002; TNI 2005). In doing so, as explored below, they reinvigorate a tripartite categorization of service delivery which undermines the "public/private" binary implicitly underlying much of the debate on neoliberalism more generally (Table 3).

As indicated in Table 3, significant differences exist between the public utility, commercial, and community governance models, despite the fact that these models overlap to some degree in practice. One important distinction is the role of the consumer: a citizen, a customer, or a community member. Each role implies different rights, responsibilities, and accountability mechanisms. Yet this tri-partite categorization tends to compartmentalize water supply into ideal types. In fact, many governments have chosen to create hybrid management models. Some have chosen, for example, to retain ownership while corporatizing water services, as in the Netherlands. In France, private-sector management of municipally owned water supply infrastructure via long-term management contracts is widespread. Other countries such as Denmark, with a long tradition of cooperative management of the local economy, prefer the coop model—provision by a non-profit users "association

Table 3: Water supply delivery models: the cooperative, the state, and the private corporation

		State	Market	Community
Resource management institutions	Primary goals	Guardian of public interest; Conformity with legislation/policy	Maximization of profit; Efficient performance	Serve community interest; Effective performance
	Regulatory framework	Command and control	Market mechanisms	Community-defined goals (not necessarily consensus based)
	Property rights	Public (state) or private property	Private property	Public (commons) or private property
Resource management organizations	Primary decision-makers	Administrators, experts, public officials	Individual households, experts, companies	Leaders and members of community organizations
	Organizational structure	Municipal department, civil service	Private company, corporation	Cooperative, association/network
	Business models	Municipally owned utility	Private corporate utility	Community cooperative
Resource governance	Accountability mechanism	Hierarchy	Contract	Community norms
	Key incentives	Voter/ratepayer opinion	Price signals (share movements or bond ratings), customer opinion	Community opinion
	Key sanctions	Political process via elections, litigation	Financial loss, takeover, litigation	Livelihood needs, social pressure, litigation (in some cases)
	Consumer role	User and citizen	User and customer	User and community member
	Participation of consumers	Collective, top-down	Individualistic	Collective, bottom-up

in which local accountability is a key incentive". Moreover, this tripartite classification is clearly inadequate when applied to the global South, where "public" water supply systems often supply only wealthier neighbourhoods in urban areas, leaving poor and rural areas to self-organize through community cooperatives or informal, private, for-profit provision by water vendors, often at volumetric rates much higher than those available through the public water supply system. Indeed, most residents use multiple sources of water in the home, and rely on a mix of networked and artisanal water supply sources, through both state and private sector delivery systems, using a combination of household piped network water connections, shallow and deep wells, public hydrants, and water vendors for their water supply needs (see, for example, Swyngedouw 2004). A public/private binary, even where it admits to the possibility of a third "cooperative" alternative, is clearly insufficient for capturing the complexity of water provision in cities in the South (Swyngedouw 2004). Alternative community economies of water do, in fact, already exist in many cities in the South (Table 4), and represent "actually existing alternatives" to neoliberalism which activists have sought to interrogate, protect, and replicate through networks such as the "Blue Planet Project", "Octubre Azul", World Social Fora (Ponniah 2004; Ponniah and Fisher 2003) and alternative "world water fora".[16]

In opening up space for the conceptual acknowledgement of alternative community economies (cf Gibson-Graham 2006), this tactic is to be welcomed. Yet caution is also merited, insofar as appeals to the commons run the risk of romanticizing community control. Much activism in favour of collective, community-based forms of water supply management tends to romanticize communities as coherent, relatively equitable social structures, despite the fact that inequitable power relations and resource allocation exist within communities (McCarthy 2005; Mehta 2001; Mehta, Leach and Scoones 2001). Although research has demonstrated how cooperative management institutions for water common pool resources can function effectively to avoid depletion (Ostrom 1990; Ostrom and Keohane 1995), other research points to the limitations of some of these collective action approaches in water (Cleaver 2000; Mehta 2001; Mosse 1997; Potanski and Adams 1998; St Martin 2005). Commons, in other words, can be exclusive and regressive, as well as inclusive and progressive (McCarthy 2005). Indeed, the role of the state in encouraging redistributive models of resource management, progressive social relations and redistribution is more ambivalent than those making calls for a "return to the commons" would perhaps admit.

Thus, the most progressive strategies are those that adopt a twofold tactic: reforming rather than abolishing state governance, while fostering and sharing alternative local models of resource management. In some instances, these alternative strategies tackle the anthropocentrism of neoliberalization (and "human right to water" campaigns) directly,

Table 4: Neoliberal reforms and alter-globalization alternatives

Category	Target of reform	Type of reform	Alter-globalization alternative
Resource management institutions	Property rights	Privatization	• Mutualization (re-collectivization) of asset ownership (Wales; Bakker 2004)
			• Communal water rights in village "commons" in India (Narain 2006)
	Regulatory frameworks	De-regulation	• Re-regulation by consumer-controlled NGOs such as "Customer Councils" in England (Franceys forthcoming; Page and Bakker 2005)
Resource management organizations	Asset management	Private sector "partnerships"	• Public–public partnerships (eg between Stockholm's water company (Stockholm Vatten) and water utilities in Latvia and Lithuania) (PSIRU 2006)
			• Water cooperatives in Finland (Katko 2000)
	Organizational structure	Corporatization	• Low-cost, community-owned infrastructure (eg Orangi Pilot Project, Pakistan; Zaidi 2001)
Resource governance	Resource allocation	Marketization	• Sharing of irrigation water based on customary law ("usos y costumbres") in Bolivia (Trawick 2003)
	Performance incentives/sanctions	Commercialization	• Customer corporation (with incentives structured towards maximization of customer satisfaction rather than profit or share price maximization; Kay 1996)
	User participation	Devolution or decentralization	• Community watershed boards (Canada; Alberta Environment 2003)
			• Participatory budgeting (Porto Alegre, Brazil; TNI 2005)

recognizing ecological as well as human needs, the latter being constrained through a variety of norms, whether scientifically determined "limits", eco-spiritual reverence, or eco-puritan ecological governance. In other cases, they may make strange bedfellows with some aspects of neoliberal agendas, such as decentralization, through which greater community control can be enacted (Table 4).

These models are necessarily varied; no one model of water governance can be anticipated or imposed (cf Gibson-Graham 2006). Rather, they build on local resource management and community norms, whether rural water users' customary water rights ("usos y costumbres") in the Andes (Trawick 2003); revived conceptions of Roman "res publica" and "res commmuna" in Europe (Squatriti 1998); or community norms of collective provision of irrigation in Indian "village republics" (Shiva 2002; Wade 1988). In each instance, a place-specific model of what Indian activist Vandana Shiva terms "water democracy" emerges, offering a range of responses to the neoliberalization agendas identified earlier in the paper. In other words, these "really existing" alter-globalization initiatives are a form of what Gibson-Graham terms "weak theory": deliberately organic, tentative, local, place-based, and (at least at the outset) modest.

"Weak", does not, however, imply "insignificant". These reforms are, of course, necessarily local—because water is usually consumed, managed, and disposed of at a local scale. But they are nonetheless replicable, and thus represent potentially powerful "actually existing alternatives" to neoliberalization. One example is the recent proliferation of "public public partnerships", in which public water supply utilities with expertise and resources (typically in large cities in the North) are partnered with those in the South, or with smaller urban centres in the North (PSIRU 2005, 2006; Public Citizen 2002; TNI 2005). Activists have actively promoted these strategies as a tactic of resistance to water supply privatization initiatives, while acknowledging the political pitfalls of promoting public–public partnerships in the wake of failed private sector contracts, particularly the potential for such partnerships to be promoted as a strategy for less profitable communities, allowing more limited private sector contracts to "cherry pick" profitable communities. Institutional support from multilateral agencies may soon be forthcoming, as the newly commissioned UN Secretary General's Advisory Board and Water and Sanitation has requested the UN to support the creation of an international association of public water operators.[17] Encouraged by the UN Commission on Sustainable Development's official acknowledgment of the importance of promoting public–public partnerships (TNI 2006; UNCSD 2005), and by specific campaigns by public water supply utilities—notably Porto Alegre—governments in Argentina, Bolivia, Brazil, Indonesia, Holland, Honduras, France, South Africa, and Sweden have initiated public-public partnerships, at times also entailing a radical restructuring of management–worker relationships within water supply utilities (TNI 2006).

Conclusions

As explored in this paper, the adoption of human rights discourse by private companies indicates its limitations as an anti-privatization strategy. Human rights are individualistic, anthropocentric, state-centric, and compatible with private sector provision of water supply; and as such, a limited strategy for those seeking to refute water privatization. Moreover, "rights talk" offers us an unimaginative language for thinking about new community economies, not least because pursuit of a campaign to establish water as a human right risks reinforcing the public/private binary upon which this confrontation is predicated, occluding possibilities for collective action beyond corporatist models of service provision. In contrast, the "alter-globalization" debate opened up by disrupting the public/private binary has created space for the construction of alternative community economies of water. These "alter-globalization" proposals counterpose various forms of the commons to commodity-based property and social relations. Greater progressive possibilities would appear to be inherent in the call of alter-globalization activists for radical strategies of ecological democracy predicated upon calls to decommodify public services and enact "commons" models of resource management (see, for example, Bond 2004a, 2004b; TNI 2005).

How does a more refined understanding of neoliberalization, as outlined in the typology introduced at the outset of this paper, assist in this task? First, it enables activism to be more precise in its characterization of "actually existing" neoliberalisms, and thus to develop alternatives which have more political traction. For example, the "commons" is an effective strategy for combating privatization because it correctly opposes a collective property right to private property rights. Second, in locating the application of neoliberalization in specific historically and geographically contingent contexts, it emphasizes what Sparke terms the "*dis*locatable" idealism of neoliberalism (Sparke 2006), both through generating alternatives and through demonstrating how ostensibly neoliberal reforms may be congruent with other political agendas. In so doing, it enables us to see that neoliberalism is not monolithic—and that it creates political opportunities that may be progressive. For example, some neoliberal reforms may be congruent with the goals of alterglobalization activists—such as decentralization leading to greater community control of water resources. Third, it reminds us to pay attention to the multiplicity of reforms that typically occur when "neoliberalizing nature", not all of which focus on property rights. Specifically, the typology presented in Table 1 allows us to refine our academic analyses and activist responses to different types of neoliberalization, which vary significantly, opening up the creation of a range of alternative community water economies (Table 4).

Many of these alternatives, it should be noted, are not produced in reaction to neoliberalization, but rather resuscitate or develop new approaches to governing the relationship between the hydrological cycle, and socio-natural economies and polities. Some aspects of these reforms are congruent with a neoliberal agenda, but the work of alter-globalization activists reminds us that they need not be subsumed by neoliberalization. Rather, these reforms open up new political ecological and socio-natural relationships through which an ethic of care—for non-humans as well as humans—can be developed. As this paper has argued, this "alter-globalization" agenda necessitates a refinement of our conceptual frameworks of neoliberalization, accounting for multiple modes of property rights and service provision. This conceptual reframing allows us both to accurately analyze neoliberalization in situ and also to generate politically progressive strategies with which to enact more equitable political ecologies—particularly if our definitions of prospective "commoners" are porous enough to include non-humans.

Acknowledgements

This paper benefited greatly from discussions with Brewster Kneen and other members of the Forum on Privatization and the Public Domain. Helpful comments from Jamie Peck, Becky Mansfield, Melissa Wright, Anil Naidoo, David Brooks, Oliver Brandes, and two anonymous reviewers did much to strengthen the paper and refine its argument. Thanks are also due to the insight and inspiration generated through interactions with NGOs and research/activist think tanks, including the Alternative Information and Development Center (South Africa), the Council of Canadians and affiliated Blue Planet Project (Canada), PSIRU (England), Public Citizen (US), and the Urban Social Forum (Indonesia).

Endnotes

[1] The 1992 International Conference on Water and the Environment set out what became known as the "Dublin Principles": including the principle that "water has an economic value in all its competing uses and should be recognized as an economic good". The Dublin Principles have been adopted by numerous international, multilateral and bilateral agencies. For assessments and critiques of commercialization in the water sector, see Bakker (2004), Finger and Allouche (2002), Huffaker and Whittlesey (2003), Johnstone and Wood (2001), Kaika (2003), Kijne (2001), Kloezen (1998), Kumar and Singh (2001), Landry (1998), McDonald and Ruiters (2005), Shirley (2002), Takahashi (2001), and Ward and Michelsen (2002).

[2] For an NGO perspective critical of water privatization, see the Council of Canadians Blue Planet Project (http://www.canadians.org/blueplanet/index2.html). For academic studies critical of the privatization process, with a focus on developing

countries, see the Municipal Services Project website (http://qsilver.queensu.ca/~ mspadmin). The US-based Public Citizen runs a campaign on water supply (http://www. citizen.org/cmep/Water/). The Global Water Partnership is an influential network of companies, governments, and lending agencies committed to the Rio-Dublin principles (http://www.gwpforum.org/). For an international public sector union perspective, see the PSIRU website (http://www.psiru.org).

[3] See, for example, articles in the recent special issue of *CNS* 16(1) (2005), or in the special issue of *Geoforum* on neoliberal nature (2004: 35(3)) edited by James McCarthy and Scott Prudham.

[4] The International Covenant on Economic, Social and Cultural Rights, one of the keystones of international human rights law. None of the United Nations conventions on human rights (except article 24 of the Convention on the Rights of the Child) explicitly recognizes the right to water (Morgan 2004).

[5] The Committee on Economic, Social and Cultural Rights (CESCR) is the body of independent experts that monitors implementation of the International Covenant on Economic, Social and Cultural Rights by its State parties.

[6] These declarations include the Cochabamba Declaration, the Group of Lisbon's Water Manifesto (Petrella 2001), and the Declaration of the P8 (the world's poorest eight countries, organized as a counterpart to the G8) at their fourth summit in 2000.

[7] Campaigns include the UK-based "Right to Water" (http://www.righttowater.org.uk) and "Blue October" campaigns, the Canada-based "Friends of the Right to Water Campaign", and the US-based "Water for All" campaign and "Green Cross" campaign for an international convention on the right to water (http://www.watertreaty.org).

[8] The Constitution of the Republic of South Africa guarantees the right of citizens access to sufficient water (Act 108 of 1996, section 7(2)).

[9] For example, water is defined as collective property ("waqf"), with water available free to the public, under Islam (Faruqui, Biswas and Bino 2003).

[10] As recognized by the UN Committee in its comment on the human right to water, which stated that, in permitting third parties (such as the private sector) in addition to state actors to supply water, an additional burden is placed upon regulatory frameworks, including "independent monitoring, genuine public participation, and imposition of penalties for non-compliance" (ECOSOC 2002, article 24).

[11] See Frérot (2006). Antoine Frérot was, at the time, the Director General of Veolia (one of the two largest private water companies in the world).

[12] Veolia's French language website states, for example, that "L'eau est considérée à la fois comme un bien économique, social, écologique et comme un droit humain" ["Water is considered an economic, social and ecological good as well as a human right"], http://www.veoliaeau.com/gestion-durable/gestion-durable/eau-pour-tous/bien-commun. See also the Open Forum on "Water: Property or Human Right?" at the 2004 Davos Forum, http://gaia.unit.net/wef/worldeconomicforum_ annualmeeting2006/default.aspx?sn=15810.

[13] The Ministerial Declaration of the Hague on Water Security in the twenty-first century followed the inter-ministerial meeting known as the "2nd World Water Forum" in 2000. See http://www.worldwaterforum.net.

[14] Commodification entails the creation of an economic good through the application of mechanisms to appropriate and standardize a class of goods or services, enabling them to be sold at a price determined through market exchange.

[15] The classic definition of a market failure is a case in which a market fails to efficiently allocate goods and services, due to the "failure" to meet assumptions of standard neoclassical economic models. For example, market failures occur when property rights are not clearly defined or are unenforceable, when goods are non-excludable and non-rivalrous ("public goods"), when prices do not incorporate full costs or benefits ("externalities"), when information is incomplete, or in a situation of monopoly.

[16] See, for example, the on-line chatroom at http://www.waterjustice.org; the website of the second alternative world water forum (http://www.fame2005.org).
[17] See archived meeting session history on the Advisory Board website: http://www. unsgab.org.

References

ADB (2003) *Beyond Boundaries: Extending Services to the Urban Poor*. Manila: Asian Development Bank

Alberta Environment (2003) *Water for Life: Alberta's Strategy for Sustainability*. Edmonton: Alberta Environment

Anderson T and Leal D (2001) *Free Market Environmentalism*. New York: Palgrave

Angel D (2000) The environmental regulation of privatized industry in Poland. *Environment and Planning C: Government and Policy* 18(5):575–592

Aquafed (2006) Statement on the right to water and role of local governments by Gérard Payen, during the opening session of the World Water Forum. http://www.aquafed. org/pdf/WWF4-opening_GP_RTW-LocGov_Pc_2006-03-16.pdf

Assies W (2003) David versus Goliath in Cochabamba: Water rights, neoliberalism, and the revival of social protest in Bolivia. *Latin-American-Perspectives* 30(3):14–36

Bailey R (2005) Water is a human right: How privatization gets water to the poor. *Reason Magazine* 17 August. http://www.reason.com/news/show/34992.html

Bakker K (2000) Privatizing water, producing scarcity: The Yorkshire drought of 1995. *Economic Geography* 96(1):4–27

Bakker K (2001) Paying for water: Water pricing and equity in England and Wales. *Transactions of the Institute of British Geographers* 26(2):143–164

Bakker K (2004) *An Uncooperative Commodity: Privatizing Water in England and Wales*. Oxford: Oxford University Press

Bakker K (2005) Neoliberalizing nature? Market environmentalism in water supply in England and Wales. *Annals of the Association of American Geographers* 95(3):542–565

Barlow M and Clarke T (2003) *Blue Gold: The Fight to Stop the Corporate Theft of the World's Water*. New York: Stoddart

Bauer C (1998) Slippery property rights: Multiple water uses and the neoliberal model in Chile, 1981–1995. *Natural Resources Journal* 38:109–154

Berkes F (1989) *Common Property Resources: Ecology and Community-based Sustainable Development*. London: Belhaven Press

Bernstein S (2001) *The Compromise of Liberal Environmentalism*. New York: Columbia University Press

Blokland M, Braadbaart O and Schwartz K (2001) *Private Business, Public Owners*. The Hague and Geneva: Ministry of Housing, Spatial Planning, and Development and the Water Supply and Sanitation Collaborative Council

Bond P (2002) *Unsustainable South Africa: Environment, Development, and Social Protest*. London: Merlin Press

Bond P (2004a) Water commodification and decommodification narratives: Pricing and policy debates from Johannesburg to Kyoto to Cancun and back. *Capitalism Nature Socialism* 15(1):7–25

Bond P (2004b) Decommodification and deglobalisation: Strategic challenges for African social movements. *Afriche e Oriente* 7(4)

Bradshaw M (2004) The market, Marx and sustainability in a fishery. *Antipode* 36(1):66–85

Bridge G (2004) Mapping the bonanza: Geographics of mining investment in an era of neoliberal reform. *The Professional Geographer* 56(3):406–421

Bridge G and Jonas A (2002) Governing nature: The re-regulation of resource access, production, and consumption. *Environment and Planning A* (guest editorial) 34:759–766

Bridge G, McManus P and Marsden T (2003) The next new thing? Biotechnology and its discontents. *Geoforum* 34(2):165–174

Castree N (2005) The epistemology of particulars: Human Geography, case studies, and "context". *Geoforum* 36(5):541–666

Cleaver F (2000) Moral ecological rationality, institutions, and the management of common property resources. *Development and Change* 31(2):361–383

DFID (1998) *Better Water Services in Developing Countries: Public–Private Partnership—The Way Ahead*. London: Department for International Development

Dinar A (2000) *The Political Economy of Water Pricing Reforms*. Washington: World Bank.

Dubreuil C (2005) *The Right to Water: From Concept to Implementation*. World Water Council

Dubreuil C (2006) *Synthesis on the Right to Water at the 4th World Water Forum, Mexico*. World Water Council

ECOSOC (2002) General comment 15. Geneva: United Nations Committee on Economic, Social and Cultural Rights

Estache A and Rossi C (2002) How different is the efficiency of public and private water companies in Asia? *World Bank Economic Review* 16(1):139–148

Faruqui N, Biswas A and Bino M (2003) *La gestion de l'eau selon l'Islam*. CRDI/Editions: Karthala

Finger M and Allouche J (2002) *Water Privatisation: Transnational Corporations and the Re-regulation of the Water Industry*. London: Spon Press

Franceys R (forthcoming) Customer committees, economic regulation and the Water Framework Directive. *Journal of Water Supply: Research and Technology–Aqua*

Frérot A (2006) Parce que ce droit est fondamental, il doit devenir effectif. *Le Monde* 17 March

Gandy M (2004) Rethinking urban metabolism: Water, space and the modern city. *City* 8(3):363–379

Gibbs D and Jonas A (2000) Governance and regulation in local environmental policy: The utility of a regime approach. *Geoforum* 34(3):299–313

Gibson-Graham J K (2006) *A Postcapitalist Politics*. Minneapolis: University of Minnesota Press

Glassman J (2006) Primitive accumulation, accumulation by dispossession, accumulation by "extra-economic' means. *Progress in Human Geography* 30(5):608–625

Gleick P (1998) The human right to water. *Water Policy* 1:487–503

Goldman M (2005) *Imperial Nature: The World Bank and the Making of Green Neoliberalism*. New Haven, CT: Yale University Press

Haddad B (2000) *Rivers of Gold: Designing Markets to Allocate Water in California*. Washington: Island Press

Hammer L (2004) Indigenous peoples as a catalyst for applying the human right to water. *International Journal on Minority and Group Rights* 10:131–161

Harvey D (2005) *A Short History of Neoliberalism*. Oxford: Oxford University Press

Hassan J (1998) *A History of Water in Modern England and Wales*. Manchester: Manchester University Press

Huffaker R and Whittlesey N (2003) A theoretical analysis of economic incentive policies encouraging agricultural water conservation. *International Journal of Water Resources Development* 19(1):3753

Hukka J J and Katko T S (2003) Refuting the paradigm of water services privatization. *Natural Resources Forum* 27(2):142–155

Ignatieff M (2003) *Human Rights as Politics and Idolatry*. Princeton: Princeton University Press

Johnston B R (2003) The political ecology of water: An introduction. *Capitalism Nature Socialism* 14(3):73–90

Johnston J, Gismondi M and Goodman J (2006) *Nature's Revenge: Reclaiming Sustainability in an Age of Corporate Globalization*. Toronto: Broadview Press

Johnstone N and Wood L (2001) *Private Firms and Public Water. Realising Social and Environmental Objectives in Developing Countries*. London: International Institute for Environment and Development

Kaika M (2003) The Water Framework Directive: a new directive for a changing social, political and economic European framework. *European Planning Studies* 11(3):299–316

Katko T (2000) *Water! Evolution of Water Supply and Sanitation in Finland from the mid-1800s to 2000*. Tampere: Finnish Water and Waste Water Works Association

Kay J (1996) Regulating private utilities: The customer corporation. *Journal of Co-operative Studies* 29(2):28–46

Kijne J W (2001) Lessons learned from the change from supply to demand water management in irrigated agriculture: A case study from Pakistan. *Water Policy* 3(2):109–123

Kloezen W H (1998) Water markets between Mexican water user associations. *Water Policy* 1:437–455

Kumar M D and Singh O P (2001) Market instruments for demand management in the face of scarcity and overuse of water in Gujerat, Western India. *Water Policy* 3(5):387–403

Kymlicka W (1995) *Multicultural Citizenship: A Liberal Theory of Minority Rights*. Oxford: Oxford University Press

Landry C (1998) Market transfers of water for environmental protection in the Western United States. *Water Policy* 1:457-469

Laurie N and Marvin S (1999) Globalisation, neo-liberalism and negotiated development in the Andes: Bolivian water and the Misicuni dream. *Environment and Planning A* 31:1401–1415

Laxer G and Soron D (2006) *Not for Sale: Decommodifying Public Life*. Toronto: Broadview Press

Lorrain D (1997) Introduction—the socio-economics of water services: The invisible factors. In Lorrain D (ed) *Urban Water Management—French Experience Around the World* (pp 1–30). Levallois Perret: Hydrocom

Maddock T (2004) Fragmenting regimes: How water quality regulation is changing political-economic landscapes. *Geoforum* 35(2):217–230

Mansfield B (2004a) Neoliberalism in the oceans: "Rationalization", property rights, and the commons question. *Geoforum* 35(3):313–326

Mansfield B (2004b) Rules of privatization: Contradictions in neoliberal regulation of North Pacific fisheries. *Annals of the Association of American Geographers* 94(3):565–584

McAfee K (2003) Neoliberalism on the molecular scale. Economic and genetic reductionism in biotechnology battles. *Geoforum* 34(2):203–219

McCarthy J (2004) Privatizing conditions of production: trade agreements as neoliberal environmental governance. *Geoforum* 35(3):327–341

McCarthy J (2005) Commons as counter-hegemonic projects. *Capitalism Nature Socialism* 16(1):9–24

McCarthy J and Prudham S (2004) Neoliberal nature and the nature of neoliberalism. *Geoforum* 35(3):275–283

McDonald D and Ruiters G (2005) *The Age of Commodity: Water Privatization in Southern Africa*. London: Earthscan

Mehta L (2001) Water, difference, and power: Unpacking notions of water "users" in Kutch, India. *International Journal of Water* 1(3–4)

Mehta L (2003) Problems of publicness and access rights: Perspectives from the water domain. In Kaul I, Conceicao P, Le Goulven K and Mendoza R (eds) *Providing Global Public Goods: Managing Globalization* (pp 556–575). New York: Oxford University Press and United Nations Development Program

Mehta L, Leach M and Scoones I (2001) Editorial: Environmental governance in an uncertain world. *IDS Bulletin* 32(4)

Morgan B (2004a) The regulatory face of the human right to water. *Journal of Water Law* 15(5):179–186

Morgan B (2004b) Water: frontier markets and cosmopolitan activism. *Soundings: a Journal of Politics and Culture* Issue on "The Frontier State" (27):10–24

Morgan B (2005) Social protest against privatization of water: Forging cosmopolitan citizenship? In Cordonier Seggier M C and Weeramantry J (eds) *Sustainable Justice: Reconciling International Economic, Environmental and Social Law*. The Hague: Martinus Nijhoff

Mosse D (1997) The symbolic making of a common property resource: History, ecology and locality in a tank-irrigated landscape in South India. *Development and Change* 28(3):467–504

Mutua M (2002) *Human Rights: A Political and Cultural Critique*. Philadelphia: University of Pennsylvania Press

Narain S (2006) Community-led alternatives to water management: India case study. Background paper: Human Development Report 2006. New York: United Nations Development Programme

Olivera O and Lewis T (2004) *Cochabamba! Water War in Bolivia*. Boston: South End Press

Ostrom E (1990) *Governing the Commons: The Evolution of Institutions for Collective Action*. New York: Cambridge University Press

Ostrom E and Keohane R (eds) (1995) *Local Commons and Global Interdependence: Heterogeneity and Cooperation in Two Domains*. Cambridge, MA: Harvard University, Centre for International Affairs

Page B and Bakker K (2005) Water governance and water users in a privatized water industry: Participation in policy-making and in water services provision—a case study of England and Wales. *International Journal of Water* 3(1):38–60

Perrault T (2006) From the Guerra del Agua to the Guerra del Gas: Resource governance, popular protest and social justice in Bolivia. *Antipode* 38(1):150–172

Petrella R (2001) *The Water Manifesto: Arguments for a World Water Contract*. London and New York: Zed Books

Ponniah T (2004) Democracy vs empire: Alternatives to globalization presented at the World Social Forum. *Antipode* 36(1):130–133

Ponniah T and Fisher W F (eds) (2003) *Another World is Possible: Popular Alternatives to Globalization at the World Social Forum*. New York: Zed Press

Potanski T and Adams W (1998) Water scarcity, property regimes, and irrigation management in Sonjo, Tanzania. *Journal of Development Studies* 34(4):86–116

Prudham W S (2004) Poisoning the well: Neoliberalism and the contamination of municipal water in Walkerton, Ontario. *Geoforum* 35(3):343–359

PSIRU (2005) *Public Public Partnerships in Health and Essential Services*. University of Greenwich, Public Services International Research Unit

PSIRU (2006) *Public–Public Partnerships as a Catalyst for Capacity Building and Institutional Development: Lessons from Stockholm Vatten's Experience in the Baltic Region*. University of Greenwich, Public Services International Research Unit

Public Citizen (2002) *Public–Public Partnerships: A Backgrounder on Successful Water/ Wastewater Reengineering Programs*. Washington: Public Citizen and Food and Water Watch

Robbins P (2003) Transnational corporations and the discourse of water privatization. *Journal of International Development* 15:1073-1082

Robertson M (2004) The neoliberalization of ecosystem services: Wetland mitigation banking and problems in environmental governance. *Geoforum* 35(3):361–373

Rogers P, de Silva R, et al (2002) Water is an economic good: How to use prices to promote equity, efficiency, and sustainability. *Water Policy* 4(1):1–17

Rorty R (1993) Human rights, rationality, and sentimentality. In S Shute and S Hurley (eds) *On Human Rights: The Oxford Amnesty Lectures*. New York: Basic Books

Roy A (1999) *The Cost of Living*. London: Modern Library

Salman S and McInerney-Lankford S (2004) *The Human Right to Water: Legal and Policy Dimensions*. Washington DC: World Bank

Scott J (1998) *Seeing Like a State: How Certain Schemes to Improve the Human Condition have Failed*. New Haven: Yale University Press

Segerfeldt F (2005) *Water For Sale: How Business and the Market Can Resolve the World's Water Crisis*. London: Cato Institute

Shirley M (2002) *Thirsting for Efficiency*. London: Elsevier

Shiva V (2002) *Water Wars: Privatization, Pollution and Profit*. London: Pluto Press

Smets H (2006) Diluted view of water as a right: 4th World Water Forum. *Environmental Policy and Law* 36(2):88–93

Smith L (2004) The murky waters of the second wave of neoliberalism: Corporatization as a service delivery model in Cape Town. *Geoforum* 35(3):375–393

Sparke M (2006) Political geography: Political geographies of globalization (2)— governance. *Progress in Human Geography* 30(3):357–372

Squatriti P (1998) *Water and Society in Early Medieval Italy, A.D. 400–1000*. Cambridge: Cambridge University Press

St Martin K (2005) Disrupting enclosure in the New England fisheries. *Capitalism Nature Socialism* 16(1):63–80

Susilowati I and Budiata L (2003) An introduction of co-management approach into Babon River management in Semarang, Central Java, Indonesia. *Water Science & Technology* 48(7):173–180

Swyngedouw E (2004) *Social Power and the Urbanization of Water*. Oxford: Oxford University Press

Swyngedouw E (2005) Dispossessing H_2O: The contested terrain of water privatization. *Capitalism Nature Socialism* 16(1):81–98

Takahashi K (2001) Globalization and management of water resources: Development opportunities and constraints of diversified developing countries. *International Journal of Water Resources Development* 17(4):481–488

TNI (2005) *Reclaiming Public Water: Achievements, Struggles and Visions from Around the World*. Amsterdam: Transnational Institute

TNI (2006) *Public Water for All: The Role of Public–Public Partnerships*. Amsterdam: Transnational Institute and Corporate Europe Observatory

Trawick P (2003) Against the privatization of water: An indigenous model for improving existing laws and successfully governing the commons. *World Development* 31(6):977–996

UNCSD (2005) *Report on the Thirteenth Session*. New York: UN Commission on Sustainable Development. E/CN.17/2005/12

UNDP (2003) *Millenium Development Goals: A Compact for Nations to End Human Poverty*. New York: United Nations Development Program

UNDP (2006) *Beyond Scarcity: Power, Poverty, and the Global Water Crisis: UN Human Development Report 2006*. New York: United Nations Development Programme, Human Development Report Office

UN Economic and Social Council (2003) *Economic, Social and Cultural Rights*. Report submitted to the 59th session of the Commission on Human Rights, by the Special Rapporteur on the Right to Food. E/CN.4/2003/54

UNWWAP (2006) *Water: A Shared Responsibility*. New York: United Nations World Water Assessment Program

Wade R (1998) *Village Republics: Economic Conditions for Collective Action in South India*. Cambridge: Cambridge University Press

Ward F A and Michelson A (2002) The economic value of water in agriculture: concepts and policy applications. *Water Policy* 4(5):423–446

Walker D L (1983) The effect of European Community directives on water authorities in England and Wales. *Aqua* 4:145–147

WHO (2003) *The Right to Water*. Geneva: World Health Organisation

Winpenny J (1994) *Managing Water as an Economic Resource*. London: Routledge

Winpenny J (2003) *Financing Water for All: Report of the World Panel on Financing Water Infrastructure*. Geneva: World Water Council/Global Water Partnership/Third World Water Forum.

Zaidi A (2001) *From Lane to City: The Impact of the Orangi Pilot Project's Low Cost Sanitation Model*. London: WaterAid

Chapter 3

The Polanyian Way? Voluntary Food Labels as Neoliberal Governance

Julie Guthman

Introduction

Commodities that embed ecological, social, and/or place-based values have been posed as an important form of resistance to neoliberalization because they are putatively protective, in the Polanyian sense of protecting land, other natural resources, and labor from the ravages of the market. Such commodities are especially common in the realm of food production, and are necessarily distinguished by a label, with organic, fair trade, and various geographic indicators being particularly well-known examples. They protect the "conditions of production" with specific standards of production and with verification mechanisms designed to capture and/or retain value for certain producers. It is the retention of value that eases tendencies of intensification and exploitation and thus mitigates neoliberalism's "race to the bottom". At the same time, these labels are in some respects analogs to the very things they are purported to resist, namely property rights that allow these ascribed commodities to be traded in a global market. The standards developed to substantiate these labeling claims establish boundaries of acceptable behavior, and modes of enforcement of these standards create a set of property rights to the use of the label. Producers must then prove they meet these previously agreed upon standards to cash in on any benefits that might accrue from the use of such labels. And the value inhered in this right is only realized upon exchange of a commodity.

Mutersbaugh (2005a) has recently called the labeling phenomenon "fighting standards with standards". While there is something to be said about this formulation—namely, as he says, an opportunity for social movements to "jump scales" to multilateral institutions, it nevertheless, as he also says, produces new modes of governmentality. Indeed, following Heynen and Robbins (2005) who note four dominant aspects of the neoliberalization of environmentalism (governance, privatization, enclosure, and valuation), these labels look to be typical of neoliberal regulation. They are governed by a complex array of state/private/NGO/multilateral bodies that subscribe to notions of audit/transparency as "action at a distance" (Rose 1999); they extend property rights to practices where none previously existed; they entail forms of enclosure in ways that produce scarcity; they attach economic values to ethical behaviors; and, finally, they "devolve" regulatory responsibility to consumers. In other words, not only do these labels concede the market as the locus of regulation, in keeping with neoliberalism's fetish of market mechanisms, they employ tools designed to create markets. Since Polanyi (1944) saw the role of social regulation as resisting the market, the invocation of Polanyi among those who champion these labels points to an important theoretical tension.

Politically these labels bear scrutiny, as well. For, despite my abiding skepticism of labels as a vehicle of social and environmental improvement, it may be that at this political juncture, to use Margaret Thatcher's unfortunate phrase, "there is no alternative". In that case, the important question is to what extent the contestations of neoliberalism outweigh the reinscriptions. Is it possible, that is, that they help induce "push back" at the same time that they so obviously incorporate the techniques of what Peck and Tickell (2002) call roll-out neoliberalization?

The purpose of this paper is to work through some of these contradictory aspects of protective labels. Along the way, I will discuss the mechanisms of such protection and then demonstrate that even in the ideal, different sorts of labels significantly vary as to whom and what they protect; furthermore, some labels do very little, if anything, and there are many commodities in the world that do not stand a chance of being valorized with a label at all. So, even in the best of circumstances, protection is highly uneven. At the same time, in recognition that what is hopefully a temporary foreclosure of other avenues of collective action has rendered what is necessarily an exclusionary protection thinkable, the paper will grapple with how these labels may produce political openings outside of their most proximate effects. These might include the production of new political subjectivities. First, however, I look at what is being claimed by those who are more sanguine about the political possibilities of these labels.

Labels as Protection: The Polanyian Way

Labels that describe the benefits and positive qualities of a commodity have obviously existed for a long time. For the purposes of this paper I mean voluntary adherence to standards with some measure and verification of social or ecological betterment and certification in return for a label.[1] While participation in labeling schemes may be driven by values or moral conviction, the presumption is that labels will establish a basis by which producers can be compensated for the costs of following these standards. This is a relatively novel form of agro-food regulation, with the organic standard as the likely progenitor of this trend. The last 15 years have seen a number of competing and complementary labeling schemes developed, as well as a proliferation of fair trade type labels. Even controlled origin (AOC) and certain craft labels, which well predate the emergence of organics, have been cast into a new light as an effect of these other, newer labels (eg Barham 2003). The profusion of such labels is not coincidental, I will argue, with roll-out neoliberalization.

Several scholars have theorized these labels as a modern day equivalent of Polanyi's (1944) double movement, a societal movement for self-protection as the fictitious commodities of land and labor become subjected to the "self-regulating" market. Polanyi saw the self-regulating market as fundamentally dehumanizing and in fact unable to self-regulate and posited that "society" would resist the forces of commoditization—or at least impose regulation to defend itself against the instabilities of the market (Burawoy 2003; Mansfield 2004c). Since neoliberalism fetishizes the powers of the market to regulate human behavior and is also associated with the commoditization of everything, it is not surprising that Polanyi figures prominently in efforts to theorize neoliberalism's counter movements. Insofar as protective labels modulate the effects of the market, they would be in that way consistent with Polanyi.

Accordingly, along with Mutersbaugh (2005a), Barham (1997, 2002) has been explicit in her use of Polanyi, seeing values-based labeling as "one historical manifestation of social resistance to the violation of broadly shared values by systemic aspects of 'free market capitalism'" (2002:350). While others do not invoke Polanyi per se, many other scholars make more generalized claims about how these labels counter the anomic forces of capitalism generally or the particular effects of neoliberalism. Raynolds (2000), for example, sees the fair trade movement as a way to "challenge the abstract capitalist relations that fuel exploitation in the global agro-food system" (297). Bacon (2005) claims that the fair trade movement refutes the neoliberal assumption that participation in markets will benefit everyone and shows how this imbalance of power relations has been partially rectified with higher returns for fair trade producers. Renard (1999) posits that fair trade coffee not only offers higher distributions to producers but also makes them safe from competition! Moving "beyond both celebratory as well as overly dismissive takes on fair trade", Goodman (2004:894), nevertheless, sees fair trade as an alternative form of development—driven by consumers' ethics of care rather than direct aid—that at least may partially address the inequities produced by neoliberalization. And while generally skeptical of the ability of fair trade to generate radical transformation, Shreck (2005) concedes that fair trade may offer redistribution. One theme that recurs throughout this literature is how these commodities incorporate moral values at the same time that they help retain economic value. Renting, Marsden and Banks (2003) call organic and fair trade networks "short supply chains" because they are embedded with value-laden information linking producer and consumers irrespective of the distance commodities have traveled (400).

Despite what would seem to be clearly distinguishing features between labels that inhere qualities based on process (such as organic/fair trade) and those that attach place/terroir, they are treated in remarkably similar terms. Indeed, because US-negotiating bodies have so opposed geographic indicators in trade agreements, Barham (2003) is even more sanguine about place-based labels as a way to contest neoliberal moves. In her view, the fact that geographic indicators cannot travel like other ecolabels pits them squarely against globalizing forces. She also argues thus that they are a potential tool of rural development, keeping otherwise marginal places producing profit. In a similar vein, Marsden and Smith (2005) see alternative food networks (AFNs)—trust-based marketing arrangements that deliver high-value food (eg traditional, regionally specific, organic)—as a tool of sustainable rural development in marginalized areas. What they call "value capture", efforts to retain value in local communities that would otherwise go to downstream producers, is facilitated by "dense networks", but also seems to involve some sort of label if their case studies serve as adequate examples. Here, again, this localized value capture is theorized as a defense from the devalorization processes associated with conventional production systems and "globalization". Buller and Morris (2004) also speak of market-oriented initiatives that "re-qualify foods" according to either production processes (which they parse out as traditional and or modern ecological) or territory. They, too, laud the possibility of improved market access and/or the capture of a greater proportion of value. And they add that the higher prices presumably obtained in these initiatives more closely offset the true costs (externalities included) of production (1070). So, even when these initiatives are guided by moral values, including the possibility of non-alienated work, economic value capture provides the necessary cushion to survive in the world economy.

In light of the claims being made, there is remarkably scant attention throughout this literature to the actual mechanisms that might capture and/or retain value. Nor, for that matter, do those who argue that price premiums pay for the environmental costs of conventional production that have been externalized ever make clear how it is that a premium that goes to an individual producer pays for what are clearly socialized costs of, say, pollution abatement or landscape restoration. In fact, the overall approach remains highly elusive as to how value is captured, much less where value actually comes from in the first place. As I will discuss in the following section, at the minimum protection takes boundary setting and governance of those boundaries in ways that turn out to be not so consistent with Polanyi.

How Labels Protect

Assuming "normal" conditions of competition under capitalism, for a commodity to be protective of the environment and/or classes of people, it must realize value for the targeted actors above and beyond what they would receive otherwise (or prevent against erosion of existing values received). This extra value is what provides the necessary cushion to preclude a competitive "race to the bottom". Optimally, this cushion would allow for the totality of producers' social reproduction and the replacement or renewal of used natural resources; it would, as Buller and Morris (2004) suggest, pay for re-internalizing externalities. Minimally it would create conditions less exploitive than existing arrangements. Even if the goal is not explicitly monetary, but rather, say, better working conditions or more enfranchised labor processes, it seems a necessary if not sufficient condition for protection that the unit of production retain more value to allow for lower productivity. These protective commodities, then, are inherently redistributive.[2] While they may appropriate value from other nodes of the supply chain, they are more likely to target a redistribution of income from consumers to primary commodity producers and their productive assets—and occasionally to wage laborers involved in primary production.[3]

What, then, are the mechanisms of this redistribution? The idea is that supply chains can be regulated in such a way as to shift where value is appropriated to favor some actors over others (Kaplinsky 2000). In the case of voluntary labels, this regulation involves boundary setting that is at once protective and exclusionary, with the two key elements being standard setting and verification (Guthman 2004b). Standards delineate the production processes, allowable materials, employment practices, regional boundaries, and so forth that are the basis of any sort of labeling claim. Voluntary, proactive standards must be based on demonstrable difference from conventional commodities. In addition, these qualities require some sort of external guarantee unlike qualities intrinsic to commodities, such as flavor, which can presumably be detected on their own (Mutersbaugh 2005b). As Mutersbaugh puts it, "for certified agriculture, the demands of inspectability become privileged over rapidity of turn-over time because *risk* inheres more in lack of information about location and context than in rapidity of arrival . . . in the case of quality-certified ethical (eg fair trade, organic) products, a firm's market share is based in part upon a green reputation" (391). In other words, consumers have to believe this difference, if they are to pay the difference. Verification is what makes the labeling claims believable.

Both standards and verification establish barriers to entry (Guthman 2004a). Standards-based regulation rests on the presumption that only some can meet those standards. Some labeling schemes, such as organic, are fortified with more barriers such as lengthy transition periods. The cost and hassle of the certification process, as well as the increased surveillance that verification entails, also excludes some producers from participation. In exchange for demonstrating that these rarefied standards are met, certifying bodies confer a property right to the use of that label. In turn, willing (and convinced) consumers pay a price premium for the ascribed commodity. Consumers' wages (and other income) are the source of value of the redistribution that is the basis of protection, designed to reward (or compensate) producers who do things differently. Without the construction and maintenance of quasi-monopoly conditions, competition is unleashed and the incentive disappears. In short, as with most economic protection, exclusion is what allows this sort of value transfer to transpire at all—a critical point to consider in terms of the political efficacy of labels. It would then behoove us to explore who or what is being protected by these labels as a way to understand who is being excluded.

Who Labels Protect

It has been well demonstrated that the making and enforcement of standards is highly politicized (Campbell and Liepins 2001; Guthman 2004a). In addition, operationalization of these standards imposes new work routines, uncomfortable levels of surveillance, and even economic costs that are at cross purposes to the redistributions they are supposed to encourage (Freidberg 2003; Mutersbaugh 2002). In other words, standards-based regulation produces many complications and unintended consequences. My purpose here is far simpler. It is to demonstrate that even in the ideal, the protection various labels offer is uneven and not always directed to where the need is greatest. This will then serve as a starting point to explore some of the contradictory aspects of these labels in regards to neoliberalization.

While thus far my treatment of labels has been fairly generic (reflecting to some extent how they are treated in the literature), much variation exists in regards to their purposes and operational principles. For instance, among the various claims made about labels, some are meant to protect or preserve existing arrangements while others are meant to improve them. Furthermore, some are focused on production processes, some are focused on places (to secure or relocate revenue streams), while others are explicitly redistributive to classes of people. Table 1 schematizes some of the differences among these protective labels. Within this table, I have included two types of labels aimed at processes—one at ecological processes (organic), one at labor processes (craft cheese); two aimed at place—one at specific places (terroir), the other at generic localism; and one that is explicitly redistributive (fair trade). I make no

Table 1: Taxonomy of protective labels

	Intent of standards	Focus of verification	Example	Barrier	Distributional effect
Process based	Encourage ecologically sustainable practices	Materials used, piece of land	Organic	Meeting standards, verification, 3-year transition	After transition, subject to competition, very dynamic, prices decline
	Safeguard taste/ traditional methods	Labor process	Craft cheese, PDO	Entry into craft, apprenticeship	Value retained with producer
Place based	Safeguard taste/ specific qualities	Territorial qualities of land	AOC—terroir	Access to designated land	Monopoly ground rent
	Reduce food miles, support regional development	Within designated boundary	Generic local	Marketing agreement	Inter-regional competition
Distributive	Redistribution of commodity prices	Revenue allocation along supply chain	Fair trade	Verification only	Redistributional between consumers and producers

claims that the table is exhaustive of the types of protective labels that currently exist in the world. What I want to draw out, instead, is how the intent of the standards lead to different foci for verification purposes and, hence, barriers to entry. I also want to suggest that the forms these barriers take can have quite different distributional consequences but rarely offer the sort of protection for which they are championed.

For example, those labels that aim to preserve existing conditions not surprisingly also have the strongest barriers to entry. Craft labels, such as Protected Denomination of Origin (PDO), applied to products such as Parmagiana Reggiano, arguably both protect an unalienated labor process and retain value for the cheese maker. The gatekeepers of these labels are usually those already trained in the craft who apprentice a select group of newcomers. Similarly, controlled origin labels (AOCs) purport to safeguard particular qualities of land associated with a certain taste (*terroir*). Access to such designated land is itself a formidable barrier to entry, made all the more so by the monopoly ground rents that develop when a *terroir* comes to be associated with exceptional characteristics (Guthman 2004b; Harvey 2001). Because these designations are regulated by the state and cannot freely be traded like intellectual property rights, at least in the EU (Barham 2003), these designations protect existing producers with access to land and craft, irrespective of the inevitable efforts of food industry players to produce cheaper substitutes. Such labels are hardly redistributive. Yet, some of the other labels do not offer much protection at all. Guthman (2004a, 2004b) has shown that the organic barriers have been relatively easy to skirt and, as a result, prices have declined considerably over the last decade or so, pushing many producers out of the market. The fair trade movement claims to verify the circuits of trade and not to create barriers to entry (although even certification is a barrier). While fair trade is the only major existing food label that is clearly re-distributive in its intent (Shreck 2005), its low entry barriers has brought major players into the market, including Starbucks and Nestlé, in ways that threaten either to undermine the credibility of the label or to shift verification costs onto producers. As for these generic local labels, some are governed by marketing agreements that designate who can market under a given name and thus involve some form of verification. Other products deemed "local" are governed simply by a producers' self-claims and public willingness to buy both the idea of the local and the claim. In either case, even though such generic localisms are often characterized as efforts to reduce reliance on "imports" so to improve local development prospects, they effectively cannabilize other markets and in time could induce a great deal of inter-regional competition (DuPuis and Goodman 2005).

In short, it seems impossible to have a protective label without some sort of created scarcity. And it appears that the most effective of these labels (AOC, craft cheeses) are highly exclusionary, protecting those with existing access to already-valorized land or a craft and not necessarily the most economically or socially vulnerable. While some labels, like organic or even generic localism, can offer temporary protection for more marginal producers around the world, without barriers to entry they are subject to competition. Among the labels discussed, only fair trade offers the possibility of substantive, long-term redistribution. Its efficacy on this count, however, hangs in the balance, for there are many commodities in the world and producers of those commodities that are unlikely to be valorized even with a fair trade label. So while labels might be good for some (Pollyannian?), they are hardly good for everybody (Polanyian). Furthermore, the degree to which that they produce competition and reproduce inequality—themselves benchmarks of neoliberalism—suggests a more fundamental imperative to examine these as a form of neoliberal governance.

Neoliberalizing Labels, Labeling Neoliberalisms

As stated earlier, voluntary food labels came of age more or less concurrently with the phase of neoliberalization that Peck and Tickell (2002) have dubbed "roll-out". I do not think this is coincidental. The earlier phase of "roll-back" neoliberalization (beginning in the 1980s) initiated processes most commonly associated with neoliberalism: the privatization of public resources and spaces, the minimization of labor costs, the reductions of public expenditures (at least in the areas of social welfare), and the elimination of regulations seen as unfriendly to business, all in the name of "letting the market work" as the optimal mechanism to allocate goods and services (Jessop 2002; Mansfield 2004c; McCarthy and Prudham 2004; Peck 2004; Peck and Tickell 2002). This earlier phase also put the "hollowing out of the state" into motion, as many aspects of governance began to be displaced upwards to international bodies, outwards to private firms and other civil society actors, and downwards (devolved) to local and regional governments (Jessop 2002). Roll-back neoliberalization thus left massive instabilities, inequalities, and externalities in its wake, especially insofar as the north Atlantic evisceration of Keynesian-Fordist regulatory institutions and welfare programs coincided with the retraction of the development project and the imposition of structural adjustment in the global south.

Roll-out neoliberalization has thus been theorized as multi-sited efforts to stabilize and redress some of the worst consequences of roll-out, even to "re-embed" the neoliberal market and economy (Jessop 2002)— again evoking Polanyi. Because roll-out appears less mean-spirited than roll-back (notwithstanding the Bush juggernaut and the securitization and increased state intrusion that has come hand in glove with roll-out), roll-out at times obtains softer, or "third way" status, as several scholars have noted (Jessop 2002; Mansfield 2004c; McCarthy and Prudham 2004; Peck 2004; Peck and Tickell 2002). Much of this kinder, gentler neoliberalism is achieved with "flanking mechanisms", referring to state-led encouragement of civil society institutions to provide erstwhile retracted services and other compensatory mechanisms (Castree 2005; Jessop 2002). Surely voluntary efforts to encourage more sustainable production practices, as well as the "developmental consumption" associated with fair trade labels (Goodman 2004), come under this rubric.

Two additional characteristics of neoliberalization are worth noting here. One is its process orientation, which Peck and Tickell (2002) rightly captured in using the "-ation," rather than "-ism" suffix. Because neoliberalization in many respects involves roll-backs and devolution of existing institutions rather than the imposition of new pre-conceived institutions, those institutions that emerge are necessarily undetermined and, thus, variable (Larner and Craig 2005; Peck and Tickell 2002). The other is its baroque nature. Efforts to fill in the gaps left by roll-back necessarily take place at multiple scales, by many combinations of public and private sector actors. As Peck (2004) and others have noted, even though neoliberal philosophy argues for de-regulation, in practice neoliberalization has produced significant re-regulation: new rules, new rule-making bodies, and new spheres of rule-making, one consequence of which is that scalar politics have become a key feature of contestation around neoliberalism (Mansfield 2004c; McCarthy and Prudham 2004). And as Mansfield (2004c) and Robertson (2004) have shown, old rules often remain partially in place, creating new layers of rules, a palimpsest of regulation. Lawrence (2005) has commented on a number of other complications associated with partially devolved governance, including the devolution of responsibility without power (and funding) and the creation of new layers of bureaucracy with overlapping and connected spheres of authority. Surely the infinite complexities of rule give lie to the goals of transparency and accountability, also touted by neoliberal regimes.

In both these ways, rollout neoliberalization seems a bit like a patch for a computer operating system—an always partial and incomplete attempt to keep the program from crashing altogether, but with key vulnerabilities left intact, and no one really able to figure out the code. In addition, the fact that "actually existing neoliberalisms" do not emerge lock step with the neoliberal project—that aspects have spatially variable historical precedents and path dependencies—makes the character of things that emerge in the process of neoliberalization highly complex and even contradictory (Jessop 2002; Mansfield 2004c).[4] Among other issues, it makes it very difficult to assess to what extent emerging forms reinscribe neoliberalism and to what extent they instantiate the beginning of Peck and Tickell's "push back". Nevertheless, in recognition that neoliberalism's contradictions are also dialectical possibilities, in what follows, I want to revisit labels with these concerns in mind. Following Heynen and Robbins (2005) who have noted four dominant pieces of the neoliberal environment agenda: governance, privatization, enclosure, and valuation, I will take each in turn, and then add a fifth: devolution.[5]

Governance

Neoliberalism has been associated with a shift from government to governance, where government refers to the power and rule of the state, and governance loosely refers to non-state mechanisms of regulation. Governance also implies the employment of tools that indirectly encourage subjects to act in particular ways, rather than through "command and control" or so-called coercive forms of regulation (Rose 1999). The focus on governance in part reflects a turn toward Foucauldian thinking on the micropolitics and techniques of rule that is not necessarily specific to neoliberalism, yet there is a way in which governance is, as Rose (1999) says, "of particular significance today because recent political strategies have attempted to govern neither through centrally controlled bureaucracies (hierarchies) nor through competitive interactions between producers and consumers (markets), but through such self-organizing networks" (17). While the soft face of these new "tools of governance" (Salamon 2002) makes it hard to take issue with them at face value, some (eg Larner and Craig 2005; Peck and Tickell 2002) seem to argue that this shift from anti-regulation to meta-regulation is a bait and switch, allowing the appearance of no government when, indeed, the state has grown considerably and society is more rule-bound than ever.

In any case, it is the proliferation of what McCarthy and Prudham (2004) describe as "increasingly voluntarist, neo-corporatist regulatory frameworks involving non-binding standards and rules, public–private cooperation, self-regulation, and greater participation from citizen coalitions, all with varying degrees of capacity and accountability" (276) that concerns me here. Tellingly, Buller and Morris (2004) see these modes and mechanisms of governance as a distinct third way between state regulation and the privatization-of-everything approach endorsed by "free market economists". At the same time they are cognizant of "growing penetration and importance of private rules, conventions, and market forms of regulation in sustainable food production" and an arguable "reversal of the traditional division of responsibilities to a new situation in which public policy increasingly plays the role of facilitator through support schemes and payments while market forces play a greater role in regulation" (1080). This has certainly been the case of voluntary food labels, as seen in the standard and verification process alone. To take the organic standard as one example, while some countries have standards for organic production codified into national law (including the highly contentious US standard), an international standard has been developed within the context of *codex alimentarius* which will presumably be the baseline standard for trade disputes, and many NGOs have their own standards including the internationally recognized IFOAM (International Federation of Organic Agriculture Movements). International organic trade remains guided by a patchwork of these standards, often carrying multiple certifications (see Mutersbaugh 2005a for elaboration of this point). Verification, however, is usually accomplished by non-state actors, through private second- and third-party certifiers and trade associations, some of which are run as businesses and some of which are run as nonprofit organizations. Since the establishment of a federal rule for organic production in 2001, the US federal government now accredits these certifiers—at last count there were 99 certifiers operating in the US. The federal rule, designed to harmonize and make organic regulation less complicated, appears instead to have added more layers. At the same time, it has forced certification to come under basic norms of due process, effectively making the state the arbiter of last resort. Other labels appear to be governed by a similar patchwork of state and private regulation. Many AOC designations, for example, receive state oversight but are managed through non-state governing bodies. Fair trade, meanwhile, is regulated through a complex system of private retailers, international NGOs, and peasant cooperatives. None of these are purely of the state or outside of state, and all are governed at multiple scales.

Such unevenness is clearly at odds with goals of transparency; it is also at odds with the goals of letting the market work. The myriad measurements, rules, and rule-making bodies and measurements that go into operationalizing these markets can be onerous and inefficient themselves (Mutersbaugh 2005b; Robertson 2004). They also give the lie to notions of governance that suggest that behaviors can be induced in non-political ways. The governance of the labels themselves is always highly politicized because they involve boundary setting (Campbell and Liepins 2001; DuPuis and Goodman 2005; Guthman 2004c; Mansfield 2004b). Yet these boundaries are crucial to the projects of protection and redistribution that these labels attempt. All that said, the very inscrutability, baroqueness, and political embeddedness of label governance create some interesting openings. It is possible, that is, to create labels with quite radical governance mechanisms and have them fly under the radar, so to speak.

Privatization

Most of the work on neoliberal environmental governance, including Heynen and Robbins (2005), use the term privatization to describe a transfer of some sort of good, service, or condition of production from the public to the private sector. There is little doubt that voluntary labeling shifts regulatory responsibility from the public sector to non-governmental actors. Yet, privatization can also be used to describe limiting rights of access. For example, neoliberal privatization of the North Pacific pollack fisheries involved a change in the rules of access, restricting certain fleets to particular waters, for example, and not privatization of the fishery itself. Moreover, it entailed making an already existing quota system transferable, meaning the right to fish could be bought and sold (Mansfield 2004a, 2004c). These somewhat malleable understandings of privatization follow modern property theorists, who understand property as not the thing itself, but a set of claims to a thing (MacPherson 1979), which Rose (1994) has described as a "bundle of sticks". The importance of this metaphor is that it allows not only for property to be divisible with claims held by different users, but also that such claims can be bought and sold in markets. One reading of neoliberal privatization is that the "bundle of sticks" is being debundled in unprecedented ways, including, in the case of landed property, the sale of different ecosystem services to different users (Robertson 2004). The hallmark of neoliberal privatization is, as Mansfield suggests, not so much that heretofore commons are being titled (although that takes place too), but that property rights are being invented to enforce a market rationality. For, it is the creation and assignment of tradable rights that makes nature subject to the highest bidder (McAfee 1999).

So, here I want to establish that voluntary food labels are analogs to this latter sort of privatization, not simply a shift to private sector regulation. Like ecosystem services, there is a way in which they create a property right for self-regulating. Rather than command and control regulations that nominally force all producers to abide by a set of constraints, the constraints imposed by labeling schemes are voluntary and made compensable by the establishment of that property right. What is being bought and sold through the verification process is a property right to the use of a label so as to obtain access to markets and increased values. The right itself is not directly transferable, however; a buyer cannot simply pay for the use of the label without meeting the criteria behind the label. Nevertheless, some of the rights that these labels inhere attach to landed property itself. For example, AOC and organic labels are based on claims about where certain parcels are located or how they were treated. Insofar as these claims then become the basis of monopoly rents and hence higher land values (Guthman 2004b), they potentially involve a shift of wealth to already existing landowners.

In addition, there is the question of what is being made into property. Some might argue that these labels are a type of intellectual property right (IPR). Knowledge and skill are no doubt key ingredients of a craft cheese, and some have suggested that organic production is fundamentally a distinct knowledge system (eg Morgan and Murdoch 2000). Still, since these labels have been posed as a way to redistribute (or retain) value, presumably toward the site of primary production, it would follow that the labor process is that which is not sufficiently valued, of which knowledge is only a part. If that is the case, producing a property right around a labor relation is arguably a conflation of production relations and exchange relations.[6] In effect, trade regulation substitutes for labor regulation, as with the failure to incorporate labor norms directly into WTO-sponsored international trade agreements (Boiral 2003). Extending property rights to human behaviors and institutions that heretofore were not titled is precisely the sort of thing for which many IPRs have been criticized (McCarthy 2004:530). The silver lining? Intellectual property rights can be protectionist, which is why traditional plant breeders have also fought for such rights.

Enclosure

Closely related to the question of property is that of enclosure. The establishment of property rights necessarily involves enclosure, although in this case something far less violent than the forced removal of peasants from the countryside. A well-developed area of scholarship in regards to common property resource management has shown how governance invariably involves some element of exclusion, generally to prevent the collective action problems that are presumed to exist with a scarce or desirable resource (see Mansfield 2004a for a good review and exposition as to how these scholars concede the market logic of neoliberalism).

Often that has meant producing seasonal access restrictions and/or harvest quotas. Sometimes it has meant producing spatial boundaries of where one can operate, although this has proven difficult in the case of ocean fisheries, as Mansfield argues. Not all (beneficent) enclosures are about dividing a resource commons, however; they may also involve dividing up markets. DuPuis (2001) has shown how early twentieth century milk-marketing orders relied on exclusions and boundaries, established in the spirit of orderly conduct and fairness.

Barham (2003) seems sanguine that common property management ideas can be applied to AOC and other ecolabels. Labels do require governance akin to common property management, as a way to codify who gets access to the benefits of that label and who does not. It is odd, though, that in the case of labels there is not a commons of which there is a putative tragedy, or, for that matter, a pre-given scarcity that needs to be protected. Critics of neoliberal environmental governance have already noted that attempts to privatize space to prevent the scarcities associated with the dreaded tragedy of the commons seem to produce scarcities—in water, land, and so forth (Heynen and Robbins 2005; Liverman 2004). In limiting access to a market, the scarcity that is produced is somewhat different, though. Because these enclosures produce a price premium, what becomes scarce is access to the commodity in question at more competitive prices. Labels thus create a bit of an inverse: the practical ability to farm more sustainably or justly is not scarce; the economic ability may be. The larger point is that privatizing a commons in "doing good" creates incentives that are at odds with the purpose of inducing ethical behavior more broadly. Nevertheless, it could certainly be argued that with careful attention to the boundaries created by these labels, they could protect people more vulnerable than those currently being protected.

Valuation

Neoliberal valuation rests on the presumption that the market will assign high prices to scarce resources, although, as many have noted, the valuation of eco-systemic qualities, such as "ecosystem services", air and water quality, and biodiversity proves difficult precisely because these things are not easily reducible, divisible, or fungible (Liverman 2004; Robertson 2004). The valuation problem would seem less formidable with labels, at least at first blush. After all, these are by definition attached to commodities that already flow through the market unlike, say, a wetland. Still, the valuation mechanisms behind these labels are not all that straightforward, making appropriate Liverman's inclusion of fair trade/green labeling under the commoditization-of-everything rubric.

As I have argued elsewhere, the value-added in these labels is an economic rent—an above "normal" rate of return based on some sort of scarcity.[7] As Kaplinsky (2004) notes, regulations that create industry-specific monopoly conditions, including the establishment of intellectual property rights, can be the basis of economic rent, and it is precisely these non-tangible pieces of value chains that are increasingly sources of rent in today's political economy. That said, some might argue that the price premiums associated with these labels are not rent but are simply returns that cover the internalization of costs that have been otherwise externalized (Buller and Morris 2004; Lampkin and Padel 1994). This argument has some validity; theories of rent assume that all producers operate at the lowest possible cost and this is not always the case, particularly with production systems that aim at ecological sustainability. Nevertheless, the externalities that arise from low-cost systems are generally socialized and it remains unclear how they might be "paid for" by individual producers, whose production systems happen to attract price premiums in the market.

In any case, the argument I wish to pursue here does not require that the reader buys theories of rent. For the presumption that value can be determined and shifted is itself subject to scrutiny. Besides arguments from neo-classical economics that place the origin of profit in exchange, even among scholars sympathetic to classical political economy, value is seen as more elusive than that implied in the labor theory of value and theories of rent. First of all, advocates of ethical labels assume that use values and exchange values are synonymous. And, in fact, ethical values are commodified into exchange values (Guthman 2002). Yet, as Sayer (2003), who wishes to distinguish the moral use value from the exchange value, argues, the use values of commodities can be inclusive of moral concerns, irrespective of how exchange values circulate. While Barham (2002:350) would seem to concur when she states that "value-based labels" are those that "carry explicit messages about a product's value in registers that are usually considered to be non-market by economists", her argument otherwise suggests that moral/ethical values are precisely what should be commodified in these value-based labels.

More damning is Graeber's (1996) argument that any system of value entails struggle over definition, in part because what is being exchanged is non-commensurable between two actors (although the exchange makes them so). That being obtained is an object of desire; that being let go is by definition expendable. But if value, as he says, is "something that mobilizes the desires of those who recognize it" (12), what does that suggest in a transaction when the object of desire is not just a thing but a desire to be just and ethical? Henderson (2004:491) throws in an additional wrench when he states that "values that inhere in commodities become relative to each other", and that value is always in the process of being mediated by a nonvalued or devalued force, to the extent that "value itself can be a destabilizing force". Such would seem to hold for ethical commodities; the devaluation of labor and natural resource renewal of primary producers under current conditions of neoliberalism is exactly what has to figure in their moral valuation for consumers. In such a situation, these two poles of value seem strikingly incommensurable and would certainly call into question whether the price paid by the ethical consumer can really make up the difference of that devaluation. That some of the value is conferred by inspections and certification procedures, which are themselves exchanged in markets, further complicates the matter (Mutersbaugh 2005b). What I am arguing is that labels do not or cannot represent and capture a value that maps onto the "true cost" of production. They must, however, persuade us that they are doing something like that.

Devolution: Persuading and Producing the Neoliberal Consumer

That value itself is relative in value-based labels and elsewhere raises the question of how they incite consumers to part with their own "surplus" value—that is to pay some sort of price premium. Here I would argue that standards, verification procedures, and certifying bodies do more than produce boundaries of acceptable behavior; by establishing property rights, they also convince, redolent of Rose's (1994) property as persuasion. And the proximate site of persuasion is the label itself. Labels tell consumers stories about what makes the commodities behind them important, an idea captured in Hollander's (2003) notion of "supermarket narratives" and DuPuis' (2000) "talking milk carton". Labels, in that way, interpolate the knowledgeable consumer.

In hailing the consumer, however, these labels reinforce another aspect of neoliberalism's political economic project: devolution. In actuality, these labels are devolutionary in several ways, since standards are codified and verified by multiple regional, non-state, and/or informal regulatory networks at various nodes on their supply chains. Nevertheless, perhaps the most crucial way they are devolutionary is that they put regulatory control at the site of the cash register. While such regulation gets counted as non-coercive (Salamon 2002), by choosing what sort of ethical products to buy or not to buy, consumers are making regulatory decisions about ecological and public health risk, working conditions and remuneration, and even what sort of producers of what commodities should be favored in the world market. Whether these labels produce adequate knowledge to support these important decisions is itself a concern. More significantly, to regulate at the scale of the (often privileged) consumer is hardly commensurate with the scale at which social and ecological problems are generated and is bound to be highly uneven in its effects. How can individual consumption decisions even pretend to create broad public benefit?

At this point, it is worth pausing to consider another way in which this aspect of neoliberal governance should be analyzed, following Larner's (2003) call to consider neoliberalism as a set of techniques and not only its political economic parameters. Insofar as "advanced" liberalism "does not seek to govern through 'society' but through the regulated choices of individual citizens" (Rose 1996:41), it is certainly arguable that the knowledgeable, choice-making consumer is the political subjectivity fostered by these other strategies of environmental governance. In this line of thinking, the consuming subject is an effect not a mechanism of neoliberal governance. If this is the case, it seems crucial to reflect on some of the more troubling political rationalities labels produce. Here, I think, they make crucial concessions to neoliberal ideology: that the state cannot govern, that labor is property, that property is protective, that markets can self-regulate, that consumption choices are meaningful exercises of freedom (Dean 1999; Rose 1999), and, most fundamentally, that putting a monetary value on ethical proclivities is even thinkable, as if "doing good" is one more thing to be bought and sold. These are precisely the sorts of rationalities that obscure possible paths of action outside of the market, reinforcing the politics of no alternative.

Conclusion: Is There No Alternative?

Devolving social regulation to individual consumers seems a far cry from the politics of social protection implied by Polanyi's double movement. That voluntary, protective labels work with the market—indeed extend market mechanisms into realms where they previously did not exist—seems to stray from Polanyian thinking as well. Nor do they necessarily help modulate the market's vagaries. If anything, they induce competition, and the social and ecological protections they offer are always and everywhere partial and uneven. This unevenness surely articulates with the inequality unleashed by neoliberalism's own embrace of the market. Yet, in keeping with Polanyian concerns with the anomic forces of the market, they are in some ways an expression of socially created embeddedness.

These labels are also contradictory as expressions of neoliberal roll-out. They are governed by non-transparent public–private partnerships to be sure, but such non-public governance leaves open the possibility of radical governance mechanisms. They confer a property right, but not a true privatization; and such property rights have long been the workhorse of protectionism. They entail exclusivity but so have more collectively oriented common property management regimes. And yes, they commodify ethical values but within the context of already existing commodities. Such contradictoriness is not surprising. As Peck and Tickell (2002), and Mansfield (2004c) have argued, not all facets of neoliberalism cohere. Similarly, as McCarthy and Prudham (2004) have stated with respect to environmentalism, counter-projects to neoliberalism often incorporate its elements. In part, these contradictions owe to the indeterminate nature of neoliberalism itself—always an unfolding project.

Given that neoliberalism makes neither its own ideology visible or its own transformations determinate (Jessop 2002; Peck 2004), what does all this suggest for the politics of the possible? Within the framework of "there is no alternative" it may be folly to disregard tools that have even a modicum of efficacy in mitigating the injustices and destruction of contemporary neoliberalism. Following Gibson-Graham (1996) it might be important to consider the spaces they open. At the very least, then, progenitors and advocates of these labels might pay more attention to who/what is being encouraged in the creation of these labels in hopes that labels with more radical intentions can be developed. Perhaps, that is, the exclusivity inherent to these labels can be made more purposive to leave out today's winners in the global economy, rather than selectively help a few of its losers.

Another, perhaps a better, "way out" is to consider how these labels could work within a broader dialectic. Bondi and Laurie's (2005) injunction to look at the heart of neoliberalism and not its interstices is apt here. Because while it may be the case that these labels are at best limited, and at worst perverse, their saving grace may be in their indirect consequences. So, for example, strategic use of labeling may help embarrass (or encourage) major suppliers into changing their practices as Unilever did in nearly abandoning the use of genetically engineered supplies of grain for its European market. They may make transparent corporate vulnerabilities that activists can exploit. Or they may, following Barnett et al (2005:39) "enlist ordinary people into broader projects of social change".

On that note, perhaps the best way out is a return to Polanyi. Polanyi, it should be remembered, saw the state as a site of regulation. The presumption of the double movement is that society would organize through the state to obtain social protection (Burawoy 2003). While it would be folly to read Polanyi directly onto the present, particularly in light of the putative failure of pre-neoliberal regulatory models and an understandable distrust of existing states, the point should not be lost that there are forms of governance, perhaps still unimagined, that incorporate and promote societal, public wants and needs in ways that voluntary labels could never achieve. The best hope for these labels, then, is that they could help produce more collectivist political subjects who in time would develop forms of governance more commensurate to the socialized problems before us. That would be the Polanyian way.

Acknowledgements

I am grateful for the Estes Park group (you know who you are) for planting the seeds of some of the ideas elaborated in this paper. I wish to acknowledge the specific contributions of Melanie DuPuis, James McCarthy, and Tad Mutersbaugh, as well as two anonymous reviewers for very useful suggestions at various stages of the paper's preparation.

Endnotes

[1] They are voluntary, in the sense of not being state mandated, and that they ostensibly draw consumers to a product rather than warn them off. Not all producers necessarily volunteer to come under their rubric, however; much of the growth in fair trade and organic is driven by market intermediaries.

[2] Attempts at ecological or social responsibility that are not redistributive can worsen social inequalities. For example, the new European ethical trade initiatives, such as EurepGap, are designed to have all producers conform to what are presumably higher standards (Campbell 2005). The problem is that meeting these standards is so onerous and costly, that much like ethical initiatives in Britain, they force certain producers out of the market (Freidberg 2003) or into second/illegal markets (Dunn 2003). Paradoxically, though, these sorts of standards aim for a much larger swathe of producers and their practices than the voluntary protective labels.

[3] As pointed out by one reviewer, in some respects I am glossing over important differences between petty commodity production and that based on wage labor. The fact is that few of these labels actually target wage labors as the recipients of redistributions,

although it is often presumed that marginal farmers will share the benefits obtained through a label with their employees (Brown and Getz forthcoming). As for "willing workers on organic farms" (a name that reflects an actually existing network of organic farming volunteers) they are effectively providing the subsidy (redistribution) that allows those farms to compete.

[4] For this reason, several scholars are calling for more careful enunciations of the concept and/are beginning to question the utility of it altogether (Castree 2005; Larner 2003).

[5] I use the lens of environmental governance because it is the closest programmatically to contemporary agro-food politics, but want to note that this area remains under-explored except for in regard to trade liberalization. Look for Guthman (forthcoming) for an exploration of this topic.

[6] That is, putting aside the value distribution at the site of production is itself political (between labor and land, between labor and capital, among different members of households).

[7] See Guthman (2004b) for an extended discussion of how organic regulation produces rent; also Mutersbaugh (2005a).

References

Bacon C (2005) Confronting the coffee crisis: Can fair trade, organic and specialty coffees reduce small-scale farmer vulnerability in northern Nicaragua? *World Development* 33(3):497–511

Barham E (1997) Social movements for sustainable agriculture in France: A Polanyian perspective. *Society and Natural Resources* 10(3):239–249

Barham E (2002) Towards a theory of values-based labeling. *Agriculture and Human Values* 19(4):349–260

Barham E (2003) Translating terroir: The global challenge of French AOC labeling. *Journal of Rural Studies* 19(1):127–138

Barnett C, Cloke P, Clarke N and Malpass A (2005) Consuming ethics: Articulating the subjects and spaces of ethical consumption. *Antipode* 37(1):23–45

Boiral O (2003) The certification of corporate conduct: Issues and prospects. *International Labour Review* 142(3):317

Bondi L and Laurie N (2005) Introduction: Working the spaces of neoliberal subjectivity. *Antipode* 37(3):494–401

Brown S and Getz C (forthcoming) Privatizing farm worker justice: Regulating labor through voluntary certification and labeling. *Geoforum*

Buller H and Morris C (2004) Growing goods: The market, the state, and sustainable food production. *Environment and Planning A* 36(6):1065–1084

Burawoy M (2003) For a sociological Marxism: The complementary convergence of Antonio Gramsci and Karl Polanyi. *Politics and Society* 31(2):193–261

Campbell H (2005) The rise and rise of EurepGAP: European (re)invention of colonial food relations? *International Journal of Sociology of Agriculture and Food* 13(2). http://www.csafe.org.nz/ijsaf/archive/vol13(2)_05/vol13_2.html

Campbell H and Liepins R (2001) Naming organics: Understanding organic standards in New Zealand as a discursive field. *Sociologia Ruralis* 41(1):21–39

Castree N (2005) The epistemology of particulars: Human geography, case studies, and "context". *Geoforum* 36(5):541–544

Dean M (1999). *Governmentality: Power and Rule in Modern Society*. Thousand Oaks, CA: Sage

Dunn E (2003) Trojan pig: Paradoxes of food safety regulation. *Environment and Planning A* 35(8):1493–1511

DuPuis E M (2000) Not in my body: rBGH and the rise of organic milk. *Agriculture and Human Values* 17(3):285–295

DuPuis E M (2001) *Nature's Perfect Food*. New York: New York University Press
DuPuis E M and Goodman D (2005) Should we go "home" to eat? Towards a reflexive politics of localism. *Journal of Rural Studies* 21(3):359–371
Freidberg S (2003) Cleaning up down south: Supermarkets, ethical trade, and African horticulture. *Journal of Social and Cultural Geography* 4(1):27–42
Gibson-Graham J K (1996) *The End of Capitalism (As We Knew It)*. Malden, MA: Blackwell
Goodman M K (2004) Reading fair trade: Political ecological imaginary and the moral economy of fair trade foods. *Political Geography* 23(7):891–915
Graeber D (1996) Beads and money: Notes toward a theory of wealth and power. *American Ethnologist* 23(1):4–24
Guthman J (2002) Commodified meanings, meaningful commodities: Re-thinking production–consumption links through the organic system of provision. *Sociologia Ruralis* 42(4):295–311
Guthman J (2004a) *Agrarian Dreams? The Paradox of Organic Farming in California*. Berkeley: University of California Press
Guthman J (2004b) Back to the land: The paradox of organic food standards. *Environment and Planning A* 36(3):511–528
Guthman J (2004c) The trouble with "organic lite" in California: A rejoinder to the "conventionalization" debate. *Sociologia Ruralis* 44(3):301–316
Guthman J (forthcoming) Neoliberalism and the making of food politics in California. *Geoforum*
Harvey D (2001) *Spaces of Capital*. New York: Routledge
Henderson G (2004) "Free food": The local production of worth, and the circuit of decommodification: Toward a value theory of the surplus. *Environment and Planning D: Society and Space* 22:485–512
Heynen N and Robbins P (2005) The neoliberalization of nature: Governance, privatization, enclosure and valuation. *Capitalism Nature Socialism* 16(1):5–8
Hollander G M (2003) Re-naturalizing sugar: Narratives of place, production, and consumption. *Social and Cultural Geography* 4(1):59–74
Jessop B (2002) Liberalism, neoliberalism, and urban governance: A state theoretical perspective. *Antipode* 34(3):452–472
Kaplinsky R (2000) Globalization and unequalisation: What can be learned from value chain analysis? *Journal of Development Studies* 37(2):117–146
Kaplinsky R (2004) Spreading the gains from globalization: What can be learned from value chain analysis? *Problems of Economic Transition* 47(2):74–115
Lampkin N and Padel S (eds) (1994) *The Economics of Organic Farming*. Wallingford: CAB International
Larner W (2003) Neoliberalism? *Environment and Planning D: Society and Space* 21(5):509–512
Larner W and Craig D (2005) After neoliberalism? Community activism and local partnerships in Aotearoa New Zealand. *Antipode* 37(3):402–424
Lawrence G (2005) Promoting sustainable development: The question of governance. In Buttel F H and McMichael P (eds) *New Directions in the Sociology of Global Development*. New York: Elsevier
Liverman D (2004) Who governs, at what scale and at what price? Geography, environmental governance, and the commodification of nature. *Annals of the Association of American Geographers* 94(4):734–738
MacPherson C B (ed) (1979) *Property: Mainstream and Critical Positions*. Toronto: University of Toronto Press
Mansfield B (2004a) Neoliberalism in the oceans: "Rationalization," property rights, and the commons question. *Geoforum* 35(3):313–326

Mansfield B (2004b) Organic view of nature: The debate over certification for aquatic animals. *Sociologia Ruralis* 44(2):216–232

Mansfield B (2004c) Rules of privatization: Contradictions in neoliberal regulation of North Pacific fisheries. *Annals of the Association of American Geographers* 94(3):565–584

Marsden T and Smith E (2005) Ecological entrepreneurship: Sustainable development in local communities through quality food production and local branding. *Geoforum* 36:440–451

McAfee K (1999) Selling nature to save it? Biodiversity and green developmentalism. *Environment and Planning D: Society and Space* 17:133–154

McCarthy J (2004) Privatizing conditions of production: Trade agreements and environmental governance. *Geoforum* 35(3):327–341

McCarthy J and Prudham S (2004) Neoliberal nature and the nature of neoliberalism. *Geoforum* 35(3):275–283

Morgan K and Murdoch J (2000) Organic vs. conventional agriculture: Knowledge, power and innovation in the food chain. *Geoforum* 31:159–173

Mutersbaugh T (2002) The number is the beast: A political economy of organic-coffee certification and producer unionism. *Environment and Planning A* 34(7):1165–1184

Mutersbaugh T (2005a) Fighting standards with standards: Harmonization, rents, and social accountability in certified agro-food networks. *Environment and Planning A* 37(11):2033–2051

Mutersbaugh T (2005b) Just-in-space: Certified rural products, labor of quality, and regulatory spaces. *Journal of Rural Studies* 21(4):389–402

Peck J (2004) Geography and public policy: Constructions of neoliberalism. *Progress in Human Geography* 28(3):392–405

Peck J and Tickell A (2002) Neoliberalizing space. *Antipode* 34(3):380–404

Polanyi K (1944) *The Great Transformation*. Boston: Beacon Press

Raynolds L (2000) Re-embedding global agriculture: The international organic and fair trade movements. *Agriculture and Human Values* 17(3):297–309

Renard M-C (1999) The interstices of globalization: The example of Fair Coffee. *Sociologia Ruralis* 39(4):494–500

Renting H, Marsden T and Banks J (2003) Understanding alternative food networks: Exploring the role of short food supply chains in rural development. *Environment and Planning A* 35(3):393–411

Robertson M M (2004) The neoliberalization of ecosystem services: Wetland mitigation banking and problems in environmental governance. *Geoforum* 35(3):361–373

Rose C (1994) *Property and Persuasion*. Boulder: Westview Press

Rose N (1996) Governing "advanced" liberal democracies. In Barry A, Osborne T and Rose N (eds) *Foucault and Political Reason: Liberalism, Neo-liberalism and Rationalities of Government* (pp 37–64) Chicago: University of Chicago Press

Rose N (1999). *Powers of Freedom: Reframing Political Thought*. Cambridge: Cambridge University Press

Salamon L M (2002) New governance and the tools of public action. In Salamon L M (ed) *The Tools of Government: A Guide to the New Governance* (pp 1–47). New York: Oxford University Press

Sayer A (2003) De(commodification), consumer culture, and moral economy. *Environment and Planning D: Society and Space* 21(3):341–357

Shreck A (2005) Resistance, redistribution, and power in the fair trade banana initiative. *Agriculture and Human Values* 22(1):17–29

Chapter 4

Property, Markets, and Dispossession: The Western Alaska Community Development Quota as Neoliberalism, Social Justice, Both, and Neither

Becky Mansfield

Introduction

In 1992, the United States, prodded by the State of Alaska and various community organizations, pioneered the Western Alaska Community Development Quota (CDQ). Run jointly by the State of Alaska, the US National Marine Fisheries Service (NMFS), and NMFS' regional branch the North Pacific Fishery Management Council (the Council), the aim of the CDQ is to use the voluminous fish resources of the Bering Sea to provide economic opportunities for people of coastal western Alaska. Regional fisheries for species such as Alaska pollock, Pacific cod, Pacific halibut, and king and snow crab are among the largest and most lucrative in the country and the world (NMFS 2005). Despite these resources and the large fishing and processing industry benefiting from them, the people of the region, 85% of whom are indigenous, are extremely poor, with poverty rates over 25% and local unemployment rates as high as 45% (State of Alaska 2003). Indigenous poverty amidst valuable resources that are exploited by others is not an unusual phenomenon, and as in other cases the situation stems from a history of economic, political, and cultural disenfranchisement. The "community development" part of the CDQ refers to state-led efforts to redress this ingrained set of problems by harnessing fish resources for local economic development.

The "quota" part of the CDQ refers to the central mechanism of the program. A quota of 7.5–10% of each year's total catch of fish, as set by the Council, is set aside for the CDQ. Regulators then allocate this total quota among six "CDQ groups" representing self-selected sets of communities; there are 65 communities, with a total of 27,000 people, divided unevenly among the six groups (State of Alaska 2003:6) (see Figure 1). What is innovative about the CDQ is that quota is not designed so local people benefit directly by catching and using the fish (ie use value), but instead quota is marketable (ie exchange value). CDQ groups may not sell their quota outright, but the program is designed for them to lease their quota to non-CDQ firms already active in the industry; these firms now pay CDQ groups for the right to catch fish. By the early 2000s, annual revenue for all CDQ groups combined was around US$70 million, with most income from leasing quota (State of Alaska 2003). The CDQ groups then take the profits from leasing their quota and reinvest them in fisheries development projects, and such activities have included becoming equity partners in these large fishing firms and their vessels. From 1992, when the program started, to 2002, overall assets increased from US$13 million to 227 million (State of Alaska 2003). What becomes clear, then, is that quota is a new form of property. There is debate about whether such quota is formal property—regulators claim it is not because the state can eliminate it altogether by ending the entire regulatory program (eg NMFS 1993)—but quota acts as property in that it encloses access to fish, can be transferred in the market, and was designed as capital to be invested for further accumulation.

When focusing on quota, the CDQ appears to be one more example of "neoliberalism and nature" (Bakker 2005; Heynen and Robbins 2005; McCarthy and Prudham 2004). Privatization, as a shift in ownership, is at the center of neoliberalization of nature in two senses. Privatization moves control and management of nature from the public (government) to the private (business) sector. More generally, privatization encloses nature (individual resources, natural processes, etc) as property, gener-ally conceived as private property, and brings it into capitalist markets as commodities. Privatization in both senses can be seen in the CDQ, as creating quota and treating that quota as a marketable good creates new property rights in access for fish. Quota incorporates the private sector into management decisions in new ways and encloses access to resources in the name of commercial economic development. No longer just the role of the state, resource allocation occurs through mar-ket forces. This underlying process of privatization—the enclosure and commodification of resources as private property—is what David Harvey (2003) has called the "cutting edge" of neoliberalism today. I myself have argued that all efforts at privatization are neoliberal, and one way of knowing neoliberalism when you see it is by the presence of privatization (Mansfield 2004a).

However, the structure and history of the CDQ challenge this interpre-tation of the program as just another neoliberal project. At the same time that the CDQ appears as a form of neoliberal privatization, it is also a form of protection *from* the market. Not only is it motivated by concerns about regional and racial injustice and inequity, but quota is a mechanism through which the central government redistributes resources to poor people, and does so in a way that creates an inalienable form of property. Government oversight—through the allocation procedure —protects the

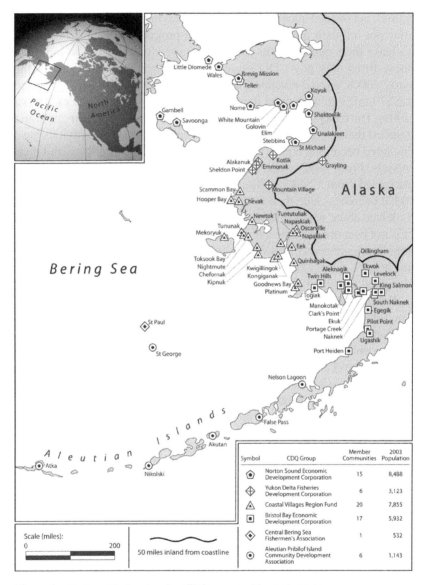

Symbol	CDQ Group	Member Communities	2003 Population
⬢	Norton Sound Economic Development Corporation	15	8,488
⬥	Yukon Delta Fisheries Development Corporation	6	3,123
△	Coastal Villages Region Fund	20	7,855
▣	Bristol Bay Economic Development Corporation	17	5,932
◈	Central Bering Sea Fishermen's Association	1	532
◉	Aleutian Pribilof Island Community Development Association	6	1,143

Scale (miles):
0   200

50 miles inland from coastline

Figure 1: Western Alaska, showing CDQ communities and groups
(source: Map by Jim DeGrand)

CDQ communities from the effects of the open market. These countervailing tendencies could be interpreted as evidence of contradictions in neoliberalism, such that the "free market" cannot exist without the very same government interventions that are considered anathema by neoliberal proponents. I have identified such contradictions in related fisheries management programs of the North Pacific region, arguing that it was state-managed protections from the market that made neoliberal privatization work (Mansfield 2004b), and related insights about re-regulation are a hallmark of geographical scholarship on neoliberalism (Brenner and Theodore 2002; Bridge and Jonas 2002; Peck and Tickell 2002). As I will show, however, the CDQ presents a different situation; protections from the market are *not* used primarily to support the market and extend neoliberal relations, but are based on quite different ideas about proper means to achieve socio-environmental goals.

This paper starts from this tension in which what seem to be quite opposed positions exist at the core of the CDQ program. It seems it should be possible to analyze the program to reveal what the CDQ "really" is. Is it a neoliberal program of capitalist expansion or is a redistributive program aimed at social justice? Is it built on the idea that ethical values cannot be counted on for achieving goals because people almost always act in their own self-interest, while the market is a great equalizer that coordinates such self-interested action into the greater good for all? Or is it built on the idea that markets produce inequity, injustice, and environmental degradation, while ethical principles can and should guide action? But the more I have analyzed the CDQ, I have found that both positions are plausible. It is not even possible to make separate lists of neoliberal and social justice aspects of the program, because for each aspect the logic of one seems to bleed into the other. That what we take as neoliberal can hybridize with what we take as non-neoliberal is certainly true in a variety of management situations, such as community forestry (McCarthy 2005). Noticing these hybrids, or "incompatibilities", without immediately resolving them can be important for destabilizing conventional categories and creating new possibilities for action (Singleton 2005). It is important, then, not simply to acknowledge incoherence, but to give attention to how it comes to be and in what ways it is generative of new potential. That is, the existence of multiple logics is not in itself a surprise (although it is interesting the extent to which the CDQ can be described equally well in almost opposite terms). What is more interesting is to ask how multiple logics are able to coexist: through what processes and mechanisms are these different logics made compatible?

For the CDQ, I have come to the conclusion that there is a deeper co-herence to the program, and it can be discerned through careful analysis of the program's property dimensions. Property is central because it is quota-as-property that animates both logics. Quota encloses access to fish and serves as capital for the CDQ groups to invest, and quota provides an inalienable resource to be used for these groups' benefit. Building on recent scholarship on property, I argue that once property is expanded beyond orthodox notions of bounded spaces of independent ownership to emphasize interdependence, obligation, and the reasons for property relations, it is possible to see that privatization in the CDQ embodies multiple logics without being incoherent. The goal of this paper is to consider privatization not only through the lens of arguments for and against neoliberalism and its economic logics, but to view privatization specifically in its property dimensions, which have multiple legal and economic aspects. To be clear, then, the surprise here is not that the CDQ is incoherent or has multiple logics, but that the property mechanism provides it with some unexpected coherence.

Analysis of the CDQ program is based on investigation of implementing regulations themselves as they have changed over time. Publications of these regulations include not only the regulatory language itself—which can be traced through time—but also various meta-commentary regarding history, rationale, summary of public comments and responses, and so on. Regulatory documents were supplemented with related documents, for example, environmental impact statements and public statements (eg in the media) by individuals involved in the CDQ in a variety of roles.

Competing Logics in the CDQ

When the CDQ started in 1992, it applied just to the Alaska pollock fishery, but the success of the initial program inspired general extension throughout the 1990s to most species regulated by the central government. As written into law and regulation during this time, the CDQ has a variety of features that shape how quota is allocated and used. Quota is provided to communities that meet eligibility criteria, including that they are adjacent to the Bering Sea, have been designated as native communities (although all residents can benefit), have limited commercial fisheries development, and depend primarily on the Bering Sea for existing activities. Communities that have met these criteria organize themselves into CDQ groups, which are corporations that receive allocation of quota on the basis of detailed business and community development plans for investing and growing their capital. Business and development activities are legally required to be related to the fish industry in some way. Government officials assess the CDQ plans when allocating the total quota among the individual groups, which also provides government oversight of the CDQ groups. This description of the program makes it seem straightforward: eligible communities receive from the state a resource they then market to generate economic benefits, which are then invested to provide further benefits. This easy description, however, masks the conceptual difficulty parsing the program, that is, difficulty figuring out the underlying logic of the mechanisms of the program.

The conceptual difficulty of the CDQ can be seen in the quota itself, which does very different things simultaneously. Quota first appears as the very definition of neoliberal privatization. It encloses a public resource—the right to catch fish—as one that is allocated to a closed set of actors (the CDQ groups). What was once legally available to all is no longer. These actors are then able to sell this resource back to those who once had free access but now are excluded (the non-CDQ fishers). Quota thus privatizes something that was once public and commodifies something that was never before a commodity (ie *fish* once caught were a commodity but the *right to go fishing* never was). In so doing, quota creates a market where once there was none, thus expanding capitalist relations. As private, transferable property that fosters market relations, quota follows the neoclassical economic argument for property (Demsetz 1967), which has become dominant in fisheries discourse over the past 50 years and is central to neoliberalization of contemporary fisheries (Mansfield 2004a; St Martin 2005; see, for example, Hannesson 2004). This economic argument is that enclosing things as private property makes them valuable, induces labor, and fosters conservation of resources, all because property owners are guaranteed to see the benefits of their action. Conversely, a lack of private property inherently generates problems, including declining profits and resource bases, because it is not in any individual's self-interest to protect a resource or refrain from inefficient economic activity (because someone else will reap the benefits of positive action). Building on this logic, over the past two decades fisheries regulators have subject the North Pacific to a program of "rationalization" that uses privatization as the central mechanism for addressing problems in the fishery, which are attributed open-access fishing regimes (Mansfield 2004a, 2006). Because the CDQ is a "limited access" program—ending open access in the fishery—it is consistent with this broad rationalization program and its conception of property, and regulators see the CDQ as a potential model for other rationalization programs. "The management experience gained through the . . . CDQ fisheries can be used to develop and assess future limited access programs for [other] fisheries" (NMFS 1998:8356). Thus, the CDQ not only creates property, but inserts this property mechanism into a market context and builds from orthodox notions about the role of property in economic systems. This is all quite consistent with a neoliberal approach to fisheries management.

Yet, the same quota mechanism also contradicts neoliberal approaches to the free market, because it is structured as a state-sponsored program of redistribution. Citizens of these communities have not bought quota on the open market, nor have they earned it through their past performance in the fishery, as is the case with other forms of fisheries privatization. For example, with individual transferable quotas (ITQs) regulators permanently allocate quota among fishers, usually on the basis of historical catch, and fishers can then use, temporarily lease, or permanently sell the quota. This is the case with the North Pacific halibut and sablefish ITQ program (known as an individual fishing quota, or IFQ). In contrast to this reliance on past performance, in the CDQ it is precisely residents' disenfranchisement that motivates the program. Quota provides a resource to those who do not have other means of acquiring it. Thus, while consistent with rationalization, the rationale of the CDQ was not to address problems related to the property regime. As the Council—which designed and still manages the program—put it, the goal was "promotion of economic stability, growth and self-sufficiency in maritime communities ... This Community Quota program redistributes the pollock resource with the objective of economic and community development" (NPFMC 1992:103, 105). In other words, redistribution occurs not through the market—the goal of neoliberal restructuring—but through the action of the state and for the explicit purpose of providing opportunities where previously they did not exist.

Despite this, many CDQ supporters explicitly distance themselves from emphasis on redistribution, emphasizing that the CDQ is not welfare (or "entitlement"). For example, NMFS countered criticism that the CDQ is a "'give-away' welfare program", by stating that the quota is "designed to provide start-up support for western Alaska communities" (NMFS 1992a), while the executive director of the Bristol Bay CDQ group, Nels Anderson Jr, testified to Congress that "this is an opportunity program, not an entitlement program" (US House of Representatives 1995). Statements such as these suggest that the CDQ is "really" motivated by neoliberalism and the market rather than justice and redistribution. Yet that such statements are necessary also suggests that quota can be seen as welfare-style redistribution. For example, in his argument against making the CDQ national law, Senator Slade Gorton from Washington (where many of the non-CDQ firms are located) stated that "the allocation-related provision in this bill that I find most objectionable is the provision mandating a permanent entitlement program for Native Alaskans through community development quotas" (US Senate 1996b). Further, a National Research Council (NRC) report on the CDQ notes that residents of CDQ communities themselves contrast the CDQ with welfare, and prefer the CDQ because it allows them self-determination in *both* market and subsistence economies (NRC 1999). That the CDQ can contribute to subsistence activities further undermines the either/or choice between neoliberalism and social justice.

Market dimensions of the program exhibit similar tensions regarding their neoliberal and social justice intentions and content. Transferable quota does extend the market. As Patience Merculief, from the Central Bering Sea CDQ group, testified to Congress, "the CDQ program has offered the alternative opportunity of real participation in the private sector [and] the transformation of the economy... to individual initiative and market forces" (US House of Representatives 2001). But this market includes a variety of limitations on who can hold and transfer quota. For example, the program is geographically limited only to the area under jurisdiction of the Council, and even within this general region communities have to meet eligibility criteria. More critically, quota is only partly marketable: CDQ groups can lease it, but they cannot sell it. As early supporters envisioned it, "the CDQs would be inalienable, that is, they could not be transferred out of the community and would be a permanent economic birthright". Inalienability is very much a part of the formal program: quota can be held *only* by the CDQ groups, which transfer *only* use-rights and *only* temporarily. The NRC describes this inalienability as "intergenerational equity" and as a special feature of the CDQ (1999:114). Such inalienability contrasts with other privatization programs, such as the halibut-sablefish IFQ, in which the ability of individuals to fully sell their quota shares is a foundational feature.

Conversely, even as the CDQ groups represent communities, they are explicitly corporations. Each of the CDQ groups is required to develop in-depth business plans that articulate both what they are going to do with their quota (how they will use it as productive capital) and what they are going to do with their revenue (how they will accumulate more capital). Seen differently, however, the corporate role of CDQ groups supports a social justice narrative, in that the corporations are accountable not to shareholders, but to citizens. As with quota, the corporation cannot be privately or publicly sold, but is inalienable to the set of communities it represents. There are also rules governing the relationship between the group and its constitutive communities; for example, the board of directors of each group must have an elected representative from each member community. [However, the NRC (1999) provided evidence that CDQ groups are not well integrated with their communities.] In sum, these limits and rules all reflect the CDQ's social justice aspects. They indicate a non-market logic in which the CDQ corporation is tied to a social goal. The CDQ is limited to a geographic location and group of citizens, and the program is designed to help these citizens by protecting them from broad-based competition and the threat of losing their quota. In other words, these limitations do not simply serve to further the market (in the sense implied by neoliberal re-regulation), but instead offer concrete protections from the market.

Contradictory impulses are also found in the allocation process. Allocation decisions—how to divide the total quota among the CDQ groups—are made by the state of Alaska in consult with NMFS, which itself highlights the ongoing role of the state. To make these decisions, the state evaluates the soundness of the business and development aspects of each group's business plan, including the potential for future success and their past track record. In one sense, allocation serves as an oversight tool through which the state can offer protections from pure market relations. This role was made especially evident in a case in the mid-1990s, when the state used its allocation power to help one CDQ group extricate itself from bad business decisions and partnerships (NRC 1999). In another sense, the allocation procedure can be interpreted as a form of neoliberal governmentality (Barry, Osborne and Rose 1996), in which government oversight disciplines the CDQ groups to the market by rewarding them for making proper business decisions, which are those that accumulate capital. Most tellingly, the allocation procedure, with its focus on business plans and capital accumulation, forces groups to compete against each other both for allocation of quota and for contracts and partnerships with non-CDQ firms. The NRC noted that oversight allows the state to "induce better performance" (1999:90). Competition was purposely built into the program and allocation procedure, and is cited as evidence that this program is not welfare. Larry Cotter of the Aleutian Pribilof Island CDQ group, who was a member of the Council when it was designing the CDQ, stated that "there was fear that the program could degenerate into a quasi-welfare program. To ensure that would not happen, the Council developed a process by which the CDQ organizations would be required to comply with rigorous planning and reporting requirements . . . The [plans] would be comprehensively evaluated, and the performance of each group reviewed. The state of Alaska would . . . ultimately make a recommendation for allocation among the six groups" (US House of Representatives 2001; see also BSFA 1998: episode 3). In these ways, government allocation and oversight provides protections from the market to a particular group of disadvantaged citizens—and demands that they turn themselves into neoliberal citizens subject to the market.

So it is that regulatory features of the program seem to add up to something quite confusing. In some interpretations, the CDQ is a neoliberal program in which establishing markets is the primary goal. Participation in markets teaches people how to behave in markets to benefit from them. In other interpretations, the CDQ is a social justice program in which social benefits are the primary goal. Market forces must be directed and risks mitigated, which means that intervention in the market is acceptable as long as it achieves the overarching goals. In one interpretation, social goals are embedded in the market; in the other, the market is embedded within social goals. The difficulty choosing between these interpretations is reflected in the small literature on the CDQ. The NRC (1999) clearly acknowledges the market-based dimensions of the program, but situates these within the community development aspects of the program. Both Tryon (1993) and Keys (1997) treat the program as a form of capital, but Tryon sees this as positive in that it expands opportunities, while Keys argues it is privatization based on "market ideology" and will therefore exacerbate inequality. Ginter (1995), Holland and Ginter (2001), and Townsend (1997) all emphasize the CDQ as a form of community-based management and common property institution, aimed specifically at economic development. Yet these authors also suggest that the CDQ is a form of privatization. Not only do they note that because the CDQ is a privatized, rights-based form of fishery management and allocation it resembles an ITQ, but they focus on the relationship among different property regimes and the role of the CDQ within these. For example, Holland and Ginter state that the CDQ (like other market-based programs) creates a new form of property interest that can end problems supposedly resulting from open access fisheries (those without property). What this means is that even though they seem to highlight community (rather than market) aspects of the CDQ, the importance of these community aspects is stated in terms of their market rationality: it is *property* that makes all the difference here. How, then, should we think about property and its relationship to the CDQ?

Purposes of Property in the CDQ

Property is the crux of the CDQ, and the logic of property that animates the program is simultaneously one of capitalism and one of protecting people from capitalism. Quota-as-property provides the means for participating in the market and serves to protect people from vagaries of the market, and both participation and protection are the means for overcoming socio-economic exclusion. These tensions raise deeper questions about property itself and encourage investigation of property in the CDQ. The past century of legal scholarship on property and rights makes clear that the orthodox notion of property—ownership of private property—is far too narrow and does not adequately describe or explain real property relations (Cohen 1927; Hohfield 1913; Macpherson 1978; Rose 1994; Singer 2000; Underkuffler 2003; Waldron 1988; in Geography, see Blomley 2004, 2005). The ownership model presumes an autonomous, individual owner who has complete control over a discrete object against the incursion of the state and society. This idea of ownership as non-interference and individual control (ie ownership as freedom) is the basis for many political and economic arguments about the importance of property. In place of this, property scholars have shown that property is a social relationship among a variety of kinds of property holders (eg individual, state, communal) and non-holders regarding allocation of different kinds of rights to things (eg rights to use and to exclude). Among these different rights, exclusion is often considered the most important (Underkuffler 2003). This expanded [or, in Blomley's (2004) terms, "unsettled"] notion of property itself illuminates the CDQ. While seemingly designed around orthodox notions about property (and especially the economic justification of property as opportunity), by the ownership standard, quota is not property. For example, it is not held by individuals, is not fully transferable, varies with each allocation cycle, and can be revoked by the state simply by eliminating the program altogether. However, when property is viewed more broadly, quota fits a basic definition of property as a social relationship in which an individual or group can use the object of the property relation, exclude others from using it, and transfer it. CDQ groups decide how to use the quota, by definition others are excluded from using quota or taking it without permission of the CDQ groups, and the CDQ groups are able to—encouraged to—transfer quota in various kinds of market arrangements.

There are, however, broader implications of this expanded notion of property. Not only are there multiple kinds of property—of which ownership of private property is just one—but "private property itself may be a good deal more complicated" than generally acknowledged (Blomley 2004:xvi). *All* forms of property involve not just non-interference, control, and freedom but simultaneously social obligations, interdependence, and regulation. Carol Rose (1994) observes that even individual private property is never an individual act but is always already cooperative. For something to be property, a claim not only has to be communicated by the claimant, but that communication has to be recognized and acknowledged by others. Social relationships that constitute property are also evident in the different kinds of rights that comprise property and ways that exercise of rights inherently imposes duties—or vulnerabilities—on others (Hohfield 1913; Singer 2000). My *right* to exclude you from using my fishing quota creates your *duty* to not use it. In practice, then, various property rights will come into conflict (Freyfogle 2003; Singer 2000). My freedom to *use* my property to have loud parties with smoky bonfires can impede your freedom to *exclude* loud noises and smoke, which can impede your freedom to *use* your property as you wish. As a wide range of case examples show, it is impossible to turn to an abstract notion of property to adjudicate such conflicts, because a claim from either side could be based on property rights (Freyfogle 2003; Singer 2000; Underkuffler 2003).

Social relationships are especially clear in the allocative, distributional aspects of property (Underkuffler 1996, 2003). The basic insight that allocation is a social relation is hardly new, but recent legal scholarship uses this to investigate the core of property. Because property is about the who, what, where, and when of control over resources, the assertion and recognition of property rights both creates duties for others and "necessarily denies or takes from another" (Underkuffler 1996:1038). Therefore, property is not a negative right (the right to non-interference by the state), but is fundamentally a positive right that protects interests of some and not others, and "social aspirations and social goals . . . are raised by the very existence of a state-enforced property regime" (Underkuffler 2003:151). Thus, property is not a sphere of individual independence, but is precisely a sphere of interdependence, which means that the freedoms (or entitlements) associated with property inherently come with obligations. As Joseph Singer argues, "the various tensions embedded in the property system require us to impose obligations on owners—obligations to use their property in a manner that is not inimical to the legitimate interests of others. Entitlement initially appears to abhor obligation, yet on reflection we can see that it requires it. Indeed, it is the tension between ownership and obligation that is the essence of property" (Singer 2000:204). The key point is that these obligations are not external to property, to be decided before and outside of property, but that property itself creates and is based on obligations as an internal relation (Singer 2000; Underkuffler 2003). It is this set of obligations, interdependencies, allocations, and positive rights—these social relations—that make property what it is. This is not a vapid statement along the lines of "everything is a social relation", but rather gives substance to the idea that property is a social relation.

Realizing that "ownership does not and cannot mean absolute power within rigid boundaries" (Singer 2000:208), but instead always already involves interdependence and obligations, undermines the idea that property has a single, overarching logic, whether taken in the positive to mean freedom and opportunity or in the negative to mean theft and dispossession. Instead, the logic of property is that it can have multiple logics. Social relations—including goals, values, and power—structure the particular arrangement of rights/freedom and obligations/vulnerabilities property provides. It is the decision to protect something, for someone, in a particular way that makes something property and determines what the content of rights to that property will be. Laura Underkuffler (2003) describes these decisions as the normative, social choices that property inevitably involves: unavoidable and deceptively difficult choices about what to protect, with what stringency, and on what time frame. The ownership model of property does not avoid these choices but only obscures them. Thus, it is important to focus attention on the reasons for choosing property and specific configurations of it. Underkuffler argues that many limitations on "absolute" property rights—such as legal restrictions, takings, and taxation for redistribution—are quite justified because the goals (what she terms "core values") of both property and restrictions on property are the same. Because of this, such conflicts are not about property and its outsides, but instead are about the insides of property; these conflicts are about what property is and what it entails. In other words, the key question is not "is it property" but "what are we protecting and why". These are "moral questions of what property *ought* to be" (Blomley 2004:74, italics original). Property—as allocation and control of resources—does provide freedoms, does generate duties and vulnerabilities, and does require obligation. *How* it does these things is determined not by its invariable nature but by its specific conception and purpose.

This attention to how mixes of entitlement and obligation are animated by the purpose behind property—the reasons for protecting certain things for certain people in certain ways—is what makes these ideas useful for thinking through the CDQ. It focuses attention not on the essence of property in the CDQ, but on what property is meant to achieve. The reasons behind property have been the crux of the seeming incoherence of the CDQ: property as means to incorporate into the market and as means to protect from the market have been combined in the quota as a way to provide opportunity and overcome past marginalization. Therefore, in using these ideas to understand the quota mechanism of the CDQ, I focus on how these different conceptions of property—configurations of what property is and can do—come together in a single instance of property. This is somewhat different than most of this scholarship (a major focus of which is case law regarding property rights and wrongs), which focuses on contrasting instances of property, for example how property relation A and B differ, or conflict among different parties over rights to a single property.

History of the CDQ: Reasons for Property

The contingent history of the CDQ provides insight into how the quota system managed to incorporate different approaches under similar goals and into the same property mechanism. Key to understanding this history are Marxian notions of primitive accumulation (or accumulation by dispossession), which is the extension of capitalist social relations by enclosing the means of production (eg access to fish) as private commodities in the hands of capitalists, thus undermining subsistence and coercing wage labor. Dispossession is not something of the past—occurring at the dawn of capitalism—but is an ongoing process that creates conditions necessary for capitalist accumulation (Harvey 2003; Perelman 2000). In one sense, the CDQ seems to be the opposite of dispossession. The CDQ certainly extends the market economy, but does so by incorporating residents of CDQ communities not primarily as wage laborers but instead as *owners*. And, because industry participants now have to pay CDQ groups for fish they once got for free, it seems that the CDQ actually takes from the rich to give to the poor. This certainly is not an example of dispossession of the poor masses! However, I show here that the CDQ *is* very much a response to ongoing processes of dispossession that accelerated during the period in which the CDQ was conceived and implemented. It is both the causes of this dispossession and responses to it (ie entitlements and the obligations they incite) that provide the reasons (Underkuffler's "core values") for quota-as-property in the CDQ, and thus manage to unite neoliberal and social justice approaches in a single property mechanism.

The idea for a program along the lines of the CDQ emerged in the late 1980s among advocates for rural development in coastal Alaska. The crucial history starts at least a decade earlier when, in 1976, the US extended jurisdiction over the oceans from 12 to 200 nautical miles from the coastline. The US spent the next decade "Americanizing" this new area by developing a domestic fishing and processing industry to displace prior foreign activity (mainly Japanese and Soviet) (Mansfield 2001a, 2001b). From California to Alaska there was excitement about gaining domestic, local control of these fisheries, thus providing jobs and generating profits in economically depressed coastal regions. In Alaska, some new processing plants were built (many by Japanese firms), and today more than twice as much fish is landed in Dutch Harbor, in the Aleutian Islands, than any other port in the US (NMFS 2005). However, most places along the Bering Sea, including in the Aleutian Islands, were bypassed as locations for processing plants. Not only were they considered too remote and without the natural conditions for easy port construction, but also fisheries development required infrastructure and capital that was absent from these parts of Alaska. The lack of local processing capacity combined with the lack of capital also meant that much of the new fishing capacity was based not in Alaska, but further south in Washington state (State of Alaska 2003).

Commentators thus noted that Americanization was not "Alaskanization" (BSFA 2006; testimony by Eugene Asicksik in US House of Representatives 1998). Americanization "tended to exacerbate the exclusion and marginalization of Alaska Natives from the commercial fishery" (NRC 1999:7, see also BSFA 1998: episodes 3, 5, 10; Hinkes 1989; State of Alaska 2003). As before, resources were right off the coast of Alaska but benefits from them went elsewhere. Before Americanization they went to Japan; after, they went to Washington state. The sense among supporters of a CDQ program was that "it's unconscionable to leave people that have been there for generations standing on the beach while other people harvest the billion dollars worth of product off their coast" (BSFA 1998: episode 6). The perception, then, was that for Alaskans Americanization became not a moment of opportunity but a moment of dispossession. The capital intensive nature of these fisheries meant that native Alaskans in the Bering Sea region, in particular, were dispossessed of the ability to benefit from local resources. Nels Anderson Jr, of the Bristol Bay CDQ group, argued that "in most cases, our people have had no access to the [fish] resource because of the high capital investment required to participate in these fisheries" (US House of Representatives 1995), and the Bering Sea Fishermen's Association—early activists for a CDQ—describes residents as "those left behind" (BSFA 2006). The State of Alaska claimed that "prosecuting the pollock fishery required large capital investments that were not practical for the residents of western Alaska. This meant that most the people living in Western Alaska . . . had no viable means of participating in these fisheries" (State of Alaska 2003:11). The CDQ, then, was promoted as a way to right this regional inequity. In this context of fisheries development, dispossession, and regional disparity, the reasons for quota-as-property are quite clear. Designing the program around quota acknowledges that fisheries development had already bypassed coastal Alaska and this would not be changed easily. Instead, quota provides a mechanism for engaging with this industrial and highly capitalized fishery—a mechanism to "get involved in . . . a fishery that's already underway" (BSFA 1998: episode 5)—in order to keep some of the benefits of the industry in Alaska and along the coast. The CDQ also builds on the perceived strengths and weaknesses of non-fisheries policy related to Alaska natives, including the 1971 Alaska Native Claims Settlement Act that had extinguished all native claims to land in exchange for title to land, which could be received only by native corporations (Keys 1997).

But the CDQ is not just about righting regional wrongs by providing capital—in the form of fishing quota—to these underprivileged regions; it was also conceived and created during a period of intense interest in privatization of fisheries, which led to the program for rationalization, as discussed earlier. Rationalization was itself fueled by Americanization, which had created problems such as overcapacity. Rather than seeing overcapacity as a normal outcome of capitalist dynamics and fisheries development efforts, fisheries managers attributed these problems simply to the irrational incentives of open access (Mansfield 2004a, 2006). Thus, facing declining returns on investment and dissipating rents, in the late 1980s managers began talking about hard decisions. This led not only to the Council's "comprehensive rationalization plan" for fisheries restructuring, but also to the plan's precursor, an "inshore–offshore allocation" for 1992–1995 that divided catch between fishing vessels delivering to inshore processors and offshore catcher–processor vessels (often known as "factory trawlers"). The original CDQ program, for pollock only, was attached to this temporary allocation program. NMFS described this move as an "interim measure" on the way toward full rationalization, and encouraged regional managers to work "as expeditiously as possible toward some other method of allocating fish among competing users, ideally one that relies on free market decisions, instead of direct government intervention" (NMFS 1992b). The CDQ was later expanded in 1995 with implementation of one of these "free market" programs, the halibut-sablefish IFQ. CDQs, therefore, were an element of specific plans for rationalizing these fisheries. Those involved make clear that this was, in part, the result of political bargaining, in which proponents of rationalization and of the CDQ traded support for each other's programs (BSFA 1998: various episodes). This suggests the extent to which the CDQ is not the same as rationalization, even as it was implemented with it. But connections go deeper as both rationalization and the CDQ were seen as limited access strategies for ending open access in these fisheries. The project of turning access to fisheries into property through quota allocation was ongoing in the North Pacific and was based on a neoliberal logic regarding property and markets. It appears, then, that while the reason for the *CDQ in general* was to redress problems of dispossession associated with Americanization, the reason for the *quota mechanism of the CDQ* can be found in neoliberal approaches to fisheries privatization.

I want to suggest, however, that the reason for the quota mechanism is not just the dominant neoliberal logic but also that many recognized that rationalization is dispossession. Viewing the situation in 1990, people realized that few residents of this region would receive quota allocation under various privatization schemes, because quota was assigned only to those already in the fishery (those with "catch history"), and the whole point was that they had not been able to enter the fishery thus far. And if before rationalization residents did not have the capital to enter the fishery (capital for vessels, technology, licenses, wages), they certainly would not have it afterward, given the cost associated with quota acquisition. Thus, there was "apprehension" that rationalization would "institutionalize and perhaps exacerbate existing patterns" in which the residents of coastal western Alaska were left out (NRC 1999:104). If they did not get in at this point in history, they never would. Paul Fuhs, mayor of Unalaska (in the Aleutian islands), asserted "as our people have no past history in the fishery, they would certainly not receive permits, or quota shares and would be legally disenfranchised from participating in the fishery" (Fuhs 1988). Alaska Senator Ted Stevens argued that quota in the IFQ program "has value and those people that have invested in business buy them and the community has lost that contact with the fishery forever" (US Senate 1996a). In other words, the CDQ was designed to address this process of dispossession as it was happening. As Fuhs later put it, "okay, you're divvying up the quota in the Bering Sea and the communities are going to get part of that" (BSFA 1998: episode 7). Hence, current managers have described the CDQ not as rationalization (despite its market mechanisms) but as one of several protections from rationalization that have been built into the rationalization process (Fina 2005).

Conclusion

From this history, it seems that use of quota was certainly shaped by the neoliberal logic of property and markets, but was also a response to it based on social justice concerns. Quota was not designed to create a separate CDQ fishery, but instead to find a way to imbricate the residents of the Bering Sea region into the recently developed, lucrative, industrial fishery. My basic argument is that the purpose of quota is to incorporate residents into the capitalist market—as owners—as a way to avoid complete dispossession through capitalist expansion brought by the combined processes of Americanization and rationalization. The property mechanism, then, is a very coherent way to meet these multiple goals. Put differently, property in the CDQ quite purposely combines entitlement with obligation. Property in the CDQ works not because it either embraces or rejects independent ownership, but because it manages to incorporate the idea that independent ownership is simultaneously social interdependence. This, then, indicates that it is the purposes of property (ie social decisions about what property is and entails) that give substance to the quota mechanism of the CDQ. If we utilize only an idealized model of property, it is possible to identify both neoliberal and social justice tendencies in the CDQ, but not to see how they come together or why. Viewing property in terms of its inherently social purposes and goals show how what seem to be opposed positions come together.

From this analytical perspective, I have refused to resolve the tension between neoliberal and social justice narratives by claiming that the CDQ is "really" one or the other of these—it is both, and therefore neither. It is clearly a privatization program that expands capitalist social relations by disciplining subjects to the market. But it is just as clearly a redistributive program that provides protections from the market to achieve social justice goals. These come together in the quota mechanism because of particular social and historical convergence of Americanization, rationalization, and political reactions to both.

What is interesting about the CDQ, then, is not that it is incoherent or inconsistent, but that the property mechanism of privatization manages to bridge seemingly contradictory goals. That policy is incoherent should be expected. This incoherence is the point of scholarship on the contradictions of neoliberalism: in practice neoliberalism will always become some kind of messy hybrid because of internal contradictions. Further, any policy (certainly not just a neoliberal one) is the outcome of political compromise and is thus a highly contingent stabilization of social relations at a particular historical juncture; policy will of necessity be a messy hybrid of different, and at times opposing, approaches. This is certainly true of the CDQ, which, as explained, was very much a political resolution between advocates for Native Alaskans and proponents of market-based fishery policy. What this paper does is push beyond these more obvious conclusions, to ask how it is that quota came to be the mechanism that can provide this political compromise. I have argued that quota is able to do this because it is a form of privatization built on creating new forms of property; property, interpreted as interdependence, allows the CDQ to fulfill conflicting goals simultaneously. The CDQ likely represents a temporary resolution of political debates, and is very much of its historical moment, but it is a logical and coherent resolution nonetheless.

The implication of this analysis is that instead of looking for alternatives to neoliberalism at its edges—trying to find the boundary between what is and is not neoliberal—we can find alternatives within neoliberalism. Instead of focusing on "margins and interstices potentially available for alternatives" this paper has been "more concerned with possibilities for the transmutation of [neoliberalism's] core" (Bondi and Laurie 2005:399). This is, in many ways, a basic deconstructive move, in which the identity of neoliberalism is shown to include much of that which it defines as its other (see Gibson-Graham 2003). Showing that even private property is never just freedom but that freedom also generates responsibilities draws on the ownership model of property to undermine it; it does not offer a completely different model of property, but shows that even the conventional model contains within it much more than expected and widely represented. This is not to say that property is not violent, as such violence is the basis for seeing allocation as a central means by which social obligation is internal to property. But just as property is not freedom in the final instance, nor is it violence; it is the complex interplay between these that makes property property, and that provides both its generative and destructive potential. As Blomley argues, property is both a tool of dispossession and a tool for challenging dispossession. Because of this, the same is true for neoliberalism; the complex social relations of property make neoliberalism complicated at its core. Once we can see property as an entitlement that serves both to extend market relations and afford protections from dispossession—and see that these may be linked goals—even neoliberal privatization can no longer be about extension of the free market. This becomes an impossibility. It is in this way that this analysis of property and its substantive content opens up space for diverse conceptions and practices *within* neoliberalism.

Acknowledgements

I would like to thank Sally Bibb, with the National Marine Fisheries Service, for her help identifying and finding materials on the CDQ, and Jason Davis, for his general research assistance.

References

Bakker K (2005) Neoliberalizing nature? Market environmentalism in water supply in England and Wales. *Annals of the Association of American Geographers* 95:542–565

Barry A, Osborne T and Rose N (1996) *Foucault and Political Reason: Liberalism, Neo-liberalism, and Rationalities of Government.* Chicago: University of Chicago Press

Blomley N (2004) *Unsettling the City: Urban Land and the Politics of Property.* New York: Routledge

Blomley N (2005) Remember property? *Progress in Human Geography* 29:125–127

Bondi L and Laurie N (2005) Introduction to Special Issue on Working the Spaces of Neoliberalism: Activism, Professionalisation and Incorporation. *Antipode* 37:394–401

Brenner N and Theodore N (2002) Cities and the geographies of "actually existing neoliberalism". *Antipode* 34:349–379

Bridge G and Jonas A E (2002) Guest editorial: Governing nature: The reregulation of resource access, production, and consumption. *Environment and Planning A* 34:759–766

BSFA (1998) *CDQ On the Air (radio broadcast of interviews on history of the CDQ)*. Bering Sea Fishermen's Association, transcription available at http://www.cdqdb.org/reading/audioontheair.htm Accessed 24 April 2006

BSFA (2006) *Community Development Quota Website: History*. Bering Sea Fishermen's Association, http://www.cdqdb.org/history/history.htm Accessed 25 April 2006

Cohen M R (1927) Property and sovereignty. *Cornell Law Quarterly* 13:8–30

Demsetz H (1967) Toward a theory of property rights. *American Economic Review* 57:347–359

Fina M (2005) Rationalization of Bering Sea and Aleutian Islands crab fisheries. *Marine Policy* 29:311–322

Freyfogle E T (2003) *The Land We Share: Private Property and the Common Good.* Washington: Island Press

Fuhs P (1988) Let's keep fishery revenues in Alaska. *The Tundra Times* 7 March, http://www.cdqdb.org/reading/news/tundra.htm Accessed 25April 2006

Gibson-Graham J K (2003) Poststructural interventions. In Sheppard E and Barnes T (eds) *A Companion to Economic Geography* (pp 95–110). Oxford: Blackwell

Ginter J J C (1995) The Alaska Community Development Quota Fisheries Management Program. *Ocean and Coastal Management* 28:147–163

Hannesson R (2004) *The Privatization of the Oceans.* Cambridge, MA: MIT Press

Harvey D (2003) *The New Imperialism.* Oxford: Oxford University Press

Heynen N and Robbins P (2005) Symposium: The neoliberalization of nature: Governance, privatization, enclosure and valuation. *Capitalism, Nature, Socialism* 16:5–8

Hinkes C (1989) Binkley's Magnuson Act amendment could help coastal village fishermen. *Tundra Drums* 21 September, http://www.cdqdb.org/reading/news/tundrums.htm Accessed 25 April 2006

Hohfield W N (1913) Some fundamental legal conceptions as applied in juridical reasoning. *Yale Law Journal* 23:16–59

Holland D S and Ginter J J C (2001) Common property institutions in the Alaskan groundfish fisheries. *Marine Policy* 25:33–42

Keys K C (1997) The Community Development Quota program: Inequity and failure in privatization policy. *American Indian Culture and Research Journal* 21:31–71

Macpherson C B (1978) *Property: Mainstream and Critical Positions.* Toronto: University of Toronto Press

Mansfield B (2001a) Property regime or development policy? Explaining growth in the US Pacific groundfish fishery. *Professional Geographer* 53:384–397

Mansfield B (2001b) Thinking through scale: The role of state governance in globalizing North Pacific fisheries. *Environment and Planning A* 33:1807–1827; erratum 34(1)

Mansfield B (2004a) Neoliberalism in the oceans: "Rationalization," property rights, and the commons question. *Geoforum* 35:313–326

Mansfield B (2004b) Rules of privatization: Contradictions in neoliberal regulation of North Pacific fisheries. *Annals of the Association of American Geographers* 94:565–584

Mansfield B (2006) Assessing market-based environmental policy using a case study of North Pacific fisheries. *Global Environmental Change* 16:29–39

McCarthy J (2005) Devolution in the woods: Community forestry as hybrid neoliberalism. *Environment and Planning A* 37:995–1014

McCarthy J and Prudham S (2004) Neoliberal nature and the nature of neoliberalism. *Geoforum* 35:275–283

NMFS (1992a) Groundfish Fishery of the Bering Sea and Aleutian Islands Area. *Federal Register* 57:54936

NMFS (1992b) Groundfish of the Gulf of Alaska; Groundfish Fishery of the Bering Sea and Aleutian Islands. *Federal Register* 57:23321

NMFS (1993) Pacific Halibut Fisheries; Groundfish of the Gulf of Alaska; Groundfish of the Bering Sea and Aleutian Islands; Limited Access Management of Fisheries off Alaska. *Federal Register* 58:59375

NMFS (1998) Multispecies Community Development Quota Program. *Federal Register* 63:8356

NMFS (2005) *Fisheries of the United States 2004.* Silver Spring, MD: National Marine Fisheries Service

NPFMC (1992) *Final Supplemental Environmental Impact Statement of Proposed In-shore/Offshore Allocation Alternatives to the Fishery Management Plans for the Groundfish Fishery of the Bering Sea and Aleutian Islands the Gulf of Alaska.* Anchorage: North Pacific Fishery Management Council

NRC (1999) *The Community Development Quota Program in Alaska.* Washington DC: National Research Council, National Academy Press

Peck J and Tickell A (2002) Neoliberalizing space. *Antipode* 34:380–404

Perelman M (2000) *The Invention of Capitalism: Classical Political Economy and the Secret History of Primitive Accumulation.* Durham: Duke University Press

Rose C M (1994) *Property and Persuasion: Essays on the History, Theory, and Rhetoric of Ownership.* Boulder: Westview Press

Singer J W (2000) *Entitlement: The Paradoxes of Property.* New Haven: Yale University Press

Singleton V (2005) The promise of public health: Vulnerable policy and lazy citizens. *Environment and Planning D: Society and Space* 23:771–786

St Martin K (2005) Mapping economic diversity in the First World: The case of fisheries. *Environment and Planning A* 37:959–979

State of Alaska (2003) *Western Alaska Community Development Quota Handbook.* Juneau: State of Alaska

Townsend R E (1997) Fisheries management implications of Alaskan community development quotas. In Pálsson G and Pétursdóttir G (eds) *Social Implications of Quota Systems in Fisheries* (pp 279–296). Copenhagen: Nordic Council of Ministers

Tryon L E (1993) An overview of the CDQ Fishery Program for Western Alaskan Native Communities. *Coastal Management* 21:315–325

Underkuffler L S (1996) Property: A special right. *Notre Dame Law Review* 71:1033–1047

Underkuffler L S (2003) *The Idea of Property: Its Meaning and Power.* Oxford: Oxford University Press

US House of Representatives (1995) *Improving Fisheries Management in Magnuson Act.* 104-1, 25 February, CIS# 96-H651-10. Committee on Resources

US House of Representatives (1998) *Oversight Hearing on U.S. Ownership of Fishing Vessels.* 105-2, 4 June, CIS# 99-H651-1. Committee on Resources

US House of Representatives (2001) *Western Alaska and Western Pacific Community Development Quota Programs, and H.R. 553, the Western Alaska Community Development Quota Program Implementation Improvement Act of 2001.* 107-1, 19 July, CIS# 2002-H651-46. Committee on Resources

US Senate (1996a) *Hearing of the Commerce, Science, and Transportation Committee, Markup and Nominations.* 104-2, 28 March

US Senate (1996b) *Sustainable Fisheries Act. Congressional Record – Senate* 104-2:10794–10827

Waldron J (1988) *The Right to Private Property.* Oxford: Clarendon Press

Chapter 5

Discovering Price in All the Wrong Places: The Work of Commodity Definition and Price under Neoliberal Environmental Policy

Morgan Robertson

If you think prices come from markets, then you think milk comes from bottles. (Dan Bromley[1])

Introduction

On a hot July day in Washington, DC in 2005, a forum of environmental policy-makers and private-sector stakeholders convened at the Carnegie Endowment for International Peace to begin building a new market. Over the past decade, the US Environmental Protection Agency (EPA) and the US Department of Agriculture (USDA) have made increasingly determined attempts to create the necessary institutional support for trading water quality credits. In this, they have been buoyed by the success of other "regulatory markets" such as those for air pollution and wetlands, and their efforts have recently reached a new pitch with three major workshops in 2005–2006 and the issuance of a joint memorandum on the subject (EPA and USDA 2006). And yet, to the growing frustration of headquarters staff and managers, no market has emerged. The urgency of the matter comes from the fact that the 1977 Clean Water Act (CWA) forbids facilities from discharging pollutants into water without a permit; obtaining such a permit has come to entail such delay and technological sophistication that overwhelming political pressure now bears on the project of making CWA compliance cheaper and faster. Since the late 1980s, the efficiency of markets at finding least-cost solutions has been the main rubric of American environmental policy reform (EPA EITF 1991). At the Carnegie conference, after some introductory remarks by a political appointee touching on the nonpartisan and inevitable nature of market-based environmental policy and the power of citizens in free markets to effect beneficial social change, a University of Maryland economist stood up to say what nobody wanted to hear.

He announced a profound skepticism about the ability of strictly free markets to meet environmental regulatory goals, such as the goal of limiting contaminants in rivers and streams. His skepticism stemmed from the fact that, as has been pointed out by many resource economists, demand and supply in such regulatory markets are entirely controlled—entirely *created*—by regulatory directives rather than the utility functions of individual market participants. The supply of the commodity "water quality", he noted, is a function of the regulatory standards applied to the measurement of improvements in water quality: "You can always make the supply and demand curves cross if you can get the regulator to water down the scoring criteria".[2] Crucially, and for maximum rhetorical effect, his critique was aimed specifically at that icon of equilibrium economics, the supply/demand curve. Suggesting that the market-clearing price produced by this curve is *not* the product of exogenous human desires constituted an outright attack on the two fundamental theorems of welfare economics[3] which underpin neoliberal thinking, and quick action was needed to save the day for market enthusiasts. Fortunately, another political appointee was on hand, and leapt quickly up to offer the simple bromide of Say's Law: supply will create its own sufficient demand. As this was considered self-evidently true, it cleared the furrowed brows of the assembled experts.

Say's Law, in its "pure" form (a form never actually articulated by the 19th-century economist Jean-Baptiste Say; Rosenberg 1992) serves as a sort of narrative underpinning for the centrality of equilibrium analysis and the price theory of value in modern mainstream economics.[4] It is one of those delicious omphalic credos that lie at the heart of many a sprawling research paradigm. While it is mainly of historical interest to most economists, its simplicity allows it to persist in popular rhetoric as an ideological invocation, entreating a level of demand to issue forth from the black box of individual utility within us all sufficient to consume available supply. Leon Walras' two theorems of 1874, elegantly mathematized in the Arrow-Debreu proof of 1953 (Mirowski 2001:268), expanded upon Say's Law and required *price* to be the mechanism which coordinates this balance between demand and supply to the point of Pareto-optimality, where no further increase in net social welfare is possible through market exchange (Rosenberg 1992:99). When harnessed to the postwar neoclassical economists' methodological commitment to individualism and rational actors, the macroeconomic imperatives of Say and Walras were brought down to the scale of the mind of each market agent.

The stakes are thus very high, as the theoretical rationale for neoliberal capitalism has been erected on individual rationality and Walrasian equilibrium. For Walras' equilibrium theory to work, price signals must serve as the information that allows rational actors in a free market to take stock of their own desires against the resources needed to satisfy them. Thus price is theorized in classical liberal economics as the purest expression of value. For mainstream economists,[5] achieving social welfare becomes, in part, a process of facilitating accurate price discovery, of providing rational market actors with enough and sufficiently accurate information to respond to price signals. Of the many lines of criticism which come to bear on this claim, one in particular points out that Walras' and Say's principles apply only to markets in equilibrium, which is a condition that is almost never observed. Hodgson notes the cop-out, calling Walras' solution a *deux ex machina* which is premised on a forgetting of history, experience, and common sense about price behavior: "In neoclassical theory the only kind of price norm is the *ex post* equilibrium price. It is presumed to be formed after an extensive process of market adjustment and price signaling in logical rather than historical time" (1988:182). As the very name "discovery" implies, it is expected to emerge fully-formed from its cache.

But what about new markets? Markets where there is not only no extended history of price discovery, but in which the very identity of the commodity requiring a price is still in flux? This paper is concerned with observing the emergence of commodity identity and price in such a market—prices that, we are assured after-the-fact by the partisan representatives of the neoliberal capitalist state, emerged from the unmediated expression of human desires. While these are quite specialized markets that are called forth to achieve the regulatory goals of the CWA, they may also be similar to the nascent markets that are arguably commonplace all around us, but about which the dominant theorems driving economic research programs have virtually nothing to say. Observing the difficult birth of one such market, I found Say's Law pulled into service to dispel anxiety rather than to explain observed data: we need not fear for the future of a market in tradable water quality credits, for Say's Law tells us that buyers will appear if credits are produced. And although the theorems of welfare economics were not named as such in these forums (presumably due to the inside-the-beltway polysemy of "welfare"), their messages were constantly invoked to reassure us that the market price for credits will coordinate supply and demand such that optimal social welfare is achieved.

The point is not that facile misreadings of Say and Walras do injustice to the original thinkers themselves, but rather that such invocations are the ideological wheels on which neoliberal capitalism achieves its expansionist dynamic. This tendency on the part of market advocates is particularly clear in the recent effort to bootstrap "ecosystem services" markets into existence (Costanza et al 1997; Daily 1997; Daily and Ellison 2002; EPA 2003; McAfee 1999; NRC 2005; Turner et al 2003). By casting elements of the environment as "services" which provide value to human societies, they hope to stimulate environmental conservation through privatization and ownership. Following a line of logic that runs from Locke through Walras to Coase, the main thrust of these efforts has been to define new elements of the environment as property, distribute the rights to its ownership, and hope that markets and prices follow as rain follows the plow. There is every reason to suspect, however, that this latest round of the commodification of nature will experience the same contradictions as any attempt to establish markets in what Karl Polanyi (1944) termed "fictitious commodities" (Castree 1995, 2002; J O'Connor 1994; M O'Connor 1994).

But my aim here is not to fire a theoretical broadside concerning the fundamental instabilities and injuries of capital; the claim that neoliberal economic policy makes unrealistic assumptions is by now heavily belabored and exhaustively documented. My wish here is instead to observe neoliberal capitalism in situ in the context of a specific engagement with environmental policy, to show how these precepts force actual market participants into logical conundra, and how they do or do not work themselves out. The creation of new markets in novel kinds of commodities is a moment of particular importance in the definition of new kinds of property and the expansion of neoliberal capitalism, and I examine this moment through an ethnographic approach to the definition of tradable property in environmental services, and the measure of these properties through price. The material in this paper was gathered through interviews with the producers, consumers, and regulators of regional markets in wetland credits and of the prospective markets in water quality credits, as well as through participation in three national workshops on the subject of challenges to the development of water quality markets.

Work documenting the on-the-ground overcoming (or not) of the contradictions of capitalism will lead to finer-grained understandings, and can provide a tonic against the depressing tendency to see capital as unitary and omnipotent (Gibson-Graham 1993; McAfee 2003). Bakker (2005), for example, provides an excellent taxonomy in the course of suggesting that much of what we refer to using the blanket term "commodification of nature" actually consists of three interrelated moments: privatization (efforts to change ownership), commercialization (efforts to introduce efficiency and standardize production and measurement) and commodification (efforts to construct a market and make products fungible). Throughout this paper, it will be possible to observe these processes as overlapping, at times abandoned, and not understood as separate by the participants. It is also significant that participants in these debates do not even perceive these consistently as tasks to be accomplished at all: specifically, the market builders assume the automatic achievement of two important tasks which are actually an expansive and time-consuming task of institutional construction: the definition of the commodity and the discovery of price (which might fit into Bakker's typology as components of commercialization and commodification, respectively). The work of achieving these two tasks was actually eminently visible at the table in the July workshop, but to formally recognize such work would be to undercut the conceptual apparatus that sustains neoliberalism and minimizes the role of government. A hallmark of neoliberal policy is that it seeks to move *outside* of the formal apparatus of the state—castigated as ossified and insufficiently democratic—to achieve policy aims through the institutions of civil society (Amin and Thrift 1995; Peck and Tickell 2002) and an effective, direct and inherently democratic free market (Huber 1999). But, in practice, efforts to develop neoliberal environmental policy have led to endless numbers of "stakeholder forums", in which to achieve the outcome and effect of market-led environmental govern*ance*, we had to avert our eyes from the actual acts of govern*ment* occurring at a table crowded with bureaucrats.

Say What? New Commodities

I will focus my discussion on two developing markets: a planned market in water quality credits, and a young but extant market in wetland credits. Both have been promoted heavily by recent Administrations as private-sector solutions to the regulatory burdens imposed by the CWA of 1972 (EPA 2003; USACOE and EPA 2006; WHOEP 1993).

Wetland credits have been created and sold by entrepreneurial providers since 1992, in response to the CWA requirement that wetland impacts be compensated for by the party applying for a permit to fill wetlands; compensation usually consists of an equal or greater acreage of restored or created wetlands. Throughout the 1980s, nearly all compensation sites were constructed by the permit holder, and the highly uneven environmental results are a matter of record (NRC 2001). Since the early 1990s, however, regulators have been encouraging the development of both public and private "wetland banks", large pre-constructed acreages of restored wetland, which can be certified as containing a certain number of credits for sale to permit holders. Purchase of such credits satisfies permittees' CWA obligations. Wetland banks, although ecologically problematic in many ways, provide greater assurance of ultimate regulatory success than permittee-built compensation sites; banking has received some support among the environmental and regulatory community despite ingrained suspicion that wetland bank entrepreneurs "make a profit" off of wetland destruction (ELI 2002; Sibbing 2005; SWS 2005). Banks also have been specifically promoted by both the Clinton and GW Bush administrations as a market-led way to reduce the cost of regulatory burdens (EPA 2005; USACOE et al 1995). There are currently several hundred entrepreneurial providers of wetland credits around the nation, and price-based competition among them is said to exist in many areas. They have formed a national lobby (http://www.mitigationbanking.com) and have become quite influential as a self-described pro-environment constituent within the larger land development industry.

In the case of water quality trading, the limits placed on point-source (piped) inputs of pollutants into rivers have successfully reduced the level of pollutants entering the nation's waters, but the development of new polluting facilities challenges these limits. Rather than demanding ever-increasing levels of pollution control (which faces technical barriers and achieves diminishing environmental returns past a certain point), regulators have attempted to arrange for trades to occur between point-source polluters and the large population of unregulated "non-point-source" polluters[6], mainly agricultural operations, which can cheaply and easily reduce their contribution to water pollution. Participation in such markets in the role of "credit providers" is voluntary on the part of farmers. However, it is usually less expensive for farmers to reduce pollutant runoff from their fields into rivers than it is for, say, an urban water treatment plant to squeeze another increment of pollutant reduction out of an already very clean process. Market enthusiasts, always alert to such gaping differences in marginal cost, have argued that allowing polluters to buy pollution reduction credits from farmers can dramatically lower the cost of compliance for point-source polluters. An urban sewage treatment plant can buy a reduction in pounds of nitrogen much more cheaply from a farmer willing to change tillage practices than it can by retrofitting its system once again.

Given the obvious economic efficiency, it has stumped regulators and economists alike that, after nearly a decade of promotion by the EPA, a market in water quality trading (WQT) has failed to emerge. Hoping to inject a note of practical achievements on-the-ground into the prospects for WQT, the organizers of the Carnegie conference in Washington offered a chance for WQT to "learn from" the established success of wetland bank credit markets. The ensuing debate (as well as the discussions dominating a follow-up forum in Chicago in February of 2006; EPA ORD forthcoming) was strong on highly abstract questions of commodity definition and the invocation of economic platitudes, but could not come to grips with specific interventions. To the jaundiced eye of institutional and Marxist economics, it was a theatre demonstrating the consequences of neoliberal economics' formal blindness to the complexity of social structures which underlie and support markets. The forums on WQT were so thick with ad hoc and unsteady retellings of the fundamentals of welfare economics that participants were reduced to invoking "free-market-based, you know, supply-and-demand, capitalism, whatever you want to call it".[7] Having been assured that Say's Law would provide demand for, and accurately price, whatever WQT credits were supplied, regulators and entrepreneurs found themselves unable to comfortably specify and justify the actual interventions required to establish a market.

Demand Will Appear . . . But For What?

> How do we [plan a production strategy] in Water Quality Trading? We *can't* do this! The *market* will do this. If you've got your command-and-control hat on, take it off, put it in the back. (Tony Prato, economist[8])

> What you have is a commodity that you can't really observe. (Jim Shortle, agricultural economist[9])

Whereas the Walrasian "auctioneer" (an avatar of the market who plays a coordinating role in connecting buyers with sellers) is theoretically a costless and effortless creation (Boyer 1997), agreement on the actual coordinating institutions of water quality trading has proven to be intractable. Prato's epigram above suggests the tension in the room: on the one hand, the scientists and bureaucrats were admonished to be humble in the face of the power of the market to automatically discover appropriate products, prices, and production strategies. On the other hand, why had they been assembled if not to provide precisely such guidance? The paralysis this produced was palpable.

In this section I want to analyze one institution-building aspect of the debate which unfolded over the two conferences: *what* is the new property, the commodity being traded? "Water quality", said the title of the forum, but what is it and how is it measured? Considerable energetic debate explored the various ways of defining and measuring the commodity, but each potential resolution posed obstacles.

In a WQT market, someone who makes efforts that improve water quality can receive credit for those efforts, and then sell that credit to another party who wishes to degrade water quality in the same waterway to the same degree. It is therefore not a way to reduce pollution, but rather a way to allow the operation of comparative advantage to lower costs. Typically, an urban water treatment plant will purchase such credits from upstream farmers, so that the treatment plant may exceed the nitrogen limits imposed on them by the EPA. Such farmers may take measures (known as "best management practices", or BMPs), such as conservation tillage, which are known to reduce the runoff of nitrogen from farm fields.

Crucial questions arise immediately. Must the farmer's actions actually produce a measurable reduction in nitrogen loads downstream, or is installation of the BMPs sufficient to generate credit? How is an improvement to be certified and warranted? How can a regulatory agency document that pollution reductions are due to a farmer's BMP, given the dynamism of the entire landscape in contributing nitrogen to that stream? The answers to such measurement questions give shape to the commodity, and the lack of clear answers means that the commodity has a somewhat ethereal existence. For example, even if the nitrogen levels are measured a mile downstream from the farmer's field, the specific change produced by the farmer's BMPs will be hard to detect among the "noise" of other changes in the landscape. Such difficulties stimulated participants to find proxy measures that bypassed highly uncertain measurement methods. But if a WQT credit is not measured as a quantity of contaminant abatement downstream of the credit provider's facility, what *is* the identity of the commodity? Many answers were offered.

Functional Lift

Ecologists at the conference claimed that the most direct and scientific way of measuring the WQT commodity is as an increment of change at the site where abatement activities are carried out. This is often termed "functional lift"; that is, the credit represents the increase in environmental quality or function (in terms of decreased nitrogen contribution to a waterway near the farmer's land) compared with what the farmer's land would have contributed without the abatement activities (the "baseline"). Although this is a common-sensical method suggested by many at the conference, immense problems of measurement present themselves to conceiving of the commodity in this way. Firstly, ecologists objected that the baseline is a speculative condition that would change over time in unknowable ways. They also questioned the ability to quantify the lift provided by various BMPs. As ecologists described the intensive monitoring regime necessary to defensibly document "lift", economists and regulators began to protest that such certainty would be too time- and labor-intensive to achieve. Their objections were revealing. Economists viewed such information gathering as excessive because the credit purchaser's utility is fulfilled *without* knowing the exact ecological state of the abatement measure. Regulators viewed such information gathering as excessive because it would provide more data than the regulatory staff could absorb in making a determination that the farmer is in compliance.

Regulatory Relief

Some conference participants referred to the commodity as a unit of regulatory relief, measurable as "velocity through a regulatory system". This definition has the advantage of complete frankness: both credit producers and credit purchasers are completely disinterested in the ecological outcomes of their transactions. Credit purchasers desire only the rapid resolution of their encounter with the CWA permit program. The mercenary nature of this definition makes some PR-conscious market enthusiasts nervous, and has stimulated economists to use game theory to model markets where utility of both buyers and sellers is maximized by collaborating to force the market regulators to lower certification standards (King and Kuch 2003). That is, if credit producers can make subpar credits cheaply, and sell them cheaply to purchasers, without triggering regulatory compliance measures, a market mechanism will function admirably while failing to produce improved environmental conditions.

Liability

A similar way of speaking about the commodity—but one that didn't trigger such unease—was to refer to it as a purchasable transfer of liability. That is, WQT credit providers take on, for a fee, the responsibility of and liability for complying with the effluent limitations that a credit purchaser wishes to exceed. While a market in "regulatory relief" remains metaphorical, a market in transferable liability has clear precedent in the insurance and financial bonding industries. However, a commodity measured in "liability" has no closer a relationship to the ecological status of abatement sites than one measured in "regulatory relief", and faced similar strong opposition from environmentalist and scientific interest groups.

Time

The purpose of the Carnegie forum was for WQT to absorb the lessons of the successful wetland credit market, but a crucial difference emerged on the issue of commodity measurement. WQT credits, as property, have a temporal dimension and can expire: the purchase of lift, relief or liability is tied to the duration of the purchaser's need to exceed their own effluent limitations and thus must be expressed in units of lift/time, relief/time and liability/time, rather than just lift, relief or liability. Once the purchaser no longer needs the abatement, it can be bought by another purchaser. Wetland credits, by contrast, are sold to *permanently* compensate for impacts to wetlands. This essential difference prompted one wetland credit producer to repeatedly claim, "I am in the graveyard business!": like the sale of a graveyard plot, the sale of his commodity permanently retires its value. As fundamental as this difference is, it was not immediately appreciated by conference participants that adding a temporal dimension to the definition of the commodity might call for entirely different production strategies and initial rights allocations.

Probability

A fifth way in which the potential commodity was defined was in terms of the *probability* of its existence. Given the overwhelming problems of measurement and confirmation posed by ground-verifying the existence of hundreds (or thousands) of water quality abatement sites, on scattered farmsteads, prototype markets in water quality such as the South Nation River watershed in Ontario[10] and the Greater Miami River Watershed Water Quality Trading Program in Ohio[11] have encouraged the use of remote sensing and random sampling to certify the existence of the commodity. This gives the commodity a distinctly stochastic definition; in the Carnegie forum, it was proposed by an economist that perhaps 10% of all WQT credit-generating sites should be evaluated per year, and that the statistical Law of Large Numbers will guarantee that, in the aggregate, sufficient water quality abatement would be achieved to meet regulatory requirements.[12] This use of the Law of Large Numbers, much like the use of Say's Law, ventured far beyond the limits imposed by the Law's formal assumptions and served mainly to attempt closure of the debate on the nature of the commodity.

How far this babel of commodity definitions is from Say's confident predictions of demand! It is undeniably a little silly to be beating up on Say at this point in history, but his prominent invocation suggests that he cannot rest and must be continually invoked to first settle, and then obliterate the memory of, such debates. WQT is proving to be a tough case for equilibrium economics, however, and the nature of the three-way chicken-and-egg debate is now clear: of the institutional perspectives represented at the table, neither bureaucrats nor capitalists nor scientists wanted to claim responsibility for making the hard foundational choices about what would constitute the object of utility, desire and property in this market. More precisely, bureaucrats and scientists tossed the hot potato between them, while economists insisted that the game is futile. Representatives of the regulatory state insisted, in varying language, that "the science will tell us what is required to certify that water quality improvements are real and therefore fungible". Scientists responded with equal vigor that "we could tell you a universe of things about water quality, but only regulation can place parameters on the discussion such that our information is useful". Finally, economists insist that such parameterizing can only be done by the invisible hand: the market is capable of producing only optimal social welfare, and neither science nor policy can engineer its results without destroying its identity as a market.[13]

Let's Talk About Price

> The fiction of a minimalist state is belied by the reality of the state as entrepreneur, banker, distorter of prices, capitalist policeman and promoter of capitalist networks. (Michael Watts 1994:380)

The prospective market in WQT credits is at such a nascent stage that debates such as the one outlined above do not yet show a trajectory toward resolution. Lacking even a stable commodity identity, a whole suite of follow-on questions cannot even be asked, making the invocation of Say's Law particularly premature. Let us now look at the wetland banking market, which is slightly further down the road and has (however contingently) resolved the debate over the identity of the property being traded. Banking provides a window on the next struggle: the effort to discover a market-clearing price. This is really the moment where Say's Law is supposed to earn its keep, where the automatic, effortless coordination of supply and demand, with only the lightest of guidance from a minimalist state, is supposed to produce a market-clearing price that fully reflects the value of the commodity to society. Experience tells the skeptical observer that a great deal of work will be required, and then effaced, in achieving this. It is therefore interesting to examine how economists talk about price in wetland banking markets, in comparison with how the banking entrepreneurs themselves actually set price, and explain that action to themselves and others.

Economic Theorists

it does not matter whether the economic system is named capitalist or socialist. It all amounts to whether the pricing policy is based on marginalist principals, which will lead to the optimum allocation of resources. (Tjalling Koopmans 1945, in Mirowski 2001:244)

Economists who work on wetland credit markets acknowledge that these markets are not self-regulating, and that they are fully dependent on strong state regulatory power in the generation of all demand and supply (King and Herbert 1997; Oates 2006; Scodari and Shabman 1995). And yet, agentless price discovery surfaces repeatedly in their analysis as the social-welfare-maximizing tool which justifies market-based policies. To be fair, this is the only acceptable way within mainstream economics to theorize the existence of prices for wetland credits—and they do exist, apparently negotiated between buyer and seller with no interference from regulators, a fact which intoxicates the most cautious neoliberal economist. A world of acknowledged evidence that the market runs on regulation and not price is thrown aside.

Resource economists' enthusiasm over the wetland credit market's ability to produce prices is understandable. The history of theoretical writing on market environmentalism amounts to a sustained lamentation over the lack of prices which would give market participants enough information to engage in rational choices. Hahn in 1983 described the fundamental task in constructing an ecosystem service market as a question of eliciting price: "the basic objectives are to design a market that will elicit a price signal, induce efficient abatement decisions and satisfy considerations of equity" (88). Likewise, Shabman and Batie expressed cynicism about the conservation efforts of the 1970s because of the lack of price:

Because property rights for these ecological services are ill-defined, and because costs of transacting between owners of wetlands and beneficiaries of ecological services are high, there are no markets where owners of wetlands can sell ecological services to willing buyers. As a result, the market price for wetlands will not reflect the value of these ecological services. (Shabman and Batie 1980:3)

There has thus been considerable celebration that the actual value of wetland ecosystems had finally been revealed in wetland banking markets:

The value of a [wetland] credit can be determined by looking at costs faced by an applicant that has no credits ... An applicant will pay at least [the option cost] for available credits. The holder of the credits knows what it costs to produce those credits. If the applicant who needs the credits offers the holder of the credits an acceptable rate of return, a sale will be made. Once a sale has occurred, a value has been determined. (Zagata 1992)

The tantalizing existence of prices did not cause economists to forget the complicated regulatory architecture that created supply and demand, but it did cause them to make rather unguarded and optimistic predictions. The following restatement of the welfare economics credo announced, in a very widely cited policy work on wetland banking, that wetland credit commodities could be expected to behave as any other commodity: "it is the interaction of supply and demand within each region that establishes credit prices and the number of credits needing to be supplied" (Shabman, Scodari and King 1994). This statement is followed by an extended narrative scenario in which economically rational actors arrive at different prices given different initial distribution of rights. It is a modern and specific retelling of the two theorems of welfare economics accompanied, in a subsequent report from the same series, by a diagram that achieves much the same effect (Figure 1). "Yes", it seems to say, "there are a multitude of contingent and inconvenient factors that may interfere with the ability of the market mechanism to deliver the promised maximal social welfare". But they are graphically dismissed. As if the Hudson River school had tackled a box-and-arrow diagram, the wilderness of regulatory and non-market influences gives way to the ordered and civilized simplicity of the supply and demand curve: at the bottom of the diagram—to which all boxes point their arrows—sits our old friend the market-clearing price.

In more earthbound moments, economists talk frankly about the potential for perverse and persistent regulatory policies to interfere in the price mechanism, such that it may inevitably produce irrational results. Such problems had been predicted since the early observations of price in air pollution credit markets in the early 1980s:

there are many cases where exchanges occur without money passing hands; where exchanges occur but they are not freely entered

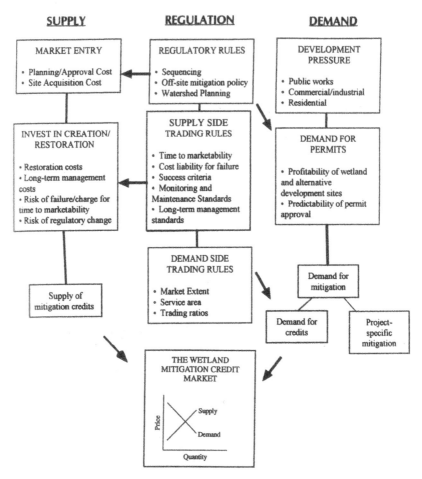

Figure 1: Diagram of the operation of a wetland credit market (source: Shabman, Scodari and King 1996)

into; where exchanges are so constrained by institutional rules that it would be dubious to infer that the terms were satisfactory; and where imperfections in the conditions of exchange would lead us to conclude that the price ratios do not reflect a corporate social judgments about values. Each of these cases gives rise to deficiencies in the use of existing price data as the basis of evaluation of input or outputs. (Shabman and Batie 1980:5)

This concern is familiar in the wetland credit market of 2006, but takes on an urgently pragmatic tone: now that we finally have the capacity to generate prices, economists say, the goal of policy must be to ensure that regulatory and non-market factors don't interfere with the generation of accurate price signals. All such interference, by definition, is exogenous to the market and to the intimate dance by which buyer and seller determine price. Left alone, this process will be rational and generate the promised social welfare. Price distortions, and therefore market failures, are to be explained in terms of regulatory interference, spatial monopolies, or inelastic demand—anything but problems with the fundamental capacity of a buyer to recognize a manufactured commodity as an object that increases his or her utility, and to purchase it at a price which reflects that utility with crystalline accuracy. In fact, the pellucid transparency of the unfettered market is frequently invoked in both WQT and wetland banking forums: "The transparency of the market helps create the clarity that is needed", and requires only "that a willing buyer and a willing seller know what they're buying, what the price is, and that they can count on the product".[14] The various fetters placed on markets, and problems in defining commodities and discovering prices, can create the impression of hopeless entanglement with extra-market social forces. Nevertheless,

> Before we submit to this incubus of complexity, however, we might seek comfort in the reflection that the great virtue of a pricing system is that it solves, avoids, mediates, or somehow manages to dispel, all sorts of complexities, particularly those that arise from various interdependencies between uses and users of goods. (Dales 1968:792)

Belief in the market-clearing price can, in other words, be tested, wrestled with, raged against, and can generate schisms, but will in the end reward faith with grace.

Entrepreneurial Bankers

This optimism is why, in dispensing advice to his fellow wetland bank entrepreneurs, Michael Rolband can cast the basic challenge of banking in terms of price:

> As for any product, classical supply/demand relationships will determine the appropriate price of mitigation credits ... The fundamental economic test that a wetland bank must meet is the ability to sell credits at a price that exceeds expected costs and investor return requirements. (Rolband et al 2000:203–210)

As a national figure in the industry, it is Rolband's prerogative to invoke such abstractions from the pulpit of a major policy publication. But his advice offers little practical guidance, and few bankers join him in these sentiments when discussing the task of setting price in actual transactions. In asking entrepreneurial bankers what their actual practice is in setting price, I am doing something deeply irrational by the lights of mainstream economic theorists. Since the Chicago-school economists led by Milton Friedman dismissed the need for empirical verification of the models of quantitative economics, the investigation of actual thoughts and opinions of market participants have been considered somewhat quaint and certainly irrelevant in the face of nearly universal acceptance of aggregate rationality (Mäki 2000; Mirowski 2001:198; Rosenberg 1992:88). Asking individuals for their personal justifications of their own actions is thus akin to asking the roulette ball why it fell on 33.

Nonetheless, if we fail to insist that the way people think about, talk about, and act out the supposed iron imperatives of the market, we would be conceding to Friedman, vacating without contest the forums in which the invisible hand materializes in the bodies and actions of men and women. In that spirit, I have observed that wetland bankers do not tend to behave as if they were being puppetted by market forces, or seeking some demand-coordinating auctioneer, or even particularly interested in the market-clearing price. They are reflective, irrational, conflicted about their many possible roles, and apparently incapable— even if the institutions of the market allowed for perfect exchange— of arriving at Pareto-optimal outcomes. Four trends are evident in the practices by which entrepreneurial bankers set their credit prices; they are exemplified below, in excerpts from interviews conducted in 2001 and 2002.

Don't Consider the Economic Situation of the Customer, or Even Negotiate over Prices

MR: How do you set your prices?

S36: We do it by what the market will bear.

MR: Just ask the customer?

S36: Well, we just set it . . . we said $25,000. They didn't baulk. And I figured, you know, the back of the envelope . . . figured that we could do that and maybe make a little money . . .

(Chicago banker[15])

The market-clearing calculus that is supposed to produce a price is nowhere apparent in this banker's account of setting a price. If the "discovery" of accurate price is composed of thousands of such moments, the Law of Large Numbers cannot help us since this banker is not using the "appropriate" criteria to set a price. Even the faintest interest in the capacity of a given client, or a class of clients, to pay a higher price would give the economist some scrap of hope for a Pareto-optimal outcome, but this banker was adamant that extensive negotiation over prices was extraneous to his business model. The back of his envelope contained no information about the economic situation of his customer, instead containing an entirely one-sided calculus concerning his own economy: what price would clear him a reasonable profit? The customer "not baulking" is the only moment of negotiation. Such asymmetry is quite common in many markets (think of the lack of negotiation over prices next time you visit the grocery store), but is still somewhat scandalous to neoclassical economic purists. Price discovery in the classical sense should proceed from this point until the customer *does* baulk, but the trade magazine *Chicago Business* noted without evident concern that this is not the standard practice in the banking industry: "Wetlands Initiative Senior Vice President Donald Hey says developers don't negotiate the price per credit. 'Nobody has asked for a reduction,' he says" (Murphy 2002).

Consider Extra-economic Factors in Setting Price

MR: So how do you come up with a price?

S40: Yeah, initially we looked at our costs, and what we anticipated our long-term costs would be, and arrived at a price that way.

MR: Would you consider the means of the customer?

S40: Yeah, I mean, you know, you kind of get a soft spot for some of those people, you know ... I just felt so sorry for that lady, I couldn't believe it.

(Minnesota banker[16])

There are two significant departures from the two theorems of welfare economics encapsulated here. Once again, this banker is setting his price with reference mainly to his cost of production rather than the ability of the customer to pay for the commodity. But in this case, while not considering economic means of the customer, he is clearly and strongly influenced by the distressing predicament of a client. The case involved a dairy farmer who had been "turned in" to the federal regulators by recreational hunters for filling in a small section of wetland, building a road to allow her cows to access land where the hunters preferred to shoot. The state issued a cease-and-desist order, ordered the road removed, and required that the farmer purchase wetland credits as compensatory mitigation. The wetland banker, a dairy farmer himself, was strongly influenced to offer a very low price both by feelings of solidarity against the state and by a degree of class antagonism against leisure hunters. These factors go considerably beyond the individual interest-based calculus of *homo economicus*.

Conduct No Market Research

MR: How did you arrive at 30 cents a square foot?

S9: I get calls, and some character called me from up by Thief River Falls and wants a price, and—you know, what the hell, you can't tell him that its 18,000 dollars an acre. So, I mean, you'd visit with 'em, and that's how I did my research, when people called me.

(Minnesota banker[17])

The active, agent-led moment in price discovery, if there can be said to be one in the classical formulation, might occur in efforts at market research. Commodity producers attempting to trim their production scheme to the winds of consumer preference and trends in price typically spend some effort in finding out what their commodity is trading for in neighboring markets, or what other producers are charging. While the banker above, unlike the previous examples, *does* engage in negotiation over price, he is not atypical in his impatience with these activities. This is probably because he, like many other bankers throughout the country, conducts his business as an adjunct to his primary occupation of residential development. Although there are no data on this matter, it is clear that many entrepreneurial bankers do not draw all of their income from credit sales, and many probably do not consider themselves to be "bankers" primarily or at all. This makes their individual identity in a market, and their collective identity as a fraction of capital, uncertain to say the least. If a banker's action in a market is not informed by their self-identification as a producer of wetland credits, it becomes entirely unclear which actions qualify as rational and which don't. Welfare economics has no concepts to deal with such complicated notions of agency.

Take Opportunities to Collude

MR: How will you set a price?

S26: Oh ... I have a friend of mine that's doing the same thing, and he kind of found out from me or he knew about it, so he's doing it too. Yeah, he's a neighbor ... So we get together, we go golfing once in a while and stuff. But he's doing it too, and we have kind of a gentleman's agreement, we come up with a price.

(Minnesota banker[18])

This kind of casual anti-competitive behavior goes hand-in-hand with the general lack of concern for maximizing (rather than simply attaining) profit. Market participants seem to prioritize ensuring stability across a broader set of social relations, within which the wetland credit market exists alongside other concerns. Social bonds that go far beyond the transaction are vital in wetland credit trading not only in situations where the producer's identity overflows the category of "banker", as we have seen, but also in more conventional scenarios of agency. One banker, who conducts his business as his sole source of revenue, expresses clearly that competition is less a matter of price than of the cultivation of networks:

> I know a large share of the development community, I know them well, and so I've been able to put together more deals than [I might have]. If one does not have such affiliations with people, and all you're trying to do is compete on price or whatever, that hasn't proved to be as beneficial. (Entrepreneurial banker[19])

I have suggested elsewhere (Robertson 2006) that the wetland banking industry is one in which prioritizing the maintenance of social networks over profit maximization is adaptive in the face of dramatic instability in the regulatory conditions which create demand. Regulatory changes at many scales, entirely exogenous to the market, can have a dramatic effect on production strategy (Robertson 2004); in such a situation, maintaining a flexible entrepreneurial strategy means tending to the social connections which can keep a banker afloat in steep seas rather than expending resources in a quixotic pursuit of the best possible price. This leaves us with a question that can have thunderous implications for neoliberal strategy, if taken seriously: what do "price signals" signal when market participants act in a way informed by any one, if not all four, of the complicating factors above?

But I do not wish to overstate the case. The above excerpts are not meant to imply that there are *no* bankers who negotiate extensively over prices, conduct market research, forego collusion or retain a professional disinterest in the personal lives of clients. Recognizable forms of negotiation over price, good-faith attempts to balance the utilities of producer and customer, in fact, happen every day in this market. But, as in this extended excerpt, they tend to affirm the pervasive role of regulatory force in shaping individual utility functions:

> If I sat down with a builder and said, "look, it's gonna cost you 250 thousand dollars to buy credits from me", and he says, "Jeez, you know, my engineer says I can [build a wetland myself] for 200 thousand" I said, "Look. Ninety days from now, you're gonna have paid me 250 thousand in full, you're gonna get a letter from the Corps of Engineers, South Florida Water Management District, and Broward County Department of Environmental Protection saying that you never have to worry about this again. Your engineer thinks it's gonna cost 200 thousand including the value of the land". I said, "You know and I know ... that you have a five-year obligation, you have to hire a contractor to do the work, things don't always go as planned; in five years, you may have to remediate once or twice or three times. You're on the hook, you may have to put a bond up". I said, "Is it worth 50 thousand dollars to have this contingent liability, and you haven't even started to build this wetland yet, versus ninety days from now, writing me a check and forgetting about it for*ever*?" It wound up being a good sales tool. (Florida banker[20])

The point of this section is not to suggest that wetland banking is fundamentally different than other commodity markets—although this argument can certainly be made. Rather it is to observe that price discovery is *always* a task achieved by complex agents whose identities exceed the economic, embedded in networks that extend beyond the breadth of the wetland credit market. This complexity cannot be wished or theorized away; it can only be undone by the conscious choices of agents who *choose*—contingently—to behave in economically rational ways. I have observed that bankers often seek stability within these larger networks, rather than maximizing their transaction-by-transaction profit. Setting price is only one of many, many decisions they have to make about achieving financial stability and other forms of non-economic satisfaction, decisions made more numerous because often the banker's economic identity is not firmly that of "producer of credits". Complex identities create complex price calculations, and price signals that are simply uninterpretable within the assumptions of neoliberal economics.

Neoliberal economists recognize this, to a certain degree. To the extent that they recognize agency as relevant at all, their impulse is usually to colonize these elements of noneconomic difference within market participants' identities by drawing such decisions within the realm of economic calculus. Rabin (1998:13) begins with admirable candor, that "[I]t is sometimes misleading to conceptualize people as attempting to maximize a coherent, stable, and accurately perceived $U(x)$", but then—in a rhetorical move similar to Shabman's graphical one in Figure 1—he returns to the arms of economic dogma: "economists ought to become aware of the shortcomings of our models, regret these shortcomings, and keep our eyes open for ways to remedy them". These arguments always end up in deeply functionalist places, and when presented with unmodelable departures from *homo economicus*, economists may become rather impatient:

> Claims about that evidence inconsistent with our traditional model of human behavior can be neglected because the evidence derives from observations of people insufficiently motivated to behave themselves according to economic assumptions, or because it fails to bear sufficiently great burdens of proof, or because the implied behavior is unlikely to matter in the types of (market) settings that economists care about. (Rabin 1998:41)

Resource economists have long lamented that the lack of actual markets in ecosystem services such as clean water and wetlands biodiversity means that their estimation of the value of these services must rely on methods of dubious reliability such as "willingness-to-pay" surveys or hedonic analysis. The arrival of actual markets heralds the generation of "straightforward, readily estimable values" in the form of price (Turner et al. 2003, 497). This is seen to be somewhat less tidy in practice, as market actors refuse to be confined within market-rational conceptions of agency, and price is thus heavily overdetermined.

Consequences for Market Environmentalism

> I don't see anything in Water Quality Trading that I don't have something in my [economic theory] bag to pull out and address it with. (Economist Tony Prato[21])

While neoliberal economists tend to view market dynamics without seeing the people who create those dynamics, critics of neoliberalism should not make the same mistake. Too often, resistance to neoliberal strategy is theorized as contingent, rich with diverse agency, and fruitfully multivocal, while the forces that advance neoliberal strategy are described in agency-flattening and even structural terms. The people who strive to create new markets after the principles of neoliberal economics are given a difficult task, and the potential regulators, consumers, and producers of new kinds of commodities are given little practical guidance in resolving some of the key obstacles. What they *are* given, and which must not be discounted, is the benevolent embrace of the state, promises of subsidy and research, and warm assurances by political figures that they are "part of the army of citizen conservationists"[22] who will lead this nation out of the morass of 1970s environmental policy errors into a neoliberal utopia. But these same leaders steadfastly refuse to lead, constantly invoking governance over government: "You are the experts!"[23] conjures one to an audience of prospective entrepreneurs, and another desires only to "comport . . . with the changes that have already taken place in the hearts and minds of the American people".[24] In places, the "neoliberal rollout" (Peck and Tickell 2002) looks as fractured and uncoordinated as resistance to it, with market actors' identities exceeding the economic, state fractions tripping over themselves, and economists producing policy prescriptions that make entrepreneurial practitioners gnash their teeth in frustration. This can largely be traced back to the fact that, while neoliberal policy must be enacted by particular agents in specific locations, neoliberalism in its purer forms declines to theorize either agency *or* location.

Understanding the close texture of individual neoliberal capitalist strategies reveals not only that are there ample openings for resistance and redirection, but that rollout and resistance may be embodied in the same policy and in fact the same person. All of the attendees at the WQT forums were active, and for the most part enthusiastic, participants in the creation of new neoliberal economic forms, and yet there was a good deal of open conflict on the specifics of market design, conflict that continues to threaten the integrity of the entire policy initiative and to which few effective responses are offered. Economists, when asked for specific information on how best to set price or stimulate production, respond unhelpfully with Say's Law, the Law of Large Numbers, and other abstractions in the form of normative fables. Prato's epigram above is one such fable: WQT and wetland banking are not new under the sun, and require no retooling of the basics of neoliberal economic policy. The state tells a parallel fable: the privatization of nature is going to interpellate all of us as producers or consumers in a marketplace of ideas, services, and other commodities. As the state informed us at the opening session of a recent national conference on water quality trading: "No matter where you said you're from when you stood up for the roll call this morning, you're in here as business innovators".[25]

The emptiness of these fables is dangerous, because under neoliberal capitalism we have accepted the role of price as a principal guarantor of democracy. Liberal economics was (and is) embraced politically not only because it advanced capitalism, but because it promised a way to replace the visible violence of political struggle with the invisible violence of economic struggle, to reduce differences to preferences (Harvey 1990; Lefebvre [1974] 1991:396). If people can be rendered as different only in our utility functions, then these differences can be reconciled in a market rather than a battlefield. This is the political context in which, increasingly, "democratic choice" has been defined as "choice in a market", an arrangement that makes a price mechanism working smoothly enough to reach Pareto-optimality the guarantor of democracy. Evidence that the price mechanism fails to operate as desired strikes at the heart of the political rationale for neoliberalism and points towards neoliberalism's failure on its own terms.

In short, price in emerging markets for poorly defined commodities doesn't work the way neoliberal theory needs it to in order to deliver on its promise of market-led democracy. As we are evidently in a period of market expansion into new kinds of property and commodities, such situations may be assumed to be relatively common, and we should pay particular attention to the justification of initiatives to commodify "ecosystem services" such as clean air and biodiversity. Were economists not impervious to a world of countervailing data, this should be disturbing to them; but while doing this kind of ground-truthing on neoliberal claims is valuable, it is not going to convince economists insulated by Friedman's methodology. They will never be the audience that matters; efforts to fact-check neoliberal claims are much more potent when inserted directly into the political and policy realm. A little grey geography goes a long way (Peck 1999) when economists have ceded the field of providing specific answers and suggestions instead of laws. It can be very effective to produce answers that recognize the actual conditions under which entrepreneurs and consumers make decisions, using venues and language likely to engage rather than repel their interest (Robertson 2006 is one very modest attempt). It can also be illustrative to demonstrate the emptiness of welfare economic precepts, eg by pushing them to *ad absurdum* limits in the context of stakeholder forums. Such work requires that we understand the agents of neoliberal capitalism as complex and conflicted identities rather than as automatons.

On the ground, price discovery and commodity identities are results of people muddling through, and these producers, consumers and regulators are seeking guidance:

> Sociology enters the equation in the problem of how actors produce a social world stable enough that they can sell those goods and services at a price at which the organization will survive. Managing people and uncertain environments to produce stability is a sizable task. Those who do it every day often demonstrate great skill and creativity as they lurch from crisis to crisis. (Fligstein 2001:18)

Neoliberal theorists are necessarily blind to many of the spaces where such issues are hammered out; I have only gestured at the deep tripartite disconnect between economic theorists, neoliberal policy advocates, and actual entrepreneurs on how neoliberal capitalism should be rolled out. Some of the people muddling through are in farm fields in Minnesota, some work at sewage treatment plants in Durango, and some are in think tanks in Washington DC. They are waiting for answers that critical geographers can provide. What *is* the commodity? How *do* we set price? The answers they get can help advance neoliberal strategy, redirect it, or drive it toward the rocks of its own contradictions.

Acknowledgements

I am grateful for the extremely helpful comments of Joel Wainwright, Dan Bromley, Jamie Peck, Nik Heynen and two anonymous reviewers, although all errors remain my own. This paper was completed with support from a Doctoral Dissertation Research Improvement Grant from the NSF, a Dissertation Writing Fellowship from the University of Wisconsin, and a fellowship from the Oak Ridge Institute for Science and Education. The views represented in this paper are the author's alone and do not necessarily represent those of the Environmental Protection Agency.

Endnotes

[1] Daniel Bromley, University of Wisconsin Department of Agricultural and Applied Economics, personal communication, May 2000. See also his book *Sufficient Reason* (2006).
[2] Dennis King, University of Maryland Department of Economics, 7 November 2005, speaking at the National Forum on Synergies Between Water Quality Trading and Wetland Mitigation Banking, Carnegie Endowment for International Peace, Washington, DC. The proceedings are detailed in ELI (2005).

[3] The two theorems state, in short, that (1) markets in competitive equilibrium produce optimal social welfare (ie Pareto-optimality), and (2) any initial distribution of resources can lead to equilibrium.

[4] When I discuss Say's Law, it is not with the intention of erecting a straw man. A normal-science reading of economics regards Say's Law as irrelevant: students of demand-side economics were taught that the Law was superseded by Keynesianism, and students of supply-side economics were taught that it was superseded by the Arrow-Debreu proof. These traditions aside, what concerns me here is that the Law itself is still cited authoritatively in the actual forums in which decisions are made concerning how to construct markets.

[5] I use "mainstream economics" in a way that overlaps with "neoclassical economics" or "classical liberal economics" to indicate the utility-based methodologically individualist approach to economics that has become so hegemonic in the United States since World War II that it can barely conceive of coherent opposition to its precepts.

[6] "Point-source" and "non-point-source" pollution in water are legal terms of art: any discrete conveyance that can be said to resemble a pipe, delivering concentrated effluent, is regulated under Section 302 of the CWA. The diffuse entry of pollutants (say, from farm-field runoff) is not (Findley and Farber 1999:375).

[7] Susan Burke, Idaho Department of Environmental Quality, at the Second National Water Quality Trading Conference, Pittsburgh, PA, 24 May 2006.

[8] Tony Prato, University of Missouri Department of Economics, comment at the US EPA Research Planning Conference on Wetlands and Water Quality Trading, 16 February 2006, Chicago, IL. The proceedings are detailed in EPA ORD (forthcoming).

[9] James Shortle, Pennsylvania State University Department of Agricultural Economics, comment at the Second National Water Quality Trading Conference, 23 May 2006, Pittsburgh, PA.

[10] The South Nation Conservancy website encourages landowners to apply for SNC's grants program as a source of funding for projects which will improve water quality. However, the site does not reveal that the SNC accumulates "water quality credits" thereby, which will be purchased by polluters: http://www.nation.on.ca/English/CleanWater.htm.

[11] http://www.miamiconservancy.org/water/quality_credit.asp

[12] Dennis King, University of Maryland Department of Economics, 11 July 2005, speaking at the National Forum on Synergies Between Water Quality Trading and Wetland Mitigation Banking, Carnegie Endowment for International Peace, Washington, DC. The proceedings are detailed in ELI 2005. The Law of Large Numbers, in its weak form, states that given an infinite sequence of uncorrelated random variables, where all have the same expected value and variance, the sample average will tend to converge on the expected value. King's use was inappropriate because it assumes identical expected values and variance for all BMP implementations.

[13] The positions in this paragraph paraphrase a three-way discussion between Iowa State University ecologist William Crumpton, University of Missouri economist Tony Prato, and EPA staffer Sue Elston at the 2006 Chicago forum.

[14] The Hon Bruce Knight, chief of USDA's Natural Resource Conservation Service, 25 May 2006, speaking at the Second National Water Quality Trading Conference, Pittsburgh, PA.

[15] Interview conducted 4 December 2002.

[16] Interview conducted 7 November 2002. While many Minnesota bankers are non-entrepreneurial in their identity as wetland bankers, and the banking community nationwide tends to dismiss Minnesota on this ground, this interviewee *is* thoroughly entrepreneurial in his approach and has participated in moderately successful attempts to organize Minnesota wetland bankers into a self-identified fraction of capital.

[17] Interview conducted 19 July 2001.

[18] Interview conducted 12 February 2003.

[19] Interview conducted 25 July 2001.

[20] Interview conducted 27 February 2002.

[21] Tony Prato, University of Missouri Department of Economics, comment at the US EPA Research Planning Conference on Wetlands and Water Quality Trading, 16 February 2006, Chicago, IL. The proceedings are detailed in EPA ORD (forthcoming).

[22] The Hon George Dunlop, Deputy Assistant Secretary of the Army for Civil Works, 26 April 2006, speaking at the Ninth National Mitigation and Conservation Banking Conference, Portland, OR. Dunlop is the political appointee in charge of the regulatory branch of the US Army Corps of Engineers.

[23] Brent Fewell, USEPA Deputy Assistant Administrator for Water, 25 May 2006, speaking at the Second National Water Quality Trading Conference, Pittsburgh, PA.

[24] The Hon George Dunlop, Deputy Assistant Secretary of the Army for Civil Works, 26 April 2006, speaking at the Ninth National Mitigation and Conservation Banking Conference, Portland, OR.

[25] Bryon Griffith, chief of the US EPA Gulf of Mexico Program, 23 May 2006, speaking at the Second National Water Quality Trading Conference, Pittsburgh, PA.

References

Amin A and Thrift N (1995) Institutional issues for the European regions: From markets and plans to socioeconomics and powers of association. *Economy and Society* 24(1):41–66

Bakker K (2005) Neoliberalizing nature? Market environmentalism in water supply in England and Wales. *Annals of the Association of American Geographers* 95(3):542–565

Boyer R (1997) The variety and unequal performance of really existing markets: Farewell to Doctor Pangloss? In J R Hollingsworth and R Boyer (eds) *Contemporary Capitalism: The Embeddedness of Institutions* (pp 55–93). Cambridge: Cambridge University Press

Bromley D (2006) *Sufficient Reason: Volitional Pragmatism and the Meaning of Economic Institutions.* Princeton, NJ: Princeton University Press

Castree N (1995) The nature of produced nature: Materiality and knowledge construction in Marxism. *Antipode* 27(1):12–48

Castree N (2002) False antitheses? Marxism, nature and actor-networks. *Antipode* 34(1):111–146

Costanza R, d'Arge R, de Groot R, Farber S, Grasso M, Hannon B, Limburg K, Naeem S, O'Neill R V, Paruelo J, Raskin R G, Sutton P and van den Belt M (1997) The value of the world's ecosystem services and natural capital. *Science* 387(6630):253–260

Daily G C (1997) Introduction: What are ecosystem services? In G C Daily (ed) *Nature's Services: Societal Dependence on Natural Ecosystems* (pp 1–10). Washington, DC: Island Press

Daily G C and Ellison K (2002) *The New Economy of Nature: The Quest to Make Conservation Profitable.* Washington, DC: Island Press

Dales J H (1968) Land, water, and ownership. *Canadian Journal of Economics* 1(4):791–804

Environmental Law Institute (ELI) (2002) *Banks and Fees: The Status of Off-Site Wetland Mitigation in the United States.* Washington, DC: Environmental Law Institute

Environmental Law Institute (ELI) (2005) *National Forum on Synergies Between Water Quality Trading and Wetland Mitigation Banking: Forum Report.* Washington: ELI

Environmental Protection Agency (EPA) (2003) Final water quality trading policy, 13 January, http://www.epa.gov/owow/watershed/trading/finalpolicy2003.html

Environmental Protection Agency (EPA) (2005) Mitigation banking factsheet, 28 November, http://www.epa.gov/owow/wetlands/facts/fact16.html

Environmental Protection Agency (EPA) and United States Department of Agriculture (USDA) (2006) Partnership agreement between the United States Department of Agriculture Natural Resources Conservation Service and the United States Environment Protection Agency Office of Water, signed 13 October, http://www.epa.gov/owow/watershed/trading/mou061013.pdf

Environmental Protection Agency Economic Incentives Task Force (EPA EITF) (1991) *Economic Incentives: Options for Environmental Protection*, March. Washington, DC: USEPA

Environmental Protection Agency Office of Research and Development (EPA ORD) (forthcoming) *Proceedings of US EPA Research Planning Conference on the Role of Wetlands in Water Quality Trading*

Findley R W and Farber D A (1999) *Cases and Materials on Environmental Law*. 5th ed. St Paul, MN: West Group

Fligstein N (2001) *The Architecture of Markets: An Economic Sociology of Twenty-first Century Capitalist Societies*. Princeton, NJ: Princeton University Press

Gibson-Graham J K (1993) Waiting for the revolution, or how to smash capitalism while working at home in your spare time. *Rethinking Marxism* 6(2):10–24

Hahn R W (1983) Designing markets in transferable property rights: A practitioner's guide. In E F Joeres and M H David (eds) *Buying a Better Environment: Cost-effective Regulation through Permit Trading* (pp 83–97). Madison, WI: University of Wisconsin Press

Harvey D (1990) *The Condition of Postmodernity: An Enquiry into the Origins of Cultural Change*. Cambridge, MA: Blackwell

Hodgson G (1988) *Economics and Institutions*. Cambridge: Polity Press

Huber P W (1999) *Hard Green: Saving the Environment from the Environmentalists*. New York: Basic Books

King D M and Herbert L W (1997) The fungibility of wetlands. *National Wetlands Newsletter* 19(5):10–13

King D M and Kuch P (2003) Will nutrient credit trading ever work? An assessment of supply problems, demand problems, and institutional obstacles. *Environmental Law Reporter* 33:10352–10368

Lefebvre H ([1974] 1991) *The Production of Space*. Cambridge, MA: Blackwell

Mäki U (2000) Kinds of assumptions and their truth: Shaking an untwisted F-twist. *Kyklos* 53(3):317–335

McAfee K (1999) Selling nature to save it? Biodiversity and green developmentalism. *Environment and Planning D: Society and Space* 17:133–154

McAfee K (2003) Neoliberalism on the molecular scale. Economic and genetic reductionism in biotechnology battles. *Geoforum* 34:203–219

Mirowski P (2001) *Machine Dreams: Economics Becomes a Cyborg Science*. Cambridge: Cambridge University Press

Murphy H L (2002) Wetlands no longer soak plans for many builders. *Crain's Chicago Business* 23 September

National Research Council (NRC) (2001) *Compensating for Wetland Losses under the Clean Water Act*. Washington, DC: National Academy Press

National Research Council (NRC) (2005) *Valuing Ecosystem Services: Toward Better Environmental Decision-making*. Washington, DC: National Academy Press

Oates W E (2006) An economic perspective on environmental and resource management: An introduction. In W E Oates (ed) *The RFF Reader in Environmental and Resource Policy* (pp xv–xx). Washington, DC: Resources for the Future

O'Connor J (1994) Is sustainable capitalism possible? In M O'Connor (ed) *Is Capitalism Sustainable?: Political Economy and the Politics of Ecology* (pp 152–175). New York: Guilford

O'Connor M (1994) On the misadventures of capitalist nature. In M O'Connor (ed) *Is Capitalism Sustainable? Political Economy and the Politics of Ecology* (pp 125–151). New York: Guilford

Peck J A (1999) Editorial: Grey geography? *Transactions of the Institute of British Geographers, New Series* 24:131–135

Peck J A and Tickell A (2002) Neoliberalizing space. *Antipode* 34(3):380–404

Polanyi K (1944) *The Great Transformation: The Political and Economic Origins of Our Time*. Boston: Beacon Press

Rabin M (1998) Psychology and economics. *Journal of Economic Literature* 36: 11–46

Robertson M M (2004) The neoliberalization of ecosystem services: Wetland mitigation banking and problems in environmental governance. *Geoforum* 35: 361–373

Robertson M M (2006) Emerging ecosystem service markets: Trends in a decade of entrepreneurial wetland banking. *Frontiers in Ecology and Environmental Science* 4(6):297–302

Rolband M S, Redmond A and Kelsch T (2000) Wetland mitigation banking. In D M Kent (ed) *Applied Wetland Science and Technology* (pp 181–213). Boca Raton, FL: CRC Press

Rosenberg A (1992) *Economics: Mathematical Politics or Science of Diminishing Returns?* Chicago: University of Chicago Press

Scodari P and Shabman L A (1995) *National Wetland Mitigation Banking Study: Commercial Wetland Mitigation Credit Markets: Theory and Practice*. US Army Corps of Engineers Institute for Water Resources Report IWR 94-WMB-7. Alexandria, VA: USCOE IWR

Shabman L A and Batie S S (1980) Estimating the economic value of coastal wetlands: Conceptual issues and research needs. In V S Kennedy (ed) *Estuarine Perspectives* (pp 3–15). New York: Academic Press

Shabman L A, Scodari P and King D M (1994) *National Wetland Mitigation Banking Study: Expanding Opportunities for Successful Mitigation: The Private Credit Market Alternative*. US Army Corps of Engineers Institute for Water Resources Report IWR 94-WMB-3. Alexandria, VA: USCOE IWR

Shabman L A, Scodari P and King D (1996) Wetland mitigation banking markets. In L L Marsh, D R Porter and D A Salvesen (eds) *Mitigation Banking: Theory and Practice* (pp 109–138). Washington, DC: Island Press

Sibbing J (2005) Mitigation banking: Will the myth ever die? *National Wetlands Newsletter* 27(6):5–6, 8

Society of Wetland Scientists (SWS) (2005) Wetland mitigation banking. http://www.sws.org/wetlandconcerns/banking.htm

Turner R K, Paavola J, Cooper P, Farber S, Jessamy V and Georgiou S (2003) Valuing nature: Lessons learned and future research directions. *Ecological Economics* 46:493–510

US Army Corps of Engineers (USACOE), US Environmental Protection Agency, US Fish and Wildlife Service, Natural Resource Conservation Service, and National Oceanic and Atmospheric Administration (1995) Federal guidance for the establishment, use and operation of mitigation banks. *Federal Register* 60(228):58605–58614

US Army Corps of Engineers (USACOE) and Environmental Protection Agency (EPA) (2006) Compensatory mitigation for losses of aquatic resources: Proposed rule. *Federal Register* 71(59):15520–15556

Watts M (1994) Development II: The privatization of everything? *Progress in Human Geography* 18(3):371–384

White House Office on Environmental Policy (WHOEP) (1993) *Protecting America's Wetlands: A Fair, Flexible and Effective Approach.* Washington, DC: The White House

Zagata M D (1992) Mitigation banking: Creating a win/win situation. In J A Kusler and C Lassonde (eds) *Effective Mitigation: Mitigation Banks and Joint Projects in the Context of Wetland Mitigation Plans* (pp 61–63). Berne, NY: ASWM

Chapter 6

The Difference that Class Makes: Neoliberalization and Non-Capitalism in the Fishing Industry of New England

Kevin St. Martin

Introduction

The emerging global regime of fisheries science and management represents an ongoing and aggressive implementation of new technologies of resource governance aligned with neoliberal polices elsewhere (McCarthy and Prudham 2004). In recent years, across a variety of fisheries in several countries, a particular neoclassical understanding of fisheries has migrated from the backwater of fisheries bioeconomics textbooks to the offices of national and international resource managers. This narrow theorization of the destructive effects of fishermen's rational economic behavior in the absence of property rights formulated in the 1950s is finding new play within systems of fisheries science and management worldwide (Hannesson 2004).[1] Fisheries bioeconomics not only describes the essential cause of "overfishing", it now produces and guides the development of management schemes directly (Mansfield 2004a; St Martin 2001). Similar to other neoliberal theorizations, bio-economic models suggest solving the "problem of fishing" by privatizing access to resources, commodifying access rights, and institutionalizing markets for those rights (eg Iudicello, Weber and Wieland 1999). The institutionalization of these essentially neoliberal practices in fisheries management has been described by many as a creeping enclosure of the fisheries commons (Apostle, McCay and Mikalsen 2002; Clay 1994; Mansfield 2004b; St Martin 2006).

Once the trope of enclosure is deployed, it is not then difficult to imagine fisheries as in the midst of a fundamental and sweeping economic and class transformation with a trajectory and inevitability paralleling that of capitalist development generally (St Martin 2005b). In the case of fisheries, the establishment of property rights, read as enclosure, signals an irreversible transformation of the mode of production reminiscent of enclosures past, albeit delayed by the difficulties of inscribing and appropriating "ocean space" (cf Mann Borgese 2000; Steinberg 2001). The nature of this economic transformation is from some "pre-capitalism" to capitalism or, in fisheries, from "livelihood harvesting" practices to a new regime of "accumulation harvesting" (Davis 1996).

While this movement suggests a vital point of resistance—the struggle against private property rights—it also makes difficult an imaginary of an alternative (ie non-capitalist) economy of fisheries that is not already archaic or, in the neoclassical story, deficient. Indeed, the non-capitalism from which capitalism emerges does not have to be specified. In this sense, even critiques of enclosure aid in the erasure of alternative economies by leaving them undocumented and devoid of possibility. The details of the economic present—how surplus is produced, appropriated, and distributed amongst fishermen and within fishing communities—remain unexplored. It would seem that the processes we associate with neoliberalism, including enclosure, garner their power and popularity via the elimination of any alternative.

The goal of this paper, via the class analysis presented below, is to recast the economy of fishing as a unique non-capitalist formation *within* an economy conceptualized as diverse (cf Gibson-Graham et al 2000, 2001). Rather than relegate economic difference to a fading past or distant location (St Martin 2005a), a present and proximate fishing economy is here valorized and produced as a site of non-capitalist potential rather than always a capitalist becoming. The analysis also serves as a means by which to better understand the effectivity of neoliberal policy implementations, specifically the institutionalization of property rights in fisheries, in terms of its ability (and inability) to transform class processes.

This paper proceeds by pointing to the persistence of non-capitalism in the fisheries of New England despite decades of economic theorization that insist upon recreating capitalist relations of production, particularly property relations, in fisheries. It looks briefly at the origins of that theorization to document just how fisheries economists saw the economy of fishing as containing a number of barriers to capitalism. Using evidence from interviews,[2] the barriers are then recast as the foundations of an alternative economy. The paper specifies the nature of that alternative form of economy and subsequently re-reads the economic dynamic in fishing, fishermen's subjectivity, and the possibilities for the economic future of fishing.

The Persistence of Non-Capitalism

With the passage of the Magnuson Act in 1976, the United States set up a system of fisheries management whereby regional councils would produce regulations to govern the fishing industry. The establishment of the council system coincided with the US enlargement of its "exclusive

economic zone" (EEZ) out to 200 miles from the coast, an unprecedented but inevitable nationalization of what had been international waters (Eckert 1979; Hanna et al 2000; Steinberg 2001; Watt 1979). The
institutionalization of the EEZ was closely aligned with the central tenets
of a fisheries bioeconomics that emerged first with the publication of
Gordon's (1954) article that suggested the essential problem in fishing
was rent dissipation due to an absence of property rights.[3] The first move
toward the repair of the fishing economy would be a territorialization of
previously international waters.

> A great extension of territorial waters recognized in international law
> would convert international fisheries into national ones and to that
> extent it would ease some of the practical problems of fisheries man-
> agement. (Gordon 1957:72)

The goal of the councils, each responsible for discrete management
zones, was to manage the massive fisheries resources that were newly
claimed by the United States federal government. With the imposition
of the EEZ, the "open access" fisheries commons of the continental
shelf became a common pool resource or, in fisheries economics terms,
"sole owned" (Scott 1955). To take advantage of this resource and to
build a domestic fishing fleet where foreign factory trawlers once domi-
nated (NOAA 2006), the federal government supplied development and
capital improvement loans to the commercial fishing industry of the
Northeast. Despite the call to limit access such that rents could be realized
rather than dispersed, what transpired was an enlargement of access for
domestic fishermen, a modernization, Americanization, and expansion
of fishing fleets, fishermen, and fishing capacity (Dewar 1983; Hanna
et al 2000).

The new regime had the curious effect of expanding precisely the
economy of fisheries that enclosure was to transform. In New England, the management regime that emerged in the 1970s and 1980s,
which was explicitly designed to restrict foreign exploitation of fisheries
resources within the EEZ, produced the conditions of existence for an
expansion of local, family-owned, and community-based fishing enterprises (Doeringer et al 1986a, 1986b; Terkla, Doeringer and Moss
1988). The establishment of the EEZ was seen by the authorities as a
way to bolster the domestic industry and to secure the borders of the US
during the Cold War; it was seen by economic theorists as the first move
toward privatization; and it was seen by fisheries scientists as the first
step toward controlling harvesting pressure on the resource. It was, however, seen by many fishermen as a means by which fisheries resources
could be reallocated from corporate factory trawlers to family-owned
and community-based enterprises.[4]

While the domestic and small-scale businesses that emerged in the
late 1970s and 1980s clearly made money for boat owners and were, in

this respect, similar to other small businesses where fixed capital presumes a right to surplus, they were distinct insofar as the right to surplus was (culturally and legally) shared by crewmembers and, indeed, surplus was distributed to crewmembers and, by extension, fishing communities via a share rather than a wage system of compensation. In addition to this unique class process of surplus production, appropriation, and distribution, a variety of cultural understandings and social practices served to differentiate fishing from standard models of capitalist enterprise (cf Kayatekin 1997, 2001). While fisheries did continue to expand, modernize, and increase capacity tremendously (which would eventually create new problems for the alternative economy), there remained a common property system where labor was compensated via shares rather than wages and capital was locally embedded within fishing communities.

The expansion of the domestic fishing effort contributed to the overexploitation of fish stock and the degradation of fisheries habitat in New England. The overexploitation of fisheries, despite being produced by a range of processes, not the least of which was the encouragement of the federal government (cf Mansfield 2006), is read by many as a confirmation of the "tragedy of the commons" thesis (Hardin 1968) and its attendant assumptions of individualist behavior (eg Hannesson 2004; Iudicello, Weber and Wieland 1999). To address the crisis in fishing, the New England council has focused primarily upon effort controls such as moratoria on licenses, limitations of the allowable days at sea (DAS), area closures, and minimum net mesh size. To fisheries bioeconomists such measures are necessarily flawed since fishermen will eventually find other ways to increase their catch efforts (Dupont 1991). As a result, bioeconomics and, increasingly, a host of institutions informed by bioeconomics call for "output controls" that would limit harvesting directly though the imposition of fishing quotas. Such quotas represent the formation of property rights in fishing and are, in a sense, the logical outcome of the enactment of bioeconomic theories in fisheries management (Mansfield 2004b; St Martin 2001). While quota management can take many forms, it is generally assumed to be some variation of individual fisheries quotas (IFQs) that give to boat owners the right to harvest a particular quantity of fish on an annual basis.

The push and consistent story of fisheries bioeconomics that insists upon the establishment of property rights in fisheries has been in effect since its formulation in the 1950s, has contributed to the legitimation of the federal government's "enclosure" of once open access fisheries in the 1970s, and has, more recently, found expression in the establishment of IFQ systems of management in Iceland (Palsson and Helgason 1994), New Zealand, and select fisheries of the US (McCay and Brant 2001; see also Bernal, Aliaga and Morales 1999; Garcia et al 1999; Symes and Crean 1995). Despite this history and hegemony of fisheries bioeconomics and its call for property rights in fisheries, the fishing communities of New England continue to resist the neoliberalization of their economy; decades of the "development" of domestic fisheries has failed to produce capitalism.

Economic Barriers or Economic Foundations?

Both the processes of enclosure and, more broadly, neoliberalization rely upon an erasure of economic difference and/or the negation of the viability of any alternative economy; in so doing they remove existing barriers to and produce the conditions of existence for capitalism. Within the discourse of fisheries science and management, this process is made clear by the constant reference to existing fishing economies as problematic, deficient, and invariably tending toward a chronic "overfishing" as well as a host of attendant environmental problems (eg habitat loss, bycatch of charismatic marine fauna, fishing down the food chain, etc).

Yet, the fisheries economics that emerged in the 1950s saw the problem of fishing as distinctly one of rent dissipation rather than a problem of environmental degradation per se (eg Gordon 1954; Scott 1955). In addition, the problematic of lost rent was compounded by, in particular, the existence of the share system of compensation in fisheries and an inherent immobility of capital.

> Hence we see that the allocation of resources to the fishery may be too generous for three reasons: the share system, low mobility, and common-property. If the economy is to put the fisherman and the farmer on the same bases, methods must be found for adjusting all three of these matters. Common-property is certainly not a good thing, but neither is it the only factor making for poverty. (Scott 1957:44)

This characterization of the economic problematic of fisheries suggests that there existed in fisheries not just the absence of property rights, but a variety of processes that constituted an economy unlike that of capitalism and whose properties were a barrier to capital accumulation: fisheries was an economy where compensation was through shares rather than wages, where capital was not mobile but tied to places, and where resources were common rather than privately owned.

When the variety of barriers that impede capital accumulation in fisheries are considered, in particular the alternative system of compensation /distribution, the class nature of the reforms called for by fisheries economists are laid bare. For example, when Scott calls for the institutionalization of "sole ownership" in fisheries (see also Scott 1955) to capture lost rent, he muses on how such rent might be redistributed.

> A large amount of the rent would be recaptured by the government, in bids for privileges: in perfect competition all the rent would be recaptured. It does not matter what is done with these funds. At the outset they might be used to resettle displaced and disappointed fishermen, or merely to compensate them, over a given period, for the loss of their

traditional livelihood. In later years, and generations, the money could be redistributed among the privileged fishermen . . . Or, the state could keep the rent, as landlord. I know of no ethical reason why either of these courses should be preferred, but if it is desired to put fishermen as much as possible in the same position as farmers, the redistribution among the privileged few would be the preferred course. This method would keep the rent of fishing among fishermen, just as the rent of agricultural land is responsible for making many farmers wealthy. (Scott 1957:54)

Unearthing the question of distribution suggests that what fisheries economists are calling for is a class transformation. Here, the movement from "livelihood" to "accumulation" harvesting (after Davis 1996) is also clearly a movement toward a new class division where "fishermen" become both the "privileged few", what Scott also refers to in the same article as "capitalist[s] in the usual sense", who will profit from a new property regime and the "hired men" who will work for them.

He [the capitalist] would presumably hire the boats on the fishery, rather than chartering them. Indeed, in the limiting case, he would own them and would hire the crews just as a farmer employs hired men. If he was a strong bargainer, the fishermen would, just as now, receive only their opportunity costs, and would not necessarily benefit from the change in arrangement (Scott 1957:55).

This scenario, which lies at the core of fisheries bioeconomics and is repeated and elaborated throughout its history, points to new economic actors that will emerge along with the institutionalization of property rights and, importantly, the removal of other barriers to capital accumulation such as the share system of compensation and capital immobility. The institution of private property rights is, here, clearly a condition of existence of capitalism but it does not alone constitute capitalism as, perhaps, Scott recognized.

Like Scott, I too want to incorporate the question of compensation. I too want to suggest that what fisheries economics is working toward is not the institutionalization of property rights per se but a more fundamental economic transformation that involves not only the institutionalization of property rights but a new pattern of the distribution of surplus via wage relations and capital mobility. Unlike Scott, I am explicitly interested in producing an ethical consideration of how surplus might be both appropriated and distributed, and its embeddedness within communities maintained rather than displaced (Gibson-Graham 2003, 2005, 2006). Also, unlike Scott and, indeed, unlike a host of researchers looking exclusively at the "solution" of privatization, I am here interested in focusing upon the *persistence* of the barriers to capital accumulation and to recast them as evidence of an alternative economy. The share system of compensation, the immobility of capital, and common property suggest the presence of an alternative "livelihood" economy where surpluses generated from common resources are "shared" amongst fishermen within specific places.

To re-imagine the barriers to capitalism in fisheries as the building blocks of an alternative economy requires an understanding of the economy as diverse rather than as monolithic (cf Emery and Pierce 2005; Leyshon, Lee and Williams 2003; Oberhauser 2005; Pavlovskaya 2004; Smith and Stenning 2006) and non-capitalism as possible and proximate rather than historic or distant (Callari 2005; Gibson-Graham 1996; in fisheries, St Martin 2005a, 2005b). It will also require a definition of capitalism as a particular class process of surplus production, appropriation, and distribution rather than an overarching system of economy corresponding to the presence of markets, competition, or private property (Amariglio and Ruccio 2001; Gibson-Graham et al 2001; Resnick and Wolff 1987). From a diverse economies perspective that sees economic processes as other than relative to capitalism, we might re-conceptualize the barriers to capitalism found in fisheries as foundations of an alternative economy (cf Gabriel 1990). Rather than vestiges to be swept away by enclosure and a capitalist becoming, the unique characteristics of fisheries economies, which are found throughout the world and represent the conditions under which millions of people labor, might become the conditions of existence of alternative economic futures.

The Alternative Economy

> the conditions of existence of non-capitalist societies, serve as the antithesis to the conditions of existence of capitalist society. (Gabriel 1990:92)

The alternative economy in New England fishing is constituted by, amongst other things, those processes thought to be barriers to the formation of capitalism: the share system of compensation, the immobility of capital, and a common property resource. A close examination of these processes will expose the economic dynamic of the alternative economy in fisheries. The share system of compensation provides a useful entry point by which we can begin to specify that dynamic. An analysis of the class process points to the connections between these "barriers" and recasts them as the interwoven elements of an alternative economy, albeit one threatened by the pressures of neoliberalization and privatization.

Sharing Fish

The share system is best characterized by the rules that govern the distribution of fish catches amongst boats and crewmembers. The set of rules that specifies how shares of the total catch for a given fishing trip will be distributed are referred to as the "lay". Differences within the industry such as boat unionization, crew and owner ethnicity, boat size, gear type, and port of origin will determine the details of the lay. In general, when catches are large, boat owners and all crewmembers involved benefit according to an agreed upon set of proportions, and, when catches are small, all suffer the same relative loss.

The share system's existence in fishing is traditionally explained as an adaptation to the uncertainty and cyclic nature of fishing: fluctuations in fish stock necessitate a share system that will spread financial risk and responsibility as much as possible (Doeringer et al 1986b). Other explanations include the problem of labor discipline given an (often) absentee boat owner (Matthiasson 1997; McConnell and Price 2006). There has, however, been very little research on the share system from fisheries economists (McConnell and Price 2006; for exceptions see Anderson 1982; Matthiasson 1996, 1997). The question of the distribution of costs and revenues, of capital and labor, has been largely ignored by a dominant economic discourse preoccupied with solving the problem of rent dissipation.

While the share system can take a variety of forms, there are two general types in New England: a "clear lay" and a "broken lay". Under a clear lay the total catch revenue is immediately divided into two parts, one for the boat and one for the crew. In the case of a broken lay, operating expenses are first deducted from the total revenue and then the remainder is divided amongst boat and crew. Table 1 is the trip settlement sheet for a fishing boat out of the port of New Bedford, MA that harvests scallops and uses a clear lay. Settlements are typically managed by settlement houses that act as a third party accounting service for individual boats (Kaplan 1999).[5] They receive the revenues from each trip and immediately distribute shares to the boat, captain, other crewmembers, and lumpers.[6] These distributions are clearly indicated on settlement sheets that are available to all parties.

In the example, the boat's share is 43% of the gross stock (total value of the catch) while the crew's share is 57%. The only shared expenses are the "pers", small bonuses typically given to mates or cooks, and docking fees. This boat pays a bonus to the captain equal to 10% of the boat's share as well as some contribution to the food. The crew's share is used to pay for such items as food, water, fuel, or ice—the operating expenses for a given trip. The remainder of the crew's share is divided amongst crewmembers using a share per person formula. In this example all crewmembers (including the captain) receive one full share (of the crew's net share) except for one individual who gets a three-quarters share probably because he or she is a novice. Significant differences in compensation can, however, occur due to variations in overall catch, the lay percentages for crew and boat, and the number of crew on a given trip. In general, operating with a clear lay will not stop the boat's net share from varying with catch but it will ensure that it does not vary to the same degree as the crew's net share.

Table 1: Example of a clear lay, scallop boat from New Bedford (anonymous examples provided by Edie & Marie Settlement House, New Bedford, MA)

Date 4 August 1997	Sail date 18 July 1997	Settlement date 4 August 1997
Gross pounds 6755	Gross stock US$50,817.00	Trip length 17 days

Shared expenses ($)		Crew expenses ($)		Boat expenses ($)	
Pers	152.46	Food	1744.61	Captain	2165.68
		Fuel1	8250.00	Food	425.00
		Fuel2	344.31		
		Ice	1386.00		
		Water	50.00		
		Bags	114.00		
Fee	150.00	Tel	137.53		
Dock	150.00	Gear	105.00		
		GearKitty	150.00		
		Unload	200.00		
Total	452.46	Total	12,481.45	Total	2590.68
		Crew (%)	57.00	Boat (%)	43.00
Gross		Gross crew	$28,707.00	Gross boat	$21,656.81
stock	$50,817.00	share	$28,707.00	share	$21,656.81
Shared	$452.46	Crew	$2590.68	Boat	$2,590.68
expenses	$452.46	expenses	$2590.68	expenses	$2,590.68
Net	$50,364.54	Net crew	$16,226.28	Net boat	$19,066.13
stock	$50,364.54	share	$16,226.28	share	$19,066.13

Crew payroll section

Title	Share ($)	Pers ($)	Total ($)	Net ($)
Captain	3416.06	2165.68	5581.74	5581.74
Crew	3416.06		3416.06	3416.06
Mate	3416.06	152.46	3568.52	3568.52
Crew	3416.06		3416.06	3416.06
Crew	2562.04		2562.04	2562.04
Crew totals	16,226.28	2318.14	18,544.42	18,544.42

Lumper payroll section

Title	Share	Pers	Total	Net
Lumper	$0.00	$0.00	$0.00	$0.00
Final totals	$16,226.28	$2318.14	$18,544.42	$18,544.42

Settlements such as the above do not depict all of the costs of fishing. There are, undoubtedly, many costs related to the boat that are covered by the boat's share but not itemized as part of the settlement. Nevertheless, the accounting that is obvious on trip settlement sheets make clearer some of the variety of economic positions occupied by "fishermen", and the importance of those positions relative to the distribution of revenues from each trip (cf Hopwood and Miller 1994; see also Davis and Jentoft 1989). Within the share system of accounting, "fishermen" may hold the position of boat owner as represented in settlement sheets by the boat itself. They may be in the position of captain, making the fisherman a crewmember and, often, a boat owner. Or, they may be in the position of a non-captain crewmember that may or may not also be an owner. In addition, within the category of crewmember there may be small differences in positions depending upon job specificity where extra pers are given to mates or cooks.

Sustaining Livelihoods

The share system works to distribute both the benefits and losses of fish harvesting between boat owners and crewmembers. In so doing, it greatly limits the mobility of capital and, instead, facilitates forms of investment tied to communities and the common resource areas upon which they depend. The share system presents a deterrent to entry into the industry because any windfall profits accruing to capital during boom times are tempered by the sharing of all surplus with labor. In addition, any individual or corporation seeking sustained returns on investments must do so within the context of the possibility of (often dramatic) changes in fish availability. In the absence of a predictable resource and the inability to suppress "wages", mobile capital will invest in other industries; capital investment in fisheries is typically locally generated and locally embedded.

Similarly, exit from the industry during times of scarcity does not fit a model of capital mobility. When fish are scarce (for any of a variety of reasons) family owned boats will continue to operate beyond what is economically rational (Doeringer et al 1986a). Fishermen will cut back on crews, forego expensive insurance, and sacrifice their safety to pursue their "livelihoods".

> We know for a fact that the government will never issue new licenses. We know in the future it's going to get worse because if a boat goes down [ie sinks], the guy isn't going to have the backing to go into it again ... If he has insurance, God willing, he'll get out. If he doesn't have insurance, he'll lose everything ... That's how I'm running right now, [with] no insurance. Me and my brother and my uncle, family, that's it. I've got an 86-foot boat. I've spent six months with just two guys—just me and my brother. A guy in the Coast Guard comes aboard, they look and say, "Where's everybody else?" "You're looking at them!" (Gloucester fisherman).

Such cost-cutting measures are particularly possible when boats are run as family enterprises (Marks 2005). Fishermen who cannot insure crew members, guarantee their safety, or promise a minimum level of compensation can rely upon their extended families to sustain the boat and the business during bad times. Such conditions, however, presume a share system, usually in the form of a broken lay where trip expenses are shared by the boat and the crew.

Interviewer: "You take your expenses off the top?"

Fisherman: "Yeah, [we] take everything out and then divide ... The other way [meaning a clear lay], they used to take out a few things. Maybe oil and that is it. Just oil and the rest would come out of the crew expenses ... So it was a little hard. We couldn't do it. I had my uncle; I had my son; he had his brother; he had his cousins—it was a family boat. What are you gonna do? I'm gonna steal from my son, my uncle, my cousins?"(Gloucester fisherman).

In the case of fisheries, family run enterprises are typically embedded within fishing communities where networks of fishermen and the people who support them (eg a variety of service providers) are vital to the success of fishing (Hall-Arber et al 2001; Jentoft 2000; Olson 2005). Indeed, fishermen running boats whose crews are not family or kinship based are, nevertheless, also highly dependent upon communities of fishermen whether they are place based, ethnic, or "virtual". The immobility of capital suggests not so much a "barrier" to accumulation but the presence of a localized and community-based economy in fisheries where the exploitation of labor by boat owners, both of whom are always "fishermen", is difficult at best.

The "livelihood" or "community economy" (cf Community Economies Collective 2001; Gibson-Graham 2006) of fisheries in New England is not only a product of the share system and capital immobility, but of the common property resource of fisheries themselves. Communities are linked directly to the common resources insofar as each crewmember's livelihood as well as that of the boat owner is a function of the health of the resource unmediated by a wage relation (see also St Martin 2006). There is, in a sense, a direct flow of wealth from the resource to the community that is otherwise obfuscated by private ownership of resources and capitalist social relations. The "commons" presumes a location and resource that is shared by a community; indeed, the commons and the community (economy) are mutually constitutive (Gudeman and Rivera-Gutiérrez 2002).

Interviewed fishermen often link together their fears of privatization, typically in the form of IFQs, with the demise of community, local economies, and the transformation of fishing from small family-owned enterprises to large corporate enterprises.

When it rebounds, these big companies are going to come in and go to that new system they're talking about [IFQs] and buy up all the licenses. It's going to be factory ships out there—that's what's going to happen. (Gloucester fisherman).

That's what the other big scare is—what is the economic impact [of IFQs] going to do to these fishermen around here? A company can come in; they have the money (Gloucester fisherman).

This joining of concerns points to the fact that these processes are intimately connected and that a change in one can affect another. While fisheries economics dissects the alternative economy and represents it as a series of individual barriers to capital accumulation (cf Mitchell 2005), fishermen consistently respond to neoliberal (particularly privatization) initiatives by referencing the entirety of what might be undermined: community, local economies, small businesses, and their "livelihoods". Within the confines of the dominant discourse, such rhetoric often has the effect of relegating the concerns of fishermen and fishing communities, as expressed, for example, in management council meetings and other public fora, to a romantic or archaic vision of fishing communities; it is only when we step outside that discourse that we can re-read the concerns of fishermen as expressions of fear relative to the demise of an alternative community economy and the potential for a class transformation.

Constituting Non-Capitalism

The share system divides the revenues generated from each trip between the crew and the boat and represents a potential division between non-owning crewmembers and boat owners. It is tempting to use this ownership division as the basis for an ontological separation of fishermen into two separate "classes" parallel to capitalists and proletariat (eg Fairley 1985). Here, however, the concept of class is understood not as a grouping of individuals but as the process of the production and appropriation of surplus (Resnick and Wolff 1987). The class analysis that follows is restricted, however, to processes associated with "the boat" as a site of production. My intention is not to essentialize this site of production (other sites such as households, churches, bars, and the radio are all important constituent elements of local fishing economies) but to use it as an entry point into the alternative nature of fishing communities.

The analysis re-reads the economy of fisheries as constituted by a unique non-capitalist class process defined by a crew or team production, appropriation, and distribution of surplus. The class process in fishing will be referred to as a *lay class process* after the name of the system of sharing revenues found in New England. This conceptualization is, in a sense, a proposition that builds upon the communal logic of the share system and the settlement house, and is intended to provide an alternative framework by which to understand what is at stake given the threat of privatization, how a transformation from the lay class process to a capitalist class process might occur, and what are the potentials of the existing community economy. Within the flow of surplus from fishing grounds to fishing communities there exist many possibilities for re-thinking the economy of fisheries outside of a "capitalocentric" frame (Gibson-Graham 1996). To understand just how the lay class process can be a distinctly non-capitalist (or non-feudal, or non-ancient) class process, we turn to an exploration of the variety of its determinants.

Identity, Hierarchy, and Class

Social and cultural practices of hierarchy have the potential to determine the class process. For example, Kayatekin (2004) notes that hierarchy and race constituted a feudal class process in sharecropping in the post-bellum southern US. In fishing there is a very high premium on the notion of fairness and independence. Indeed, independence is formalized by the federal government which defines fishermen as self-employed "co-venturers" in fishing (Matthaisson 1997). Strict hierarchies or an institutionalized separation between crewmembers or boat owners and crewmembers, which have occasionally existed in fishing (O'Leary 1996), do not currently characterize fishing in New England. Rather, both boat owners and crewmembers continue to identify as "fishermen" and all crewmembers are legally independent "co-venturers". In addition, boat owners are often crewmembers themselves or have worked as such at one time, and crewmembers typically aspire to and sometimes expect to be boat owners themselves.

Also in fishing, unlike feudal sharecropping, the production of surplus, its appropriation, and its distribution is not seasonal or annual but occurs on a trip-by-trip basis. The length of relationships between crewmembers and owners may be long but the mechanisms for the exchange of surplus are very short. Unlike feudal sharecroppers indebted to landowners, crewmembers do not enter into any long-term contracts and their terms of employment are more likely to have been negotiated by the captain rather than the boat owner. The long time period and contractual relationship between worker and owner required for the establishment and maintenance of feudal relationships does not typically exist in fishing.

The lay class process might also be usefully contrasted with capitalism or, more specifically, capitalist manufacturing where the exploitation of labor requires surveillance performed by a management hierarchy. No such mechanism is evident in fishing; captains (the only position analogous to a manager) are hired for their harvesting skills and not for their management skills. Indeed, the share system suggests that crewmembers will work together toward the common goal of harvesting and will discipline themselves (Matthaisson 1997; McConnell and Price 2006). Also, under a clear lay, crewmembers rather than boat owners directly pay for the services of the captain.

The ideals of independence and fairness important to fishermen are directly related to the lay class process in fishing insofar as they characterize it as outside of systems of hierarchy that might define it as either feudal or capitalist. The linking of "independence" and "fairness" to the lay class process is also vital as these are precisely the attributes that have been assumed by neoliberal rhetoric and conflated with an individualist desire to maximize utility and thereby legitimate privatization and the move toward a capitalist economy.

Who Owns the Fish?

The "problem" of common property in fisheries is, clearly, the essential focus of fisheries bioeconomics and related neoliberal schemes designed to institute property rights where there were none previously. From a class perspective, however, the issue of property is closely associated with that of surplus appropriation and ownership not only of the means of production (the fish) but the product that is produced. Ownership of fish after capture is here examined as a constituent element of the lay class process; it is also relevant, as we shall see, to the imposition of property rights in fishing via Individual Fishing Quotas (IFQs).

When asked who owns the catch between the moments of capture and sale, interviewed fishermen and settlement house employees referred to the catch as belonging to "the boat". Neither, however, would agree that "the boat" was equivalent to the boat owner as the sole owner of the catch (see also St Martin 2006). In practice, the catch is brought in by the captain and sometimes the mate, neither of whom is necessarily the owner of the boat, who then negotiates the sale of the catch with buyers. Once a buyer is found and the catch purchased, a check is written to "the boat" and typically carried to the settlement house where bills are paid and shares distributed.

In common and statutory law, the catch, between the moments of capture and sale, belongs to the possessor of the catch who is, undoubtedly, "the boat". In this case, "the boat" can be seen to be the boat owner. In admiralty law, however, "seamen" working for a share of the catch are entitled to put a Maritime Lien on the boat if they do not receive their share. In addition, in the case where there are several stakeholders making claims (eg when a boat goes bankrupt with outstanding bills on the mortgage, repairs, and equipment) admiralty law establishes the seamen's claims as superior (personal communication with Maritime lawyer).

In terms of class, the issue of first appropriation of surplus is closely linked to ownership of the product. Kayatekin (2001) has noted that it is exactly this issue that had to be legally settled in favor of landlords in the post-bellum US South in order for sharecropping to continue in a feudal rather than ancient mode of production. An analysis of catch ownership in fishing reveals a complexity that hampers the reduction of ownership to the boat owner since both boat owners and crewmembers have legal claim to the catch and both receive distributions of the catch via the settlement house. The shared ownership by all participants points to an appropriation of surplus that is also shared.

Property, Subjectivity, and Class Transformation

As noted above, the bioeconomic/neoliberal movement toward property rights in fishing is primarily a move toward Individual Fishing Quotas (IFQs). IFQs do not, however, literally enclose the commons in a spatial sense, they do not constitute property rights in the resource itself (ie fish). Rather, IFQs privatize (and, in the case of Individual Transferable Quotas or ITQs, commodify) access to fisheries by giving to "individuals" a right to a portion of the fish that can be harvested in a given year from a management region. In this case, ownership of resources as a condition of class process, as in feudalism or capitalism, must, in fisheries, be recast in terms of the ownership of a right to harvest. While IFQs do not confer property rights on fish before capture, the right to access is clearly a condition for an assumption of property rights *after* the moment of capture contrary to the discussion of ownership of catch above. Fish, in the sea, remain technically common but the institution of IFQs constitutes them as virtually private property, which is, of course, the very reason for IFQs.

This is reflected in the legislation establishing IFQs, the Magnuson Act of 1976 and its more recent amendments and renewals. In the Act, IFQs are defined such that the right to access a given portion of the TAC assumes "exclusive use" by the IFQ holder.

> The term "individual fishing quota" means a Federal permit under a limited access system to harvest a quantity of fish, expressed by a unit or units representing a percentage of the total allowable catch of a fishery that may be received or held for exclusive use by a person. [Section 3 definitions 16 USC 1802(21)]

The quota holder is clearly assumed to be the "person" with exclusive rights to the catch, but the holder/owner does not necessarily reduce to the boat owner or even an individual.

> The term "person" means any individual . . . any corporation, partnership, association, or other entity (whether or not organized or existing under the laws of any State), and any. . . government or any entity of any such government. [Section 3 definitions 16 USC 1802 (31)]

While federal law assumes the quota holder also has exclusive rights to the fish caught, the specification of who will receive quotas and who will not is left up to regional councils. At the council level, when IFQs are proposed/discussed, they are invariably assumed to be the eventual possession of "fishermen" who invariably reduce to boat owners.

IFQs are deeply resisted by many fishermen (see above) who perceive them as fundamentally transforming the fishing industry. In particular, they often claim that IFQs will lead to the demise of community, an ethic of "everyone out for themselves", or a "takeover" by big business. Other regulatory forms that limit effort, while also disruptive to many fishing communities (Hall-Arber et al 2001), are not so clearly associated with a class transformation. The fears of fishermen as well as the penchant of academics to refer to IFQs as "enclosure", point to an alteration in the conditions of production, appropriation, and distribution of surplus as a result of the formation of a legal right to catch a given quantity of fish.

Removing the Barriers to Capital Accumulation

While there is no necessity for IFQs to transform the class process in fishing, they do remove several "barriers" to capital accumulation and thereby open the door to capitalism itself (see above). IFQs are most clearly aimed at the "problem" of common property and work to create property rights to access that substitute, very effectively, for property rights in the resource itself. IFQs are, however, only possible within intensive systems of resource monitoring and management designed precisely to remove the variability and unpredictability of fish harvesting. They, therefore, represent a stabilization of fishing which makes harvesting attractive to new forms of capital that are neither necessarily local nor family based; IFQs offer the possibility of "accumulation harvesting" and increase capital mobility.

IFQs also threaten to solve the problem of the share system by transforming it into a wage system of compensation. Once ownership of a known quantity of fish is established, the possibility of stabilizing and reducing labor costs emerges. Boat owners (as quota holders), under these conditions, adopt the economic position of utility maximizers competing with other boat owners (cf Davis 1991; Davis and Jentoft, 1989) and thereby differentiate themselves from crewmembers such that a new class division is born. It may be that privatization (via IFQs) removes not one but three barriers to capital accumulation (ie the share system, the immobility of capital, and common property) and thereby undermines the lay class process in fisheries.

The above story links the formation of property rights (IFQs) with a potential for class transformation in fisheries. It does so by following a possible chain of events from the institutionalization of rights to access a portion of TAC, to the removal of the barriers to capital accumulation, to a shift in the appropriation and distribution of surplus. As was clear from the discussion of the lay class process earlier, class processes are, however, constituted by more than just the formation of property (or its absence) (Resnick and Wolff 1987). Other processes, in particular those of identity and subjectivity, also determine the nature of class and the potential for its transformation (Gibson-Graham 1996; Castree 1999).[7] While federal law makes possible the forging of neoliberal and ultimately capitalist subject positions within fisheries via the implementation of IFQs, there remains the question of the inhabitation of those subject positions by fishermen themselves.

Becoming Neoliberal Subjects

The dominant bioeconomic models deployed in fisheries science and management insist upon a particular subject and space that aligns with the ongoing neoliberalization of fisheries (St Martin 2001). The assumed subject of fisheries (the utility maximizing competitive individual) and the space within which that subject operates (the open access commons) have the effect of erasing and/or displacing the cooperative and territorial practices of fishermen embedded within fishing communities. Previous empirical research in New England has focused on documenting how fishermen's behavior (social and spatial) and desires contradict those assumed by dominant models of fisheries (St Martin 2001). This work suggests that there exist foundations for forms of fisheries management based on cooperation and community precisely where individual competition is thought to reign. Yet, fishermen also exhibit the behavior and desires of the bioeconomic/neoliberal subject even as they engage in processes of community and territory (St Martin 2005b). For example, they insist upon a self-identity that includes notions of independence, fairness/equity, freedom/mobility, and a self-determination captured by their "way of life".

Fishermen, who can be read as either competitive or cooperative, as individuals or community members, are called by neoliberal discourse (and the logic of bioeconomics implemented as fisheries management) to become capitalist subjects (cf McCarthy 2006), indeed, to become "capitalists in the usual sense" (Scott 1957). Larner (2003) suggests that we not only document and describe the nature of the neoliberal subject but explain how that subject is actualized and adopted as a way to explain the "tenacity" of neoliberalization. In fisheries, we can explain the attraction of the neoliberal subject position to fishermen in two ways.

First, neoliberal discourse monopolizes the attributes that fishermen ascribe to themselves (eg independence, mobility, fairness, etc) as attributes of the neoliberal subject and, ultimately, the capitalist economy. Fishermen's notion of self, at times, corresponds with and even explains the "complex appeal of [neoliberal] concepts such as 'freedom,' 'empowerment,' and 'choice'" (Larner 2003:511). As a result, other models of being a fisherman that might oppose the dominant model posit fishermen as cooperative community members, as "artisanal" and exhibiting a nature opposite that of the neoliberal subject (eg Bernal, Aliaga and Morales 1999). Alternative models of subjectivity rarely accommodate or explain fishermen's desires for independence, mobility, fairness, etc; these, it would seem, are conceded to neoliberal theorizations.

Second, neoliberalism negates any other alternative economy by depicting economic processes that deviate from capitalism as essential flaws, problems, or barriers. In fisheries, the open access commons, the share system of compensation, and capital immobility are not the elements of an alternative economy (with its own potentials and possibilities) so much as they are the barriers to an efficient and rational capitalist economy. In addition, the erasure of any alternative economy (existing or future) denies the possibility of any alternative economic subjectivity that might align with the self-image of fishermen or might differently negotiate the axes of cooperation/competition or individual/community. In the absence of any alternative, the (non-artisanal) fisherman has no option but to become the neoliberal subject trapped within a pre-modern/flawed economy, where, barring transformation to capitalism, their behavior will necessarily lead to the irrational use of resources and the undermining of the "fisherman" him/herself.[8]

Conclusion

> The existence of certain notions *of property or of self* may ... constitute anti-conditions of existence of capitalist exploitation. (Gabriel 1990:102, emphasis added)

The analysis above has focused on the question of property rights and economic subjectivity in fisheries as a way to explore the difference that class makes to our stories of neoliberalization. In the case of fisheries, it is clear that there is an ongoing neoliberalization that champions property rights, but discussions of that neoliberalization have focused primarily on how fisheries are becoming capitalist. For example, recent work has specified the imposition of a capitalist subjectivity and spatiality (eg St Martin 2001, 2005a), has characterized the trajectory of fisheries management as enclosure (eg Apostle, McCay and Mikalsen 2002), and has documented emerging social relations amongst fishermen as aligned with neoliberalization (eg Mansfield 2004b). While these are important and vital studies by which we can better understand the formation of capitalist futures in fisheries, they tell us little about the existing and persistent non-capitalist economy of fisheries and its potentials, nor do they tell us what, precisely, is lost with the transition to capitalism or how that transition happens in terms of class processes or economic subjectivities.

Privatization of resources or, in the case of fisheries, access rights to harvest via IFQs does not alone constitute capitalism. The movement from non-capitalism to capitalism requires a displacement of the former not only in material practice but in discourse. Narratives of enclosure, whether originating from those advocating privatization or from those critiquing it, powerfully displace the presence of non-capitalist economies. In the case of fisheries, existing economic activities, to the degree they are examined, are invariably represented as pre-capitalist, deficient, problematic, or as a series of barriers to be removed rather than as an alternative economy with its own strengths and potentials.

Privatization (and capitalism) appears logical and inevitable because "there is no alternative" economy either described or offered.

Class analysis exposes alternative economies and details their constitution (eg Pavlovskaya 2005) and/or becoming (eg Gibson-Graham 2005). The analysis above focused on the questions of property and subjectivity as constituent elements of the class process in fisheries. The lay class process was described as being the effect of both a tradition of common property in fisheries (coincident with a share system of compensation) and an image of "fishermen" as inherently independent and interested in fairness and equity. While the latter is typically associated with a neoliberal subject aligned with the capitalist economy, "fishermen" were here repositioned as community subjects aligned with a community economy.

The lay class process, while persistent, is threatened by an ongoing neoliberalization. A class analysis clearly points to the ways that the lay process might be undermined and transformed. In so doing, it reveals not only the constituent elements of class and the potential for transformation but the variety of sites where resistance to transformation is possible. One form of resistance is to identify and foster alternative economic understandings, practices, and possibilities. The case of fisheries is but one example of an existing alternative economy whose explication via a class analysis reminds us of the possibility and proximity of non-hierarchical forms of compensation, an ethic of sharing, a transparent distribution of surplus, and an economy centered upon a community well-being.

Endnotes

[1] The term "fisherman" will be used throughout to refer to persons directly involved in fish harvesting. While not gender neutral, it is the preferred term by both men and women who work as harvesters of fish.

[2] This article relies primarily upon interview and participant observation data gathered over several years within the fishing communities of New England. Specific research projects where fishermen, fisheries scientists, and fisheries managers were interviewed in-depth include "Oral History Project to Collect Traditional Ecological Knowledge and Develop an Historical Record of Fishermen/Scientist Interactions" (S-K Grant 96-NER-166, 1997–1998); "An Atlas-based Audit of Fishing Territories, Local Knowledge, and the Potential for Community Participation in Fisheries Science and Management" (NOAA/Northeast Consortium #06-028, 2002–2006) and "Examining the Fate of Experience Based Knowledge in a Science Policy Process" (NSF #0322570 and NSF #0349907, 2004–2007).

[3] Rent dissipation refers to the tendency, in an open access resource harvesting regime, for costs to equal revenues. In the case where there are profits but no limitations on access, new entrants will increase until costs again equal revenues (Rees 1985).

[4] This statement represents the sentiments of fishermen interviewed in the late 1990s, most of whom had been in the industry since the 1970s.

[5] In addition to fishermen, settlment house employees were interviewed. The latter contributed several "representative" settlement sheets (vessel names removed) for this

research. Settlement houses emerged in New Bedford as local and industry derived solutions to some of the problems of fisheries (Kaplan 1999). While they may be particular to New England, indeed New Bedford, the share system of compensation that settlement sheets document is widespread.

[6] Lumpers are dockside workers who unload fish for a small share of the revenues from the catch.

[7] See the special issue on "subjects of economy" in *Rethinking Marxism* 18(2) 2006.

[8] Both are explicitly discussed in Hardin's "The tragedy of the commons" (1968). There, the rational individual subject acting in his best interest in the absence of property rights inevitably produces an overexploitation of common property resources and risks schizophrenia (p 1246; see also St Martin 2005b).

References

Amariglio J and Ruccio D F (2001) From unity to dispersion: The body in modern economic discourse. In S Cullenberg, J Amariglio and D F Ruccio (eds) *Postmodernism, Economics and Knowledge* (pp 143–165). New York: Routledge

Anderson L G (1982) The share system in open-access and optimally regulated fisheries. *Land Economics* 58(4):435

Apostle R, McCay B and Mikalsen K H (2002) *Enclosing the Commons: Individual Transferable Quotas in the Nova Scotia Fishery*. St John's, Newfoundland: Institute of Social and Economic Research

Bernal P A, Aliaga B and Morales C (1999) New regulations in Chilean Fisheries and Aquaculture: ITQ's and territorial users rights. *Ocean & Coastal Management* 42:119–142

Callari A (2004) Economics and the postcolonial other. In E O Zein-Elabdin and S Charusheela (eds) *Postcolonialism Meets Economics* (pp 113–129). New York: Routledge

Castree N (1999) Envisioning capitalism: Geography and the renewal of Marxian political economy. *Transactions of the Institute of British Geographers* 24(2):137–158

Community Economies Collective (2001) Imagining and enacting noncapitalist futures. *Socialist Review* 28(3–4):93–135

Davis A (1991) Insidious rationalities. *Maritime Anthropological Studies* 4(1):13–31

Davis A (1996) Barbed wire and bandwagons: A comment on ITQ fisheries management. *Reviews in Fish Biology and Fisheries* 6:97–107

Davis A and Jentoft S (1989) Ambivalent co-operators. *Maritime Anthropological Studies* 2(2):194–211

Dewar M (1983) *Industry in Trouble: The Federal Government and the New England Fisheries*. Philadelphia: Temple University Press

Doeringer P B, Moss P I and Terkla D G (1986a) Capitalism and kinship: Do institutions matter in the labor market? *Industrial and Labor Relations Review* 40(1):48–60

Doeringer P B, Moss P I and Terkla D G (1986b) *The New England Fishing Economy: Jobs, Income, and Kinship*. Amherst, MA: University of Massachusetts Press

Eckert R D (1979) *The Enclosure of Ocean Resources: Economics and the Law of the Sea*. Stanford, CA: Hoover Institution Press

Emery M R and Pierce A R (2005) Interrupting the telos: Locating subsistence in contemporary US forests. *Environment & Planning A* 37(6):981–993

Escobar A (1995) *Encountering Development*. Princeton, NJ: Princeton University Press

Fairley B D (1985) The struggle for capitalism in the fishing industry in Newfoundland. *Studies in Political Economy* 17:33–69

Fraad H, Resnick S and Wolff R (1994) *Bringing it all Back Home*. London: Pluto Press

Gabriel S (1990) Ancients: A Marxian theory of self-exploitation. *Rethinking Marxism* 3(1):85–106

Gibson-Graham J K (1996) *The End of Capitalism (As We Knew It): A Feminist Critique of Political Economy*. Oxford: Basil Blackwell

Gibson-Graham J K (2003) An ethics of the local. *Rethinking Marxism* 15(1):49–74

Gibson-Graham J K (2005) Surplus possibilities: Postdevelopment and community economies. *Singapore Journal of Tropical Geography* 26(1):4–26

Gibson-Graham J K (2006) *A Postcapitalist Politics*. Minneapolis: University of Minnesota Press

Gibson-Graham J K, Resnick S A and Wolff R D (2000) *Class and its Others*. Minneapolis: University of Minnisota Press

Gibson-Graham J K, Resnick S A and Wolff R D (2001) *Re/Presenting Class: Essays in Postmodern Marxism*. Durham, NC: Duke University Press

Gordon H S (1954) The economic theory of a common property resource: The fishery. *Journal of Political Economy* 62:124–142

Gordon H S (1957) Obstacles to agreement on control in the fishing industry. *The Economics of Fisheries*. Rome: FAO/UN

Gudeman S and Rivera-Gutiérrez A (2002) Neither duck nor rabbit: Sustainability, political economy, and the dialectics of economy. In J Chase (ed) *The Spaces of Neoliberalism: Land, Place and Family in Latin America* (pp 159–186). Bloomfield, CT: Kumarian Press, Inc

Hall-Arber M et al (2001) *Fishing Communities and Fishing Dependency in the Northeast Region of the United States*. MARFIN Project Final Report to NMFS

Hanna S et al (2000) *Fishing Grounds: Defining a New Era for American Fisheries Management*. Washington DC: Island Press

Hannesson R (2004) *The Privatization of the Oceans*. Cambridge, MA: The MIT Press

Hardin G (1968) The tragedy of the commons. *Science* 162:1243–1248

Hardin G (1977) Denial and disguise. In G Hardin and J Baden (eds) *Managing the Commons* (pp 45–52). San Francisco: W H Freeman

Hopwood A G and Miller P (1994) *Accounting as Social and Institutional Practice*. Cambridge: Cambridge University Press

Iudicello S, Weber M and Wieland R (1999) *Fish, Markets, and Fishermen*. Washington DC: Island Press

Jentoft S (2000) The community: A missing link of fisheries management. *Marine Policy* 24(1):53–60

Kaplan I M (1999) Suspicion, growth and co-management in the commercial fishing industry: The financial settlers of New Bedford. *Marine Policy* 23(3):227–241

Kayatekin S A (1997) Sharecropping and class: A preliminary analysis. *Rethinking Marxism* 9(1):28–57

Kayatekin S A (2001) Sharecropping and feudal class processes in the postbellum Mississippi Delta. In J K Gibson-Graham, S Resnick and R Wolff (eds) *Re/presenting Class* (pp 227–246). Durham: Duke University Press

Kayatekin S A (2004) Hegemony, ambivalence, and class subjectivity. In E O Zein-Elabdin and S Charusheela (eds) *Postcolonialism Meets Economics* (pp 235–252). New York: Routledge

Larner W (2003) Neoliberalism? *Environment and Planning D: Society and Space* 21:509–512

Leyshon A, Lee R and Williams C (2003) *Alternative Economic Spaces: Rethinking the "Economic" in Economic Geography*. London: Routledge

Mann Borgese E (2000) The economics of the common heritage. *Ocean and Coastal Management* 43:763–779

Mansfield B (2004a) Rules of privatization: Contradictions in neoliberal regulation of North Pacific fisheries. *Annals of the Association of American Geographers* 94(3):565–584

Mansfield B (2004b) Neoliberalism in the oceans: "Rationalization," property rights, and the commons question. *Geoforum* 35(3):313–326

Mansfield B (2006) Assessing market-based environmental policy using a case study of North Pacific fisheries. *Global Environmental Change* 16(1):29–39

Marks B (2005) Effects of economic restructuring on household commodity production in the Louisiana shrimp fishery. Master's Thesis, University of Arizona

Matthiasson T (1996) *Cost Sharing and Catch Sharing*. Research Papers in Economics (RePEc), http://ideas.repec.org/

Matthiasson T (1997) *Fixed Wage or Share: Contingent Contract Renewal and Skipper Motivation*. Research Papers in Economics (RePEc), http://ideas.repec.org/

McCarthy J (2004) Privatizing conditions of production: Trade agreements as neoliberal environmental governance. *Geoforum* 35:327–341

McCarthy J (2006) Neoliberalism and the politics of alternatives: Community forestry in British Columbia and the United States. *Annals of the Association of American Geographers* 96(1):84–104

McCarthy J and Prudham S (2004) Neoliberal nature and the nature of neoliberalism. *Geoforum* 35:275–283

McCay B J and Brandt S (2001) *Changes in Fleet Capacity and Ownership of Harvesting Rights in the United States Surf Clam and Ocean Quahog Fishery*. Rome: Food and Agricultural Organization of the United Nations

McConnell K E and Price M (2006) The lay system in commercial fisheries: Origin and implications. *Journal of Environmental Economics and Management* 51(3):295–307

Mitchell T (2005) The work of economics: How a discipline makes its world. *European Journal of Sociology* 46(2):297–320

NOAA (National Oceanic and Atmospheric Administration) (2006) Brief history of groundfishing in New England, cited 12 November, updated 24 November, http://www.nefsc.noaa.gov/history/stories/groundfish/grndfsh1.html

Oberhauser A M (2005) Scaling gender and diverse economies: Perspectives from Appalachia and South Africa. *Antipode* 37(5):863–874

O'Leary W M (1996) *Maine Sea Fisheries: The Rise and Fall of a Native Industry, 1830–1890*. Boston: Northeastern University Press

Olson J (2005) Re-placing the space of community: A story of cultural politics, policies, and fisheries management. *Anthropological Quarterly* 78(1):247–268

Palsson G and Helgason A (1995) Figuring fish and measuring men: The quota system in the Icelandic cod fishery. *Ocean and Coastal Management* 28(1–3):117–146

Pavlovskaya M (2004) Other transitions: Multiple economies of Moscow households in the 1990s. *Annals of the Association of American Geographers* 94(2):329–351

Rees J (1985) *Natural Resources: Allocation, Economics, and Policy*. New York: Routledge

Resnick S A and Wolff R D (1987) *Knowledge and Class*. Chicago: The University of Chicago Press

Scott A (1955) The fishery: The objectives of sole ownership. *Journal of Political Economy* 63:116–124

Scott A (1957) Optimal utilization and the control of fisheries. *The Economics of Fisheries*. Rome: FAO/UN

Smith A and Stenning A (2006) Beyond household economies: Articulations and spaces of economic practice in postsocialism. *Progress in Human Geography* 30(2):190–213

St Martin K (2001) Making space for community resource management in fisheries. *Annals of the Association of American Geographers* 91(1):122–142

St Martin K (2005a) Mapping economic diversity in the First World: The case of fisheries. *Environment and Planning A* 37:959–979

St Martin K (2005b) Disrupting enclosure in New England fisheries. *Capitalism Nature Socialism* 16(1):63–80

St Martin K (2006) The impact of "community" on fisheries management in the U.S. Northea st. *Geoforum* 37(2):169–184

Steinberg P E (2001) *The Social Construction of the Ocean.* Cambridge: Cambridge University Press

Symes D and Crean K (1995) Privatisation of the commons: The introduction of individual transferable quotas in developed fisheries. *Geoforum* 26(2):175–185

Terkla D G, Doeringer P B and Moss P I (1988) Widespread labor stickiness in the New England offshore fishing industry: Implications for adjustment and regulation. *Land Economics* 64(1):73–82

Watt D C (1979) First steps in the enclosure of the oceans. *Marine Policy* 3(3):211–224

Chapter 7

Land Reform in the Time of Neoliberalism: A Many-Splendored Thing

Wendy Wolford

Introduction

Although it may have seemed unlikely just twenty years ago, the issue of land reform – defined here as the redistribution of land from large to small properties – has re-emerged as an important political issue in the Global South.[1] After a widespread hiatus in the 1970s and 80s, actors from different ends of the ideological spectrum now claim land reform as central to their political, social and economic platforms. The two dominant approaches to land reform can be imperfectly labeled neoliberal and populist.[2] Neoliberal land reforms (often referred to as Market-Led Agrarian Reforms or MLAR) attempt to create or restore private rights to property for the purpose of improving the smooth functioning of rural markets (usually markets in land, credit and agricultural inputs) and increasing efficiency and production through security of title (Borras jr. 2003; Deininger and Feder 1998; van Zyl, Kirsten and Binswanger 1996). Populist reforms, on the other hand, attempt to create or restore the connection between peasant communities and the land, improving social justice by distributing resources to the poorest who will then contribute to balanced development and food sovereignty (freedom from dependency on world food trade, see Edelman 2002, 2003; Rosset, Patel and Courville 2006; Wright and Wolford 2003).

In this paper, I compare these two very different land reform projects to make three arguments. First, I argue that land reform has re-emerged as a relevant policy for neoliberal and popular actors in large part because underlying both of these very different perspectives is a labor theory of property that ideally attributes the fruits of labor to the laborer: land reform is all things to all people (even people on radically opposed sides of the ideological spectrum) because it is fundamentally about *labor*. Land is a good that appeals to some people and not to others, but all people *work*: the recurring struggle for land throughout the twentieth century has less to do with an agrarian idealism where land is the central element of both production and social reproduction than it has to with rights to (and control over) one's labor.[3] This theoretical position on labor that undergirds both present-day neoliberal and populist formulations of land reform can be found in John Locke's labor theory of property. Although Locke is most commonly associated with neoliberal governance and institutions that privilege the rational, self-maximizing individual with rights to accumulate private property in a variety of arenas (McCarthy and Prudham 2004), his work contains nuances that enable different political actors to find support for their platforms within. John Locke's theory of property includes both the right to property produced by labor (where property is understood in the narrow sense of land and house and in the broader sense of physical goods) *and* property rights. This labor theory of property justifies and is justified by both the neoliberal focus on individual contractual rights to property (or, the right to use that property once it is claimed) and the populist focus on "land for those who work it" (or, the right to land on which a person labors and the subsistence produced).

Second, I argue that the difference between the neoliberal and populist perspectives then lies in their interpretation of *commodification*, both as a historical process and as a generalized state. Neoliberal and populist actors may both claim land reform as a strategic tool, but their interpretations of land reform's purpose are as different as the conclusions that David Ricardo and Karl Marx drew in taking the labor theory of value (which both believed in) to its "logical" end. Ricardo's belief in labor as a key source of value would lead directly to the liberal emphasis on individuals and the ability to efficiently transact labor power on the market, while Marx's belief in labor as the source of all value would lead equally directly to the emphasis on the accumulation of fixed property rights as theft of labor value (at the level of the individual as well as labor in the abstract). In re-visiting the differences between neoliberal land policies and populist demands for access to land, we are re-visiting this classic dispute between Liberal and Marxist perspectives on the process of commodification.

In regards to land reform, the neoliberal perspective assumes that the market is the optimal mechanism for allocating property to productive individuals because property rights are a reasonable reflection of labor applied: people who own property do so because they worked for it and this relationship has to be encouraged and rewarded (or, at the very least, not actively overturned) by the State. The populist perspective, on the other hand, assumes that the market is a vehicle for theft and exploitation: people who own property do so because they possess political influence (both in the present and in the past) and power that can be effectively backed up with murder and intimidation.

For the neoliberals, if there is a need for land reform, it is because the market has been insufficiently developed and has not yet incorporated some portion of the rural and urban poor. The market thus needs to be expanded to include them. For the populists, on the other hand, reforms that go through the market are thus likely to be plagued by its very historical mal-development. In this perspective markets have been sufficiently developed, but in ways that supported the privileges of the wealthy landowning class. The state thus needs to be mobilized to carry out land reform. This is not to say, of course, that market and state are mutually exclusive. On the contrary, the state is an important institutional actor in the neoliberal vision, but it is there primarily to buttress the actions and activities of the market (for an elaboration of this argument in regards to neoliberalism more generally, see Wendy Brown 2003). Likewise, the market is a necessary aspect of populist reforms: most grassroots social movements envision a complex marketing system for land reform beneficiaries that would allow local communities to compete successfully in regional markets. But here the state is required to provide the means of production and subsistence, and its support of the market is secondary.

Third, and finally, I argue that in my case study country of Brazil both the neoliberal and the populist project have generally created conditions conducive to the execution of land reform, and they have done so in ways that emphasize a labor theory of property (a theory already present in the country's Constitution but relatively moribund until now). This emphasis on labor creates unexpected ambiguities for people who obtain access to new properties. Land reform beneficiaries who have won access to land based on a labor theory of property find it difficult to feel secure in their own ownership – unless they use their land in ways that are consistent with collective social norms regarding productivity and productive-ness. How then are those social norms defined and demonstrated, and at what point should property rights be privileged over labor rights? Drawing on material gathered from land reform settlements in northeastern Brazil over the period 1999 to 2003, I show how populist struggles for land in that country have brought into sharp relief the pre-existing legal tensions of the labor theory of property.[4] I argue that although the boundaries of the settlers' land are made relatively clear, the appropriate boundaries (or guidelines) for the application of their labor are not. New land reform beneficiaries are accordingly compelled to produce and police their own boundaries, arguing over the "proper" use of their land. In this way, they have become active participants in their own surveillance and the surveillance of those around them.

In the rest of this paper, I describe the labor theory of property and then outline the ways in which it influences both the neoliberal and the populist projects for land reform. Then I use material from Brazil to explain how land reform has been promoted by both neoliberalism and populist struggles for land. Finally, I conclude by showing how these two projects have emphasized a labor theory of property and created ambiguities on the land reform settlements of northeastern Brazil, ambiguities that the settlers have partially resolved by actively producing and policing each other's boundaries.

The Labor Theory of Property

John Locke's writings on property have been extremely influential in both political and academic arenas. His influence extended well beyond the context of his time and place (late 17th century England) to provide fuel for Liberal Enlightenment thinking more generally. Today, John Locke - like Adam Smith - is read in a rather one-sided way (on Adam Smith, see Emma Rothschild 1992). He is generally presented, particularly in critical political economies, as the father of private property and the person who advocated for the constitution of the state as a means to oversee and control the juridical elements of property ownership. As James McCarthy and Scott Prudham (2004) write, "This Lockian discourse of an atomistic society of free, equal, landed individuals, governed by a state whose main purpose is the protection of their property rights, resonates strongly with neoliberalism and a host of contemporary schemes for saving or managing nature via its commodification" (277). While it is true that Locke's writings provide theoretical support for neoliberal property reforms, his work is also marshaled by subaltern actors throughout the world. Grassroots movements have organized around Locke's argument that "land belongs to those who work it."

In his Second Treatise on Government, Book Two, Chapter Five, Locke explained this theory of property in deceptively simple terms:

> "Though the water running in the fountain be everyone's yet who can doubt but that in the pitcher is his, only who drew it out? His Labour hath taken it out of the hands of nature, where it was common, and belonged equally to all her children, and hath thereby appropriated it to himself. [. . .] And even amongst us, the hare that any one is hunting, is thought his who pursues her during the chase: for being a beast that is still looked upon as common, and no one's possession" (Locke 2002, para. 29, 30).

This theory of property suggests that people are the "workmen" (Tully 1980) of God's bounty on earth: people apply their labor to the land and reap its rewards. As simple as the labor theory of property seems to be – and as widely as it is held – it lends itself to the ambiguity described throughout the paper. The two aspects of property (labor and ownership) were not inherently contradictory for Locke (and indeed most nation-state Constitutions include provisions for both[5]), because he assumed a natural state in which abundant land existed and all persons were equal.[6]

In this natural state, a person had an uncontested right to both the means and the product of his (sic) labor.

The complexities within a Lockian labor theory of property become politically explosive, however, with the development of a market - or hereditable ownership rights - in situations characterized by either extreme inequality or resource scarcity (the two may be mutually reinforcing). As Richard Pipes (2000) writes: "As attractive and self-evident as it may appear, the labor theory of property is a two-edged sword, for it can also be used to assail property. How is one to justify inherited wealth which requires no personal effort, or the fact that farm laborers and factory workers do not own what they produce?" (p. 36). It was the market, or exchanges mediated by money, that Locke argued enabled some men to accumulate more than they could use. For Locke, fixed property lines (or rights) were "unnatural" because they did not exist in a state of nature. They could be legally upheld by the state but were not necessarily legitimate if applied to land the owner did not work. As he said, "if either the grass of his enclosure rotted on the ground or the fruit of his planting perished without gathering. . .this part of the Earth notwithstanding his enclosure was still to be looked on as waste, and might be the possession of any other" (Locke 2003, para. 38, cited in Ashcraft 1981). Locke believed that "the right which all men have to the things necessary for subsistence [is] 'property' and this is, in some sense, distinguished from 'property in' some thing which a person 'comes to have" (cited in Tully 1980: 3).

The different perspectives on property in neoliberal and populist perspectives originate in the context and evaluation of the so-called "original sin" (Marx 1977: 873) of commodification: the initial transformation of labor, land and money into commodities for sale on the market (Polanyi 1980). Whereas liberal and neoliberal political economists see this as a natural and necessary evolution of man's desire to truck, barter and trade (Smith 1997: 507-520), critical political economists (including Marx and the contemporary agrarian populists) have argued that rather than exposing the true nature of production and exchange, the development of the capitalist market mystified both: far from allowing for the just distribution of rent, profit and wages, the market unfairly extracted surplus from the only commodities that themselves produced value: labor and land (Marx 1972, 1977: 873-908; Perelman 2001; Polanyi 1980).[7] This was the history of primitive accumulation that Marx argued was "written in the annals of mankind in letters of blood and fire" (1977: 875).

In this way, although liberal/neoliberal and Marxist/populist philosophers share a focus on labor as the source of value, their different interpretations of commodification (both the "original sin" and ongoing primitive accumulation) lead them to very different policy and political positions.

The Neoliberal Version of Land Reform: Life, Liberty and the Right to Property

Over the past 15 to 20 years, land distribution and land tenure reform have come to form part of the (post)Washington Consensus. In countries across Latin America, Asia and Africa, international monetary and lending agencies have entered into the debate over distribution and attempted to influence the path that distribution will take. The World Bank, particularly, has advocated with vigor for the establishment of secure tenure rights and distribution of land, usually through a market-mechanism referred to as "willing buyer-willing seller" or Market-Led Agrarian Reform (or MLAR) to contrast it to the state-led reforms of both an earlier period and those demanded by increasingly visible peasant organizations (Borras jr. 2003). This description of market-based agrarian reforms is not intended to be comprehensive or to critique the interventions of the World Bank. It is intended to describe the ideologies governing MLAR such that it will become clear how they are both similar to and contrast with the ideals embedded in the demands made by grassroots' movements for agrarian reform.

The World Bank's lending portfolio for land tenure projects has increased dramatically over the past 15 years, and bank officials believe it will continue to rise. From 1990 to 1994, the Bank funded only three "stand-alone land projects." This increased to 19 and then 25 in the 1995-1999 and 2000-2004 periods respectively. In 2004, the Bank committed approximately 1$billion to land-related projects (a larger group than the "stand-alone projects").[8] These projects have been taken up and replicated across the so-called Third World, from Eastern Europe (where a majority of the Bank's funding projects are currently located) to China, Mexico, and South Africa. In the latter, observers of the ANC's initial attempts to implement agrarian reform argued that the debate over how best to restitute and redistribute land was dominated by "technically superior and excellent lobbyists" from the World Bank (Weideman 2004: 223). Bank officials pushed for a market-based approach to reform that focused on individual property rights (van Zyl, Kirsten and Binswanger 1996), and the ANC subsequently adopted an even more narrow approach on willing sellers and willing buyers (Lahiff 2005: 1).

The World Bank has promoted attention to secure property rights as key elements of functioning markets and economic growth. As the World Bank itself maintains, reasonable people now understand that land reforms – meaning both distribution of idle land and tenure security – are necessary for the proper functioning of markets and democracy: "Few will disagree that inappropriate land policies can constitute a serious constraint on economic and social development: Insecure land tenure, outdated regulations, and dysfunctional land institutions constrain private investment and undermine local government's ability to raise taxes in many countries." [9] That these projects are as much about labor as they are about land is clear from the principles underlying their execution. First, the most widely-accepted justification for land reform in World Bank documents is the argument that secure tenure will allow people to invest productively - and for the long term. That is, people will be able to more effectively "bank" their labor as both profit from investments and as collateral. Improving the conditions of property titles will thus improve conditions for the application of labor. As Klaus Deininger and Hans Binswanger say in an articulate and well-argued paper that summarizes thirty years of World Bank land policy (1999), "Providing farmers with residual rights to production, even if these are only tempo-rary, will increase the incentive to clear and cultivate land, as illustrated by the tremendous increases in output and productivity associated with the transition from collective to individual (usufruct) rights in China" (p. 250; see also Feder and Feeny 1991: 140).

The logic is clearly articulated and simple: if self-interested maximiz-ing land users are given title to their land without state intervention, they will respond rationally by improving their land and more efficiently allo-cating resources to work it (Borras jr. 2003: 369). Echoing Adam Smith, property rights are labor returns/rights. As Smith said of the new ten-ant farmers in England in the 1700s, "A small proprietor, however, who knows every part of his little territory, who views it all with the affection which property, especially small property, naturally inspires, and who upon that account takes pleasure not only in cultivating but in adorning it, is generally of all improvers the most industrious, the most intelligent, and the most successful" (Smith 1997, Book 3, Chapter 4, para 19).

The first corollary to this argument is that the goal of land reform is to transfer land away from unproductive people to productive ones. Again, citing Deininger and Binswanger (1999) "A third benefit is that written records of landownership improve the transferability of property. By reducing asymmetric information about landownership and quality, land transactions are less costly to implement, thus increasing the liq-uidity of the land market and making it possible to transfer land from less productive to more productive individuals" (p. 250). The second corollary to this argument, of course, is that secure property rights will allow people to profit from their labor - in fact, if markets work well, then property rights should be an indication of having labored. It is this argument that appears to discourage the use of state-based tools, such as expropriation, for land redistribution. According to World Bank doc-uments, market transactions will allow for the appropriate connection between property and labor – where there is inequality, it is most often an indication of inappropriate "political" or state-based policies.

According to Deininger and Binswanger, market reforms will cor-rect problems created by "non-market" forces. They stress "the positive impact of an egalitarian asset distribution and the scope for redistribu-tive land reform where non-market forces have led to a highly dualistic ownership and operational distribution of land, that is, a distribution characterized by very large and very small holdings" (ibid: 248). Ultimately, the market should be used to create new property rights because the "political" expropriation of property sends the wrong signal to productive owners who may feel that the connection between property and labor has been severed. As an article by Klaus Deininger and Gershon Feder (1998) for the World Bank states, "markets in which to exchange rights to land can provide a low-cost means to effect transactions that would bring this factor of production to its most productive use" (p. 1). Markets can replace alternative forms of economic transaction and governance: "Improved access to markets, infrastructure, and financial intermediation, are alternative ways to provide the benefits -in terms of insurance, diversification, and access to funds for investment-associated with communal forms of land ownership" (Ibid. 5).

All of these are arguments with which many populist actors would agree – except for the assumption that capitalist markets allow for the appropriate and non-exploitative distribution of just rewards to labor. It turns out that this exception – this alternative reading of commodification and history – is ideologically, politically and materially very important.

The Populist Version of Land Reform: Land for Those Who Work It

Even as these so-called "neoliberal land reforms" have been implemented in various places around the world, a very different sort of land reform has also been pursued as part of a growing grassroots demand for social and economic justice. Throughout the late 20th and early 21st century, new rural actors from Brazil to India to South Africa have mobilized to demand radical changes in their relationship to property and the land: landless people's movements have formed most notably in Brazil (the Movimento dos Trabalhadores Sem Terra, or MST), Bolivia (Movimento Sin Tierra), Paraguay (Movimento dos Sin Tierra), the Philippines (Kilusang Magbubukid ng Pilipinas, or KMP) and South Africa (the Landless Peoples' Movement, or LPM). Land reforms are also at the center of new left-leaning governments in Latin America: in 2005, Hugo Chavez put into motion a land reform that projected titling 100,000 new small-holders as part of a "land revolution," and in November 2006, a newly-elected Evo Morales successfully directed a radical land reform through the Bolivian Congress.

These movements and politicians are increasingly connected by umbrella organizations such as the Via Campesina, a movement begun by the radical French cheese-maker and goat farmer, José Bové. This "new revolutionary peasantry" has influenced national policies in areas ranging from agricultural production to human rights; they have created transnational networks; and they have politicized transnational "politics as usual," taking part in highly visible protests at meetings of the G8, the World Economic Forum, and the World Trade Organization.

For these movements, existing land tenure regimes – and therefore the whole concept of land ownership – are illegitimate because land was not historically acquired through the honest and equitable application of labor. When the Brazilian MST was formed in 1984, the movement's first slogan was: land for those who work it (Wright and Wolford 2003). The movement argued that both feudalism and capitalism had allowed land to be taken from the poor for and by the wealthy. When the Zapatistas declared the beginning of an armed insurgency on January 1, 1994, they did so in the name of a territory they considered theirs because of a historical attachment to both its cultural and productive aspects. Likewise, Thabo Mbeki, elected president of South Africa in 1999, said in an address to his people, "Ninety years after the passage of the 1913 Land Act, we are on the way towards meeting the demand contained in the Freedom Charter, that the land shall belong to those who work it."[10]

The connection between land and labor is so fundamental for these groups that bringing the two (land and labor) into just alignment (land for those who work it) is the key to building coherent local communities, new mechanisms of food sovereignty, and sustainable forms of economic, political and social development. As a group of national and international movements wrote in their final declaration to a 2002 International Seminar on the Negative Impacts of World Bank Market-Based Land Reform Policy, titled *Land For Those Who Work It, Not Just For Those Who Can Buy It*: "We are members of peasant, research, environmental, religious and human rights organizations that have met in Washington, DC from April 15-17. We share the struggle for a world and a society in which the guiding principle will be the human being and the full enjoyment of all human rights for all people and communities; in which the right to land of rural communities is recognized; the food sovereignty of all countries is guaranteed; the environmental sustainability of the planet is preserved and the cultural integrity of all peoples is assured."

The groups who signed the above document singled out the World Bank and particularly the World Bank's focus on the market for attack. They argued that far from being "imperfect," markets had done their job perfectly: commodification allowed for the transfer of properties from a "state of nature" and the poor to the wealthy. In this perspective, property is not a "thing." It is a norm, or a social relation - what Katherine Verdery (2003) calls a "native construct": one person's property is made possible by others either agreeing (consenting) or being coerced into accepting the distribution of rights and claims. If property is a norm that enables the social construction of a set of rights, then it is influenced by the rules of the game (the political-institutional structure), by culture, by custom, and by historical contingency (Verdery and Humphrey 2004: 2).

Understanding this perspective on the market and property helps to explain why movements like the MST argue against the practice of providing land reform beneficiaries with definitive title. They argue that titling land re-creates the dynamic of commodification that allowed (necessitated) theft in the first place: the poor gain title in order to lose it (see Mitchell 2004). Instead, the MST privileges usufruct rights guaranteed by the power of the state: the populist perspective on land reform thus relies on local communities and the state to address the historical inequalities of property ownership.

Neoliberalism, Land Reform and the Labor Theory of Property in Brazil

In Brazil, both neoliberalism (as a set of economic and political policies) and the populist struggle for land created the space for a dramatic increase in land reform. Fernando Henrique Cardoso – *the* neoliberal president in Brazil (de Onis 2000) - distributed land to approximately 580,000 families, a number higher than all of the previous administrations (generally counted from 1964 on with the creation of land reform as government policy) combined (Deere and Medeiros 2005: 20). Neoliberalism as a historical moment (coming to fruition in the 1990s, the "decade of neoliberalism" in Brazil) had five important features in Brazil that facilitated (and subsequently characterized) the implementation of land reform. The five features are divided into conjunctural, substantive, and policy. In terms of conjunctural features, there was first the twinning of neoliberalism and democracy in Brazil (Dagnino 2002; Weyland 2004). The country returned to civilian rule in 1985, and as democracy was strengthened through party formalization, new presidents from Fernando Collor de Mello (1990-2) to Fernando Henrique Cardoso (1994-2002) implemented neoliberal economic policies such as the privatization of public sectors, withdrawal of various forms of social support, reduction of trade regulations and protection and liberalization of the economy (Cardoso 1995; see also Alimonda 2000). This democratic opening led to a second conjunctural feature of neoliberalism, the rise of grassroots movements fighting for access to land, most importantly the MST. The MST's formation is of course a complex combination of events, relations and people in different regions/places of Brazil (Wolford 2004), but it was firmly articulated with the increase in political space available for resistance and civil (society) expression.

In terms of substantive features, neoliberal economic policies reduced subsidies and other protections to agricultural producers, increasing the level of competition in a globalized agro-food market. This heightened level of competition combined with a dramatic fall in inflation in 1994 (due to the new currency plan, the *Plano Real*, introduced by Cardoso) to reduce land prices by nearly 50 percent from 1994 to 1995. As land became less effective as a speculative asset, something fostered by high levels of inflation, large landholders began shedding properties and the state or national agrarian reform agencies were often the best "market."

Finally, land reform received increased attention in the 1990s as a viable land management policy in part because it fit with the broader set of neoliberal land policies being introduced or refined worldwide (Deere and Medeiros 2005: 13-20). In 1997, the World Bank provided the Brazilian government with a loan of $90 million to begin a pilot project of market-led agrarian reform. This "new model of land policy [was to be] integrated into the market and independent of the government at each stage of the process" (Cardoso 1995). The bank-led land reform was aimed towards people who had previously worked in agriculture and whose annual income did not exceed US$15,000. These self-identified and – importantly – self-organized "rural producers" were provided with loans of up to US$40,000 to help them purchase land. They were required to form association with other willing buyers and to negotiate a price for a property with a landholder. The beneficiaries then had twenty years to pay back their loan. In 1998, the Land Bank became an official program, organized in collaboration with Federal and State government funds.

The World Bank's MLAR was the immediate precursor to a new governmental policy implemented in Brazil in 1998 called *O Novo Mundo Rural* (the new rural world). This policy – implemented in part to challenge the popularity of the MST's populist approach to land reform (Deere and Medeiros 2005) - introduced what Leonilde Medeiros (2002) has called a "new institutionality" for agrarian reform where even settlers who won access to land through state-led expropriations were expected to conform to market-based measures of performance and tenure. This new rural world was introduced in the hopes that tenure reform would lead to expected reforms in efficiency, transparency, and free exchange.

At the same time, even with all of these features of neoliberalism, land reform would not have registered on the national political agenda without the mobilization of powerful populist interests, primarily (though not exclusively) the MST. Neither Collor nor Cardoso originally intended to carry out land reform – even though the latter had campaigned on the promise that he would settle 280,000 families in his first term (Deere and Medeiros 2005; Ondetti 2006). It was the substantive and conjunctural opportunities provided by the "populist forces" that would push through the agrarian reforms that Cardoso later took credit for.

The MST was formed in 1984 as the military government that had ruled since 1964 was gradually relinquishing power to civilian actors. The movement began as a coalition of individual squatters groups primarily in southern Brazil (Wright and Wolford 2003) and by the mid-1990s was arguably the largest and most well-organized grassroots social movement ever to have national representation in the country's history.

Movement activists have encouraged a widening of protests for land by mobilizing among the rural and urban poor, informing them of their rights to land under the Federal Constitution. Today the movement counts its membership at nearly 2 million people, who together have carried out thousands of land occupations. The spike in settlements – when land occupations began to turn more reliably into settlements – occurred in the late 1990s after two separate massacres of landless squatters turned national and international attention on to the plight of the rural poor in Brazil (Ondetti 2006).

The increased push for and attention to land reform in Brazil gave life to a labor theory of property that was already inherent in the country's legal system. Brazilian land law supports both the "social function" of land and rights to private property. Since 1946, the Brazilian Constitution (the highest law of the land) has included the protection of land as a social good (land for the benefit of the people). This protection was strengthened in 1964 by the military government in the *Estatuto da Terra* (Land Statute), which provided more detailed instructions for land expropriation and distribution. Although this 1964 statute never led directly to a progressive agrarian reform, it did uphold the right of the federal government to expropriate land as well as the responsibility of landholders to utilize their property in a way that satisfied the social good. In 1988, this social function was listed both as a fundamental right of Brazilian citizens (under Article 5 of the 1988 Constitution) and as a means to promote agrarian reform (under Article 186). This is the legal measure that groups like the MST call on when they occupy land and demand that the state expropriate the land for the purposes of distribution to the rural poor.

In all of its various guises, however, the "social function of land" comes into direct conflict with Statutory Law (the *Codigo Civil*, or the Civil Code), which until 2003 had only limited protection of the social function, protecting first and foremost the traditional liberal rights of *private property*—owners could use, enjoy, and dispense with their property. Adjudicating localized land struggles, judges decided on a case-by-case basis which legal system to apply, and effectively leaves resolution of the contradiction in the hands of the most notoriously conservative social group in Brazil. Judges in small rural towns are usually connected by blood, marriage, and affinity to the local land-owning elites. Because local judges who adjudicate property disputes tend to be affiliated with the landed elite, it is the Civil Code tends that is privileged at the local and state levels (Meszaros 2000).

Within both the Civil Code and the Constitution, there is a second area of ambiguity: the contradiction between squatters' rights (*posseiros*) and property-holders' rights (*possuidores*). Both bodies of law grant property rights to squatters who productively occupy 50 hectares or less of land in good faith for 5 continuous years. But property owners have the clear right to defend themselves against squatters and even to eject them violently if necessary. The disjuncture between squatters' rights and ownership rights creates a situation conducive to violence because social actors involved in land reform know that it is in their interest to generate sufficient attention—media attention, political attention, and social attention—such that the federal government will become involved and invoke Constitutional law (Alston et al. 1999).[11]

Land Reform and Property Rights in Northeastern Brazil

Even as the push for agrarian reform received support from both neoliberal and populist actors in Brazil, life on the land has been complicated for the settlers because of the ambiguities inherent in the labor theory of property. In what follows, I show how land reform beneficiaries in the northeastern town of Água Preta were forced to personally negotiate the way in which they "owned" their land: the idea that land belonged to those who worked it spilled over into the settlements to mean that land was only yours if you worked it in accordance to community norms of "proper" work input. The sense that demonstrable labor input was necessary to secure permanent property rights led the rural settlers to police their own labor as well as the labor of others around them. Social interaction around property rights now incorporated the gaze of the state in the form of both the Bank of Brazil, their primary lender, and the government land reform office.

In the town of Agua Preta, about 50 kilometers from the coast and 200 from the state capital, Recife, land reform settlements were created through the expropriation of unproductive (and usually highly indebted) sugarcane plantations. These were settlements the MST occupied in the mid-1990s, although almost as soon as the settlers received their usufruct titles (1997), agrarian reform as a whole was subsumed under the *Novo Mundo Rural*. On these settlements, the aforementioned contradictions within Brazilian land law are heightened by the way in which the settlers acquired their land and their historical relationship to both land and labor on the sugarcane plantations (Wolford forthcoming). Most of the new settlers had previously worked on the plantations or on plantations in neighboring towns. Becoming settlers fundamentally changed the former rural workers' relationship to the land, but because norms are less malleable than rights, the meanings that rural workers attached to their new status as property-holders were deeply embedded in the historical construction of property as the vehicle for political, economic, and social control over their labor. For the rural workers, their own labor had been considered someone else's property even though they were active participants in the contract, with recourse (at least in theory) to the political system and to their own mobility if property norms regarding their labor were transgressed. Land "ownership" in the sugarcane region was the means to wielding political, economic and social power, to excluding others and to enforcing one's own interpretation of the law.

On the plantations, access to land was considered a "gift" dispensed at the discretion of the owner. And it was a coveted gift, coveted as simultaneously a mark of good favor from the "master" and a source of labor stability and subsistence provision. Many settlers remembered the plantation owners who had provided them with land as "good owners" and those who did not as "bad" ones (what Lygia Siguad, 2004, describes as having "honor"). But however benevolent the plantation owner was, the contradictions of Brazilian land law were evident: the rural workers were occasionally allowed to plant annual subsistence crops on their land, but they were regularly kept from planting any crops with "long roots" that might constitute a worker's legal claim to that land. As one rural worker said, "This sugar mill where we were working never gave anyone land to plant, no, never. Even the trees that the workers planted, the mill-owner would knock them all down. They planted cane and threw the workers out. The mill didn't want to give anything to the worker because they thought that the worker would take over the land." One of the crops regularly singled out for prohibition on the plantations was bananas. Planting bananas was rarely allowed, even when the land was not being used for sugarcane. As one settler said when asked if he had planted food crops while working for the former mill owner, "We were free to plant, he just didn't want us to plant bananas. If a person planted bananas, the administrator would pull them up, so we had to plant them in secret."

This history of land and labor relations on the plantations in northeastern Brazil (and it can be generalized to other regions, although I am specifically referring to the Northeast in this example) generated a very particular relationship between settlers and their land. Their experience on the plantation legitimated a labor theory of property, simultaneously justifying the "taking" of unproductive land and establishing a legal right to property. What the settlers were not sure of was how to interpret the historical process of commodification. They did not know whether to accord priority to property ownership or to labor on the land. What follows is a brief exchange between a land reform settler in Água Preta and myself. This was a middle-aged woman who became affiliated with the MST when the movement occupied the plantation she was living on and helped to usher through its relatively rapid expropriation. She insisted that she was given her land by the government as her right; she would not have invaded the property because that was not right. At the same time, she agreed that the landless were in their rights to invade.

Researcher: How did you find out that this plantation would be expropriated?

Settler: Because first there was an invasion, and so I got land because I lived here in the mill. I had the right, because I was working legally and so I got the land by right. I tried not to invade land or anything, it's just that this invasion came and then the government bought the land.

Researcher: And what did you think of the idea?

Settler: I liked it; I don't know, on the one hand it was good because a lot of people wanted to work and they didn't have land.

What all of this means is that access to land has been predicated on and encouraged considerable ambiguity – and even tension - in property rights. Because property rights were so ambiguous on the settlements, the settlers began to take it upon themselves to actively police these rights. They sensed that access to property was open to interpretation and so they engaged in unsolicited surveillance of their neighbors' properties (or what the World Bank might call participatory surveillance). One more brief illustration of an incident on a settlement called Flora highlights these points.

July 18, 1999.

This was the date of a general meeting on the settlement. One of the key issues to be discussed was a complaint brought to the settlement association by one of the settlers: he had discovered that a man from the nearby town was planting several rows of crops and grazing a cow on the upper edge of his land. The settler was not actually using that land at that time, but he was very worried that if this person continued to plant, he might be able to demonstrate productive use of the land and eventually win rights to that area. This fear came out of the historical context in which the Brazilian legal system articulated with the moral economy of the plantation to uphold both private property rights and use rights: theoretically, if a worker on the plantation – or a squatter – could show that they had planted "root crops", crops that have long roots and take a significant amount of time to mature, on a plot of land, they could win rights to that land. These were difficult claims to make against large and powerful landowners, but the MST's actions had shown the power of re-working idle property as illegitimate and casting laboring landscapes as legitimate.

On the settlements, then, these historical ideas of root crops as signifying a laboring claim to property persisted, heightened by the MST's re-working of property rights. And so even though there has never been a case where a land reform settler lost their land – or even part of their land - because of a squatter's claim, this did not stop the settlers from worrying that their land could be taken away.

The following description of the episode is from my field notes, written only about a month after I had arrived in the region, and before I had begun interviewing any of the settlers. While these field notes do not make me appear to be a particularly sympathetic or even astute observer, I think they illustrate well the nature of the event as well as the difficulty I had in understanding how different the settlers in Água Preta were to settlers I had previously lived with and interviewed in southern Brazil (Wolford 2004).

"We went to [one of the settlers'] house today, about 15 of the men from the settlement, including Antônio and [. . .] the president of the settlement. Antônio and the president thought that Caio [my research assistant] and I should go because it would be good for us to see what they had to deal with and how they did. I didn't understand what was going to happen and was pretty annoyed because I haven't gotten any work done. It turns out that there is a man from the town who lives on the very edge of the settlement (between the settlement and the city) who has been planting a few crops and grazing two cows on the land of one of the settlers. The settler who owned the land had already gone to talk to the man who replied only that he needed the land to work on and it wasn't being used, so why couldn't he use it? This, of course, is the same justification that the MST makes in occupying unproductive land. The irony was pretty lost on the settlers. The settler whose land it was (I didn't catch his name well) said that it was time to scare the guy off his land and that he could go to [the National Agrarian Reform Agency, INCRA] to get official help. Now there's an irony if ever there was one. It gets more interesting - the man who was grazing cows actually has a brother who is settled on a land reform settlement not too far away. When this was pointed out to the man, apparently he argued that the plot was too far away from his house. A pretty reasonable argument about the cattle, harder to make for the crops. The group of settlers was divided about whether they should get guns and just go up to the man's house and force him off the land or whether they should get INCRA, or give the guy more time. Antônio, the settlement's agricultural extension agent [and MST leader] seems to be a calming force in the group – at least when he begins to talk, this has a soporific effect on the rest. As we waited by Sr. Mariano's house, the culprit in question came down – he was alone which I thought was either brave or foolhardy given the tendency towards violence that the settlers sometimes display. He was not wearing any shoes and seemed to go back and forth between treating the settlers like friends and treating them like enemies. He used their arguments of idle land right back to them and they were unfazed. After a fair bit of discussion (maybe a half an hour), Antônio promised he would visit the man the next night and they would talk more calmly. The settlement president got red in the face and argued that they should take care of the situation right now. [He] is much more basic about showing his feelings and acting on them. It began to rain hard. Everyone stood under the eaves of the house that [the settler] has almost finished building. I stepped out to take a picture and everyone looked at me like I was crazy."

As is evident from these notes and the above section, the settlers were extremely conscious of what they saw as their tentative position on the land. The ambiguous nature of use rights made them walk lightly around their land, and when confronted with uncertainty over the use of the land, they deferred to the officials in the government. The settlers now referred to the state in much the same way as they had referred to their former plantation bosses. They knew that the former plantation owner had lost the land – as had large farmers all over the country – by failing to work on it, and now they worried about "filling up" their own parcels. These concerns were aggravated by the constant reminders of money they owed the bank: the Brazilian government awarded loans to all land reform settlers for both production and investment, and non-payment was considered evidence of not working and grounds for removal of the settler from his or her land. As Antônio, the extension agent for the settlement said at a meeting in July of 1999, "More now than ever, we need to do our things correctly...we need to make sure that from now on things happen naturally, but also with competence. We have to produce this banana so that in the year 2000 we can pay the bank without having to sell our land. We are going to pay the bank with the money that the bank gave us, which was the investment credit to produce banana. I am going to begin to visit your land now, people. The bank itself is pressuring for everyone to plant banana and it puts us in a delicate situation: whoever doesn't plant bananas is not going to get the second half of the investment credit."

Conclusion

In conclusion, I have attempted to make three main arguments in this paper. First, contemporary land reforms are fundamentally labor reforms: the distribution of land appeals to people and institutions across a wide ideological spectrum because such distribution is seen as a way to effectively allocate the rewards to labor. Second, a common focus on labor can and has led to very different policy positions because of different perspectives on the process of commodification. Support for land distribution among neoliberal actors, most prominently the World Bank has focused on MLARs that will allocate labor efficiently and support the functioning of markets. Populist actors, such as the MST, argue that the state must be involved in carrying out land distribution – expropriating land and settling the poor – because without such support the market is a tool for the exploitation of the poor and landless. Finally, I argued that the widespread emphasis on labor as the avenue to property coming from both the MLAR and populist approaches has created a context in which new land reform beneficiaries must police both their own labor efforts and the efforts of those around them.

Acknowledgements

The author would like to thank Becky Mansfield, Melissa Wright and Jo Kitching for their assistance and patience. She would also like to thank the three anonymous reviewers for their insightful critiques and theoretical guidance. All errors are the author's, of course.

Endnotes

[1] Many observers pronounced the end of land reform in the 1980s as "green revolution" technologies and urban industrialization worked together to reduce agricultural bottlenecks and proletarianize/urbanize a majority of the world's population (Hobsbawm 1994, 289; de Janvry and Sadoulet 1989).

[2] There are two different definitions of populism: political populism associated with charismatic politicians who claim to speak for the people, most often associated with the semi-authoritarian governments of Juan Peron and Getúlio Vargas in Latin America; and "agrarian" populism associated with grassroots efforts to promote community and a return to the local. In this paper, I use populism in the latter sense.

[3] This was originally Henry Bernstein's point (2004: 203-6; drawing on de Janvry's conclusions from his 1981 book), but the full implications or causations of this new "agrarian question (reform) of labor" are only slowly becoming clear.

[4] Fieldwork for this paper was conducted in the municipality of Água Preta, in the southern sugarcane region of Pernambuco. I interviewed all of the families on this settlement as part of field research that included interviews with approximately 200 MST settlers throughout Brazil, as well as many MST leaders, local politicians, small farmers in the regions surrounding the settlements, agrarian reform agents and agricultural day-laborers living in urban peripheries.

[5] In 1789, the newly-created National Assembly of France adopted a similar provision in the Declaration of the Rights of Man. In 1791, the Fifth Amendment of the US Constitution was ratified, and the final line read: "nor shall private property be taken for public use, without just compensation." Thus the American Constitution protects private property at the same time as it empowers the state with eminent domain, and positions both in relation to the public good. The American Convention on Human Rights (adopted in San José, CR, on November 22, 1969) went further, arguing in Article 21 that: "everyone has the right to the use and enjoyment of his property. The law may subordinate such use and enjoyment to the interest of society" (section 1) and "no one shall be deprived of his property except upon payment of just compensation for reasons of public utility or social interest" (section 2).

[6] Hobbes first introduced the idea of rights, which was a translation from the Latin term *jus naturale* (natural law) as 'right of nature.'

[7] As Marx says in his Notes to the Gotha Programme, "Labour is *not the source* of all wealth. *Nature* is just as much the source of use values (and it is surely of such that material wealth consists!) as labour, which itself is only the manifestation of a force of nature, human labour power. The above phrase is to be found in all children's primers and is correct in so far as it is *implied* that labour is performed with the appurtenant subjects and instruments" (1972: 9).

[8] Ibid.

[9] From the World Bank Land Policy Administration website, located on April 6, 2006, at: http://lnweb18.worldbank.org/ESSD/ardext.nsf/24ByDocName/LandPolicyandAdministration

[10] From the News and Media section of the South Africa Embassy website, accessed on November 27, 2006: http://www.saembassy.org/usaembassy/NewsMedia/Whatsnew/The%20land%20should%20belong%20to%20those%20who%20work%20it..html.

[11] Perhaps the most obvious manifestation of the ambiguous nature of rights is the dispute over land occupations/invasions. It is not clear, from a legal standpoint, whether people have the right to occupy public or private properties. The Constitution states

that squatters can occupy not only public property but also up to fifty hectares of private property. If they develop the property for five consecutive years, they can obtain title through adverse possession. And yet, federal decree number 2250, passed in 1997, forbids the federal agrarian reform agency INCRA from carrying out a *vistoria* (evaluation) of properties that have been occupied within the previous two years. The contradictions manifest at the highest levels of government: Attorney General Claudio Fontenelles has argued that "people have the right to invade properties not fulfilling their social function."

References

Alimonda, H (2000) Brazilian Society and Regional Integration *Latin American Perspectives*, 27(6):27–44

Alston L, Libecap G, and Mueller B (1999) *Titles, Conflict, and Land Use: The Development of Property Rights and Land Reform on the Brazilian Amazon Frontier*. Ann Arbor: University of Michigan Press

Ashcraft R (1981) Review of J Tully (1980) in the *American Political Science Review* 75(2):484–486

Bernstein H (2004) 'Changing Before Our Very Eyes': Agrarian Questions and the Politics of Land in Capitalism Today *Journal of Agrarian Change* 4(1–2): 190–225

—— (2002) Land Reform: Taking a Long(er) View *Journal of Agrarian Change* 2(4):433–463

Borras jr. S (2003) Questioning Market-Led Agrarian Reform: Experiences from Brazil, Colombia and South Africa *Journal of Agrarian Change* 3(3):367–394

Brown W (2003) Neoliberalism and the End of Liberal Democracy *Theory and Event* 7(1).

Cardoso FH (1995) Brazil and Current Challenges, A Speech at the National Press Club, Washington, D.C. April 21

Dagnino E (2002) Sociedade Civil e Espaços Publicos no Brasil, introduction to *Sociedade Civil e Espaços Publicos no Brasil*. São Paulo: Editora Paz e Terra S/A

de Janvry A and Sadoulet E (1989) A Study in Resistance to Institutional Change: The Lost Game of Latin American Land Reform *World Development* 17: 1397–1407

de Onis J (2000) Brazil New Capitalism *Foreign Affairs* (May/June)

Deere CD and Medeiros L (2005) Agrarian Reform and Poverty Reduction: Lessons From Brazil. Paper presented to the United Nations Development Programme and the Institute for Social Studies Workshop on "Land Reform and Poverty Reduction," The Hague, February 18–19

Deininger K and Binswanger H (1999) The Evolution of the World Bank's Land Policy: Principles, Experience, and Future Challenges. *The World Bank Research Observer* 14(2): 247–76

Deininger K and Feder G (1998) Land Institutions and Land Markets. Policy Research Working Paper, no. 2014. The World Bank Development Research Group

Edelman M (2002) Toward an Anthropology of Some New Internationalisms: Small Farmers in Global Resistance Movements *Focaal – European Journal of Anthropology* 40: 103.122

—— (2003) Transnational Peasant and Farmer Movements and Networks in *Global Civil Society 2003*, eds. Helmut Anheier, Marlies Glasius, and Mary Kaldor, pp 185–220. London: Oxford University Press

Feder G and Feeny D (1991) Land Tenure and Property Rights: Theory and Implications for Development Policy *The World Bank Economic Review* 5(1):135–153

Hobsbawm E (1994) *The Age of Extremes: A History of the World, 1914–1991*. New York: Vintage Books.

Kirsten J, van Zyl J and Vink N, eds. (1998) *The Agricultural Democratization of South Africa*. Cape Town: Africa Institute for Policy Analysis and Economic Integration

Lahiff E (2005) Debating Land Reform, Natural Resources and Poverty. *PLAAS Policy Brief Series* 17

Locke J (2002) *Two Treatises of Government*, book two, chapter 5, Of Property. Copyright held by Electronic Text Center, University of Virginia

Marx K (1972) *Critique of the Gotha Programme*. Peking: Foreign Languages Press

—— (1977) *Capital: A Critique of Political Economy*, Vol.1, translated by Ben Fowkes New York: Vintage Books

McCarthy J and Prudham S (2004) Neoliberal Nature and the Nature of Neoliberalism *Geoforum* 35(3):275–283

Medeiros LS (2002) *Movimentos Sociais, disputas políticas e reforma agrária de mercado no Brasil*. Rio de Janeiro: Editora da Universidade Rural and UNRISD

Meszaros G (2000) Taking the Land into their Hands: The Landless Workers' Movement and the Brazilian State. *Journal of Law and Society* 27(4):517–41

Ondetti GA (2006) Repression, Opportunity, and Protest: Explaining the Takeoff of Brazil's Landless Movement *Latin American Politics & Society* 48(2):61–94

Perelman M (2001) *The Invention of Capitalism*. Durham: Duke University Press

Pipes R (2000) *Property and Freedom*. Vintage Press

Polanyi K (1980 [1944]) *The Great Transformation: The Political and Economic Origins of Our Times*. Beacon Press

Rosset P, Patel R and Courville M (2006) *Promised Land: Competing Visions of Agrarian Reform*. Oakland: Food First Press

Sigaud L (2004) Armadilhas da honra e do perdão: Usos sociais do direito na mata pernambucana *Mana* 101:131–163

Smith A (1997 [1776]) *An Inquiry into the Nature and Causes of the Wealth of Nations*. London: Penguin Books

Tully J (1980) *A Discourse on Property: John Locke and his Adversaries*. New York: Cambridge University Press

van Zyl J, Kirsten J, and Binswanger H, eds. (1996) *Agricultural Land Reform in South Africa: Policies, Markets and Mechanisms*. Cape Town: Oxford University Press

Verdery K (2003) *The Vanishing Hectare: Property and Value in Postsocialist Transylvania*. Ithaca: Cornell University Press

Verdery K and Humphrey C, eds. (2004) *Property in Question*: *Value Transformation in the Global Economy*. Oxford: Berg

Weideman M (2004) Who Shaped South Africa's Land Reform Policy. *Politikon* 31(2):219–238

Weyland K (2004) Critical Debates: Neoliberalism and Democracy in Latin America, a Mixed Record *Latin American Politics and Society* 46(1):135–157

Wolford W (forthcoming) *This Land is Ours Now: Social Mobilization and the Struggle for Land in Brazil*. Manuscript forthcoming with Duke University Press

—— (2004) This Land is Ours Now: A New Perspective on Social Movement Formation *Annals of the American Association of Geographers* 94(2):409–424

Wright, A and W Wolford (2003) *To Inherit the Earth: the Landless Movement and the Struggle for a New Brazil*. Oakland, CA: Food First Books

Index

Printed and bound by CPI Group (UK) Ltd, Croydon, CR0 4YY

13/04/2025

14656463-0005